Families in Crisis

Pastoral Care and Family Counselling Models

Phanenmo Kath

Christian World Imprints

First Published in 2021 by

Christian World Imprints
Christian Publishing & Books from India
C-3, Wazirpur Industrial Area
Delhi-110052
cwidelhi2017@gmail.com
www.ChristianWorldImprints.com
Phone: +91 11 41526079

ISBN: 978-93-5148-508-7 (HB) ISBN: 978-93-5148-509-4 (PB)

Cataloging in Publication Data--DK
Courtesy: D.K. Agencies (P) Ltd. <docinfo@dkagencies.com>

Rengma, Phanenmo Kath, author.
Families in crisis : pastoral care and family counselling models / Phanenmo Kath.
pages cm
Originally presented as the author's thesis (D.Th)--Senate of Serampore College (University).
Includes bibliographical references.
ISBN 9789351485087 (HB)
ISBN 9789351485094 (PB)

1. Naga (South Asian people)--Kinship--India--Nāgāland. 2. Families--India--Nāgāland. 3. Families--Religious aspects--Christianity. 4. Pastoral care--India--Nāgāland. 5. Family counseling--India--Nāgāland. I. Title.

LCC DS432.N3R46 2021 | DDC 305.800954165 23

Printed in India.

Dedication

My Mother Late Mrs Ngalu Kath though unschooled was very persistent that her youngest son excel in studies and become a resourceful person in the society.

My Father Late Rev. Wekheno Kath, an inborn counsellor inspired me to become God's Servant, motivated me to take counselling as a discipline.

This book is a dream accomplished of a mother and a father's prayer for their dearest son.

***Eja* (Mother) and *Epa* (Father)** thank you for installing in me the value of hard work, the meaning of humility and the reward of honesty.

That the book in its original form is the thesis submitted to the Senate of Serampore College (University), towards the D.Th degree and is published with written permission. The candidate is responsible for the title, contents and opinion expressed in it.

Contents

Foreword

It is a privilege for me to write the Foreword to the book "Families in Crisis: Pastoral Care and Family Counselling Models" by Asso. Prof. Rev. Dr. Phanenmo Kath. Dr. Phanen is one of the few young upcoming scholars in the discipline of Christian Ministry, specialized in the area of Counselling. He has been teaching at Eastern Theological College for the last 14 years and at present, he is the Dean of the Department of ILEMA (Institute for Leadership Enhancement and Ministry Augmentation) in the College.

The present book is an outcome of his deep commitment and sincere research of his doctoral programme. It has eight chapters, which covers some very vital aspects on the crisis families are facing in the present context, a critical analysis of the problems, and further providing solution on how to deal with the challenges. It is indeed a well-researched study with proper documentation.

In the history of theological education, engaging and participating in the initiatives and negotiating towards Peace is one of the most challenging tasks. It contributes towards life-changing and life-affirming status in the history of humanity. After systematically introducing the book, Dr. Phanen delves into thoroughly understanding 'family' and presents myriad of significant perspectives. He then methodically explains the theological understanding of family and elaborates on the much-needed family counselling and therapy. It is very apt that he bases his study on the Naga family system, backing up his information with relevant data and biosystematics studies. Further, methodological issues in family studies, socio-demographic details and statistical techniques have been meticulously presented. He has also analysed and discussed various co-relations and provided a detailed summary of the findings. Dr. Phanen's interest and contribution towards coping with the present challenges families are facing is very well reflected in this book. The special contribution of the book is towards Proposing - "the New Family Counselling Models."

It is my hope that many people will take it as a privilege to go through the pages of this resourceful book. May this book touch the hearts of the readers to commit and contribute towards the important aspect of adopting the proper means of counselling models to enable the families to confidently face the challenges of this century. May this book serve as a source of peace and understanding to many families in many more aspects than one can ever comprehend.

Rev. Dr Prof. Narola Imchen
Principal
Eastern Theological College, Jorhat

Prologue

This book investigates the impact of select correlates on the Naga Families. It attempts to advocate the importance of family counselling and also suggests family counselling models in addressing the many needs of the present day Naga families.

Family is the basic and the most fundamental unit of the society. Family, as an essential institution plays a crucial role in the healthy and smooth functioning of human society. The Naga family can be defined as those related persons who live together within a household with a profound sense of belongingness, open sharing, willingness to sacrifice for the sake of one's family members and even by having a common kitchen. Every society and community has its own distinctive culture and family values. These systems governed and sustained the Naga families over the centuries. A Naga family generally consists of a husband and a wife and their unmarried children. The husband is the head of the family. Their parents also may live with them. The joint family system is not favoured by the Nagas and as such, it is practiced rarely only when there are no alternatives, say because of poverty, physical handicaps, etc. The general practice is that as soon as a son marries and becomes the head of his family he goes out and set up his own home.

The Naga families give importance to practices such as, fellow feeling, attentiveness to kith and kin, clans and one's villagers, respect for elders and acceptance of their advice, sacrifices for common good and welfare etc. However, today there are various factors that are hindering the smooth functioning of family life, such correlates include: lack of Family Communication, Impact of Mass media, Religious adherence, Educational differences, Place of Residence (Urban-rural divide), Income level, and Gender differences.

First of all, lack of family communication and the unfavorable family environment among the Naga family members have been a great concern. In earlier time, Nagas were known for their frankness, openness, politeness, constant and active communication. However, today such virtuous practices are slowly disappearing from the Naga society. Whether or not lack of family communication has an impact on Naga family is one of the correlates that need to be taken into consideration.

Mass media has impacted a lot in today's learning process and it has transformed the entire universe into a global village. However, on the other hand mass media continues to cause a threat to the family environment as it promotes liberal and globalised lifestyle. Whether or not mass media has an impact on Naga family is one the correlates under consideration.

By nature Nagas were very religious; this was manifested by series of ritual and sacrifices, both in the traditional religion and even after embracing Christianity. To Nagas there was no difference between secular and sacred; every activity of their life was governed by religion. However, with the current trends it is rather difficult to comment whether or not there is the same intensity in the Naga's religiosity. Therefore, whether or not religious adherence or lack of it has an impact on the Naga family system is one of the correlates under consideration.

Education has played a vital role in liberating people from many superstitious beliefs and practices. With Education also came enlightenment, knowledge, and other social and economic developments. Nonetheless, educated unemployed and even the educated employed Nagas are found to be neglecting certain family values. So this study attempts to verify whether the level of education has any impact on the Naga family system.

In the recent past years there has been a shift of the Naga population from villages to towns and cities particularly in search of better job and opportunities. Predominantly, Naga community and family is a closely-knit society, displaying caring, sharing, helping, and giving. It is said that within a village, due to their closeness and openness to one another, whatever is cooked in a particular family is even known by the other families even in the remote corner of the village. However, as people shift from the villages to towns and cities they tend to develop a spirit of individualism and slowly disconnect from the closely-knit society; which contribute to the disintegration of Naga family system. This research investigates whether or not a shift from villages to towns and cities has any impact on the Naga family system.

Naga families were economically self-sufficient. Each family owned cultivable land, forest products like fruits, vegetables, and firewood were in abundance; as such, people had plenty of foodstuffs. Each Naga family produced enough food grains to last for the whole year. Along with the economic prosperity of families, there was also a good community distribution system by means of sharing their belonging and foodstuffs. Moreover, hosting of 'feast of merit' by well to do and rich families, to the entire village population was normal practice. As a result, till today, there is no beggar among the Naga society. However, with the current trend of individualistic life-style and materialistic concept of life, there is an unhealthy competition. Therefore, distinct division between rich and poor, haves and have-nots is also observed among the Naga community in the recent past. This study investigates the level of income and economic position and its impact on the Naga family and family relationship.

Women in Naga society to a great extent enjoy a respectful social status inspite of the patriarchal social set up. Writing on the Naga woman, Heimindorf states, as quoted by Horam, "many women in more civilized parts of India may envy the women of the Naga Hills, on account of their high status and their free and happy life; and if you measure the cultural level of the people by the social position and personal freedom of its women, you will think twice before looking down on the Nagas." Though comparatively Naga women may be enjoying a better social status and higher position than their counterpart in mainstream India, there are certain areas where strict restrictions and division of labour between men and women still prevails in the Naga community. This study examines whether gender difference has any impact on the Naga family system.

Consequently, there is a need of psychology to understand the dynamics of family relationship, man-woman relationship, family ties, and also examine the impact of select correlates on Naga family system. The purpose is to strengthen the family relationship and to motivate family counsellors and therapists employing various counselling models among the families. With this concern, the researcher has taken up this subject for serious consideration.

The method of study is primarily empirical research, analytical and descriptive. SPSS (Statistical Package for the Social Science) a computer application that provide statistical analysis of data was used for analysis and testing the hypotheses. Analysis of quantitative data is done through different statistical methods. The tools of analysis such as Analysis of Variance-test (ANOVA), Correlation coefficient test, Chi-Square test, Stepwise Multiple Regression, Multidimensional Scaling, Percentage Analysis, ANOVA, and Factor Analysis were used in this research.

Research Findings

On the basis of the empirical research, researcher has found out that among the Impact of the select correlates on Naga family system, there are both positive and negative impacts.

1. The study result revealed that level of communication has a high significant correlation on family. Couples and family members who experience frank and open communication enjoy a higher family life satisfaction. In this highly individualistic age, members of the same family hardly have time for sharing, fellowship, and discussion. Life will only get busier in this challenging and demanding world. Therefore, it is imperative on the part of the church to educate its members on the importance of constant family interaction, family fellowship, family outing to enhance the quality of family life.
2. Mass media play a crucial role in today's context. The impact of mass media in the life of family is enormous. The research result shows that there is high significant correlation between family life and mass media, the lesser exposure to media and balanced use of media has positive impact on family life

satisfaction, where as random and uncontrolled usage of media has adverse impact on family well-being and family functioning. Mass media has fully captured people's time that family members and even spouses do not have a quality time together to share and support each other in time of needs, which affects the social fabric and family ties.

3. In the analysis the correlation between religious adherence and family life was found to be highly significant. Religion holds a crucial factor in the life of the people. Contrary to the proposed hypothesis, that there will be no significant impact of religious adherence on family, highly significant correlation is found between religion and family life. For this reason, the essence of true religiosity and spirituality needs to be cultivated and practice by the people. More than 96% of Naga people who identify themselves as Christian, must strengthen their religious belief, as religious person seems to have a greater sense of responsibility towards family life and its affairs.
4. Levels of Education: It is revealed that the level of education has a significant impact on family life satisfaction. Level of education determine the quality of life they live. Nagas with higher level of education have acquired experience and knowledge, therefore it enhances their skills and art of managing the family, as a result their families experiences happier family life.
5. Place of Residence: Place of residence has no significant correlation with family life satisfaction. Tribal society whether in the urban or rural setting still maintains and holds on to same value system. In contrary to what is believed that people shifting from rural to urban setting tend to loss their culture and value system, the study reveals that people from rural and urban settings have similar perception, belief and practices with regard to family life and functioning.
6. Income level: The research result revealed that there is significant correlation between level of income and family life. In a materialistic and commercialized world today, life has been challenged with the concept of happiness for those who have enough means to spend, and Naga Christians are not free from this. Therefore, the concept of true riches and happiness as recorded in the scripture need to be told.
7. Gender inequality is still a big concern among the tribal community. Nagas with predominantly Christian population and patriarchal social set up also faces this issue rather seriously. Therefore, the Christian community needs to be told to practice what it preaches. Large numbers of female undergoing theological training has not really impacted the gender issue to the expected level. At the surface level it may seem like Naga women enjoys better status than most other women in the country. May be to certain extend the Naga women enjoys certain privileges, but there are still in many areas like, leadership role in the society, status in the church, and their position in the family itself; the Naga women need to be really liberated.

In order to guide and prepare the Naga families toward better understanding of family values and necessity of family communications, various Counselling methods have been suggested. Skills necessary for counsellors involve in Family counselling, are listed below:

1. Conceptual Skills
2. Technical Skills
3. Interpersonal Skills

Models of Family Therapy: There are many family counselling models. However, some of the classical models were selected for the purpose of this study.

1. The Family System Counselling Model (Murray Bowen)
2. Experiential Family Counselling Model (Virginia Satir and Carl Whitaker)
3. Strategic Family Counselling Model (Jay Haley and Cloe Madanes)
4. Structural Family Counselling Model (Minuchin Salvador)

Towards an effective family counselling the researcher has attempted to suggest some new models, however, at the same time propose some of the existing family counselling models, which the researcher feels relevant in addressing the Naga family issues.

Some of the New Family Counselling Models Include

1. Gender Sensitive Model
2. Correcting Excessive Individualism Model

The Existing Family Counselling Models Include

1. Effective Communication Model
2. Individual Family Counselling Model
3. Couple Counselling Model
4. Media Awareness Model
5. Couples' Groups Counselling
6. Group Family Counselling
7. Family Networking Model

Moreover, to effectively minister and nurture the families, the role of the Church, Pastoral care and Pastoral counselling to the families are essential and important.

1. The Role of the Church in Caring the family
2. The Role of Pastoral Care for the family
3. The Role of Pastoral Counselling

Family is a gift of God to human beings in community. We must accept this gift thankfully and live gratefully. The hallmark of a Christian family is 'unity and love,' All members of the family are knit together and held together in the cord of love to live and celebrate. Family has gone through changes from a joint system to nuclear families. The ideals of traditional family system are considered to be old fashioned and outdated by today's generation.

It is high time that we consciously think of helping families to develop healthy and meaningful families. If family has to be maintained and sustained, there should be effective family counselling models that could meaningfully address the need of the present day families.

Change is the only constant in the world today, and it is happening at an increasing pace in every society. Many inventions and discoveries in the fields of science and technology, facilitation of education for all, advancement in information technology and mass media, widespread industrialization, expanded trade and commerce, and the impact of western civilization – all have had a tremendous influence on marriage and family life.

Accordingly, age-old notions and values regarding family and marriage have undergone a drastic change. Thus every effort must be made to enable families to meet life with more adequate knowledge and resources, especially with regard to the maintenance of their marriage and family life. This can best occur through education on a widespread scale.

In this demanding and challenging era Family the bedrock and heart of a strong society should be nurtured and give utmost support. If Naga society has to move forward and experience progress and development, firstly it need to address the issues of every family only then the society can experience real change and progress, because family is the most basic unit and the bottom most block of the society's foundation.

It is anticipated that the findings and results of the present analyses done among the Naga married couples will provide deeper understanding on the tenets of family life, and may give insights in maintaining and nurturing healthy functional families in the wider context.

Acknowledgements

This book is the outcome of my D.Th thesis submitted to the Senate of Serampore. Hence, I would like to acknowledge my appreciation to the Institutions and following persons for their contribution towards the successful completion of the research work.

I would like to sincerely and gratefully acknowledge the contribution of my supervisor Rev. Dr Daniel Burnabas, for his meticulous guidance throughout this research work.

Sincere word of gratitude to Rev Prof. Narola Imchen, Principal ETC, Jorhat for writing a befitting foreword. Also big thanks to Christian World Imprints, Delhi for publishing the book.

I am thankful to Federated Faculty for Research in Religion and Culture, Kottayam, for the privilege conceded to me to be part of this esteem Federated Research Programme, especially the Registrar and faculty members of FFRRC, Kottayam.

Sincere appreciation to Rev. Dr. Abraham Kuruvilla, Rev. Dr. Isaac V. Mathew, Rev. Prof. Ezamo Murry, Rev. Prof. Wati Longchar, who assisted me in the course of finalizing my research title, and also for technical guidance during the research period.

My thankfulness also goes to Dr. Jiksy Isaac, Research Consultant and Head Department of Statistics, S.B. College Changanassery, Dr. Saji K. P, M.G. University, Kottayam, and Mr. Jabir, Cochin University, Kerala, for assisting me in the empirical data analyses.

Immeasurable gratitude is expressed to Rev. Prof. Limatula Longkumer, Dean SATHRI; Dr. Lovely Awomi James, Associate Professor, ETC, Jorhat; Jacob Kurian, Principal Emeritus, IBTS, Kottayam; Mrs. Dorothy Momin, Assistant Professor of English, JB Girl's College, Jorhat, Assam and Rev. Prof. Ezamo Murry (former Principal ETC, Jorhat, Assam) for proof reading my Dissertation and making necessary corrections and valuable suggestions in refining the research work.

I wish to express my sincere appreciation to the Principal and Librarian of Trinity Theological Seminary, Singapore; Singapore Bible College, Singapore and

Baptist Theological Seminary, Singapore, for the permission to use their Library resources for my research work. Also big thanks to Rev. Carol, Sheto and family, for taking care of my stay at Singapore during my research work.

My special appreciation to the Librarian of Cochin University, Cochin; M.G. University, Kottayam; United Theological College, Bangalore; State Library, Kohima, Nagaland; SAIACS, Bangalore; Mar Thoma Theological Seminary, Kottayam, and Orthodox Theological Seminary, Kottayam, for the permission to use their library resources.

Big thanks to Church Pastors and Association leaders in Nagaland for the valuable help during empirical studies and allowing me to have access to their church married couples who participated in the seminar and answered the questionnaire.

Immeasurable gratitude is due to my church members for their incessant support, my father late Rev. Wekheno Kath for his fervent prayer support, and all my family members and well wishers for all the encouragement and support extended to me in the course of my studies.

Above all, I thank the Almighty God, for His providence, guidance and graciousness showered upon me throughout my research.

List of Abbreviations

ANOVA	:	Analysis of Variance
BTESSE	:	The Board of Theological Education Senate of Serampore College
cf (confer)	:	Compare
Co.	:	Company
DSM-IV-R	:	Diagnostic & Statistical Manual and Mental Disorder (Fourth Edition-Revised)
Ed; eds	:	Editor, editors, edition, editions
eg (exempli gratia)	:	For example
et al (et elii)	:	And others
etc (et cetera)	:	And other, and so forth
i,e (*id est*)	:	That is to say
HIV-AIDS	:	Human Immuno Virus, Acquired Immuno Deficiency Syndrome
NCSWR	:	National Commission on Self-employed Woman Report
NEP	:	New Economic Policy
SATHRI	:	South Asian Theological Research Institute
SC	:	Scheduled Caste
SPCK	:	Society for Promoting Christian Knowledge
ISPCK	:	Indian Society for Promoting Christian Knowledge
SPSS	:	Statistical Package for the Social Science
ST	:	Scheduled Tribe
UNICEF	:	United Nations International Children's Emergency Fund
Vol; vols	:	Volume, volumes

List of Tables

Chapter 1

The Context of the Research

1. Bird's Eye View of the Research Context

In this high-tech and fast changing world, family life is being pulled from all directions. In such a context, there is a need to identify the theoretical insights about family life, and also investigate the impact of the select correlates on family. Therefore, this study basically proposes to investigate the correlation between family life and the select correlates, such as; Family Communication, Impact of Mass media, Religious Adherence, Educational level, Place of Residence, Gender and Income level through empirical research.

Present-day Naga[1] families have been affected by various factors. Therefore, this research attempts to investigate the impact of select correlates on Naga

---

1 Nagas are predominantly tribal community living in the state of Nagaland. Nagas are also found in Assam, Manipur, Arunachal Pradesh, and even in Myanmar. Nagaland is located in the north eastern part of India. The state was formed in the year 1963. The capital of the state of Nagaland is Kohima, whereas Dimapur is its largest city. It is the least populated states in the country. English is the official language in Nagaland. The people residing in Nagaland are known as Nagas. The population of Nagaland as per the 2011 census is 19,78,502. There are a total of 1,024,649 males and 953,853 females in Nagaland. As per the 2011 census, the sex ratio in Nagaland stands at 931 compared to 909 in the 2001 census. Nagaland has a literacy rate of 79.55%. The male literacy is 82.75% whereas the female literacy is 70.01%. This statistic account is taken from http://www.populationindia.com/2012/03/population-of-nagaland-2011-census.html.Cf.https://swarajyamag.com/culture/how-northeast-india-was-christianised-in-the-last-100-years Christianization of Nagaland happened mostly in the decades leading to and following the Independence. The share of Christians in the population of the state was around two percent in 1911, which increased to 13 percent in 1931 and to 46 percent in 1951. By 1991, the share of Christians reached above 87 percent. By that time, the tribal population of Nagaland was nearly fully Christianised. Of the Scheduled Tribes

families. It also tries to suggest Family Counselling Models. Hence the title is: the impact of select correlates on Naga family: implication for family counselling models.

2. An Elaboration

Family is the basic and the most fundamental unit of the society. Family as an essential institution plays a crucial role in the healthy and smooth functioning in the life of human society. The Naga family can be defined as those related persons who live together within a household with a profound sense of belongingness, open sharing, willingness to sacrifice for the sake of one's family members and having a common kitchen.[2] From the family we may get true love. Every society and community has its own distinctive culture and family value system. Those systems govern and sustain the families over the centuries. A Naga family generally consists of the husband and the wife and their unmarried children. The husband is the head of the family. His parents may also be living with them. The family lives in its own house in that part of the Naga village occupied by the clan to which the head of the household belongs. The joint family system is not preferred by the Nagas and as such it is practiced but rarely and only when there is no other alternatives, that is due to poverty, physical handicaps, etc.[3] The general practice is that as soon as a son marries and becomes the head of his family he goes and sets up a home of his own.

There was a unique Naga family system accompanied by socio-cultural distinctiveness, such as, fellow feeling, attentiveness to kins, clans and one's villagers, respect for elders and acceptance of their advice, sacrifices for common good and welfare.[4] However, today there are various factors that pose as threat to the family; such correlates include: Lack of Family Communication, Impact of Mass Media, Religious Adherence, Educational Level, Place of Residence (Urban-rural divide), Gender and Income Level.

2.1. Lack of Family Communication

Nagas were by nature very open and communicate freely with family members and strangers alike. It is observed however, among the present generation that the same intensity of open communication even within the family is missing. The absence of open sharing and candid discussion, and communication within the

---

population of 10.61 lakhs counted in that year, 10.44 lakhs were Christians, and they formed more than 98 percent of the population of the Scheduled Tribes.

2 Joseph Thong, *Head Hunter Culture: Historic Culture of Nagas,* (Tseminyu: Khenyi Woch, 1997), 48.

3 A. Nshonga, *Traditional Naga Village System and Its Transformation,* (New Delhi: Anshah Publishing House, 2009), 145. Cf. Joseph, Thong, *Head Hunter Culture: Historic Culture of Nagas...,* 49.

4 J. P. Mill, *The Rengma Nagas,* (Guwahati: Spectrum Publications, 1980), 129.

family and in the community life hampers the smooth functioning of the family and society. Therefore, whether or not the lack of family communication has an impact on the Naga family system is one of the correlates under consideration.

2.2. Impact of Mass Media

Mass media has brought a lot of insights in today's learning process and it has transformed the entire universe into a global village.[5] However, mass media continues to cause a threat to the virtues of the family system, as it promotes the liberal and globalised lifestyle and projects traditional virtues, values and practices as local, unfashionable and outdated, particularly among the youngsters. Therefore, whether or not mass media has an impact on the Naga family is one of the correlates under consideration.

2.3. Religious Adherence

By nature Nagas were very religious; this was manifested by series of rituals and sacrifices, both in the traditional primal religion and even after embracing Christianity.[6] "Yet there are many factors that have contributed to the neglect or disappearance of people's spirituality among the tribals."[7] To Nagas there was no difference between secular and sacred; every activity of their life was governed by religion.[8] However, with the current trends it is rather difficult to comment whether or not there is the same intensity in the Nagas religiosity. Therefore, whether or not religious adherence or lack of it has an impact on the Naga family system is one of the correlates under consideration.

2.4. Educational Level

Education has played a vital role in liberating people from many superstitious beliefs and practices. With Education also came enlightenment and knowledge and other social and economic developments. In terms of percentage, presently Naga women may be the highest contingent pursuing theological training in India. Still, having a large number of female going to theological studies and earning higher degrees do not solve the problem of women's issues.[9] According to Limatula Longkumer "The task of education is to remove the oppressive structures of the

5 Shimreingam Shimray, "Globalisation Process and Tribal People," in *Tribal Women and Gobalisation*, (Jorhat: Tribal Women Study Centre, 2008), 110.

6 Ezamo Murry, "Justice Motifs in Kyong Folklore: A Cry for and Community for a Community of Inclusion and Equity," in *Garnering Tribal Resources for Doing Tribal Christian Theology*, edited by Razouselie Lasetso, (Jorhat: ETC Programme Coordination, 2008), 154.

7 Wati Longchar, "The Continuity of Indigenous People in Today's World," in *Garnering Tribal Resources for Doing Tribal Christain Theology*, edited by Razouselie Lasetso, (Jorhat: ETC Programme Coordination, 2008), 32.

8 Thong, *Head Hunter Culture: Historic Culture of Nagas…*, 105.

9 Limatula Longkumer, "Naga Women in Theological Education: Problems and Perspectives," in *Side by Side: Naga Women Doing Theology in Search of Justice and Partnership*, edited

society in which humans are imprisoned and exploited."[10] In actuality, as stated by Limatula, education should help people toward broader perspective about life and liberate people from all forms of injustices, discrimination and suppression. Nonetheless, Naga educated unemployed and even among the educated employed are observed to be neglecting certain family values. This research will explore the level of education and its impact on the Naga families.

2.5. Place of Residence

In the recent years there has been a shift of the Naga population from villages to towns and cities particularly in search of better job and employment.[11] Predominantly, Naga community and family is a closely knitted society displaying caring, sharing, needs, and giving. In the Naga villages due to their closeness and openness to one another whatever is cooked in a particular family is known by the other families, even in the remote corner of the village.[12] However, as people shift from the village to towns and cities they tend to develop individualism and slowly disconnect from the closely knitted society.[13] It is presume that it contributes to the loss of family close ties and other important family principles. This study examines how much the change of residence impact family relationship.

2.6. Gender Difference

Justice was a dynamic force for the co-existence of the tribal community.[14] But today, there seems to be enormous difference and gender and justice considering the number of Naga women coming for theological education and the ratio of Naga women taking up various responsibilities in the theological educations, Christian organizations, church ministries, and other secular jobs, it may appear on the surface level that Naga society is very inclusive. Naga women may be enjoying better social status and higher position in certain areas of life, comparing to most women in Indian society. Nevertheless, there are certain areas where clear division between the role of men and women still prevails in the Naga society. This study, therefore examines whether gender difference has any impact on the Naga family system.

---

by Limatula Longkumer and Talijungla Longkumer, (Jorhat: CCA-EGY/Naga Women Theological Forum, 2004), 16-17.

10 Limatula Longkumer, *Christian Education for Transformation: Foundations, Approaches and Effective Teaching*, (Kolkata: Limatula Longkumer, 2017), 7.

11 Boholi Sema, *Parent-Children Relationship among the Naga Society towards Family Enrichment*, (Dimapur: Shikhu Scholastic Press, 2012), 9.

12 Sema, *Parent-Children Relationship among the Naga Society towards Family Enrichment*..., 9

13 Sema, *Parent-Children Relationship among the Naga Society towards Family Enrichment*..., 10.

14 Murry, "Justice Motifs in Kyong Folklore: A Cry for a Community of Inclusion and Equity," in *Garnering Tribal Resources for Doing Tribal Christian Theology*..., 145.

2.7. Income Level

Naga families were economically self-sufficient. Each family owned cultivable land, forest products like fruits, vegetables, and firewood were in abundance; as such people had plenty of food stuff. Each Naga family produced enough food grains to last for the whole year. Along with the economic prosperity of each family, there was also a good community distribution system by means of sharing their foodstuffs.[15] Moreover, there was hosting of 'feast of merit'[16] by well to do families, where rich people organised feast for the entire village population. As a result till today, there is no beggar among the Naga society. However, with the current trends of individualistic life-style and materialistic concept of life, there is an unhealthy competition. Therefore, distinct division between rich and poor, haves and have-nots is also observed among the Naga community in the recent years. As people began to gain money, power and value in their life on the basis of bank balance and wealth, family relationship and functions have been greatly affected.[17] This study investigates the level of income and economic position and its impact on the Naga family and family relationship.

2.8. *Morung* (male and female dormitory)

In the past, important characteristic of the Naga family life include, the constant training of the socio-religious and moral or ethical teachings, which were imparted through the *morung*[18] (male and female dormitory). *Morung* is a tribal Institution where all the unmarried men and women from the age group of 17 years sleep in their respective *morung*. In the *morung* they were imparted with socio-cultural, moral, religious, and cultural values and ethics. Besides they also learnt the art of weaving, cooking, handicraft, woodcarving and other necessary skills for meaningful and successful life in the community, where all the un-married young

---

15 Sema, *Parent-Children Relationship among the Naga Society towards Family Enrichment*..., 10.

16 The term *'Feast of Merit'* was introduced by anthropologists and sociologists who tried to bring out a true English equivalent of the Naga concept on the grand ceremonial feast given by the wealthy men in the village, for the acquisition of popularity and status in the community. Cf. Lovely Awomi James, *Tribal Theology: Reviewing the Naga Traditional Worldview*, (Delhi: Christian World Imprints, 2017), 58.

17 M. Horom, "Naga Religion: A Case Study" *Religion and Society of the North East India*, (New Delhi: Vikas Publishing House, 1980), 57.

18 One of the earliest definitions of the word *morung* is found in the writings of Edward Winter Clark, the first American Baptist Missionary to the Naga Hills. According to Clark, the word *murong* is derived from the Assamese word which means "a big tree drum." In the olden days it was the tradition for the Naga villages to keep a drum made of a big tree drum called log drum near the bachelor's dormitory. As the big tree drum was found in Naga villages near the bachelor's dormitory, the Assamese people called the dormitory itself *murong*. Cf. Esther Jish Rengma, *Rengma Morung System Towards Developing A Communitarian Society: An Analysis*, M.Phil Thesis, School of Social Sciences, Mahatma Gandhi University, Kottayam, Kerala, 2013.

people were taught in all important matters related to life.[19] Moreover, there were number of taboos that were observed in the life of the Nagas which were binding on socio-cultural and religious belief system. Such concept of taboo could be imparted to the present day Nagas towards meaningful living.

Hence, the researcher's intention is to address the issues like family communication, advocacy for gender equality, restore the practice of respect and care for the community, advocacy for communitarian life against individualism, and the role of family counselling in addressing these issues are the major focus of this research.

3. Importance of the Research

Family life in the contemporary society has been challenged and confronted by various issues. With the fast changing world, values are also challenged so much so that today's generations are confused about what would be good for the families. The decline of the age-old striking Naga family system in the contemporary Naga society has encouraged the researcher to critically study and analyze the concept of the Naga family system, so also to study the current issues that confront or hinder the healthy functioning of the Naga family.

The importance of this research is to investigate the impact of the select correlates such as Family Communication, Influence of Mass media, Religious adherence, Educational level, Place of Residence (Urban rural divide), Gender difference and Income level upon the Naga family system, with a view to recommend family counselling models to be practiced by pastors and trained counselors working with families, so that issues pertaining to the family is addressed and family life among the Nagas is strengthened. Thus, there is a need to understand the dynamics of family relationship, man-woman relationship, family ties, communitarian spirit, socio-cultural values, work ethics, and the Naga family system in order to reinstate and preserve the richness of the Naga family life.

The present study is undertaken with an aim to investigate the correlates of the family system in relation to family environment, religious adherence, media influence, levels of education, rural urban difference, levels of income, and gender difference. In order to accomplish this aim, the following specific objectives were framed.

1. To investigate the correlations between family system and family environment, media influence, and religious adherence.
2. To study the impact of socio-demographic variables on family system, such as level of education, rural-urban difference, and level of income, and gender difference.

19 Mar Pongener, *Murong Speaks: Cultural Values and Elements for Enrichment of Naga Christian Community*, (Mokokchung: TDCC, 2011), 15.

3. To identify counselling needs as emerging from the study.
4. To suggest relevant family counselling models.
5. To connect the families with the counsellor, church and family therapist for family enrichment programmes as an outcome of the research.

4. Hypotheses

In the light of the above discussion, the following hypotheses are proposed for the present study:

4.1. Major Hypotheses

1. There will be no significant Impact of Family Communication on family
2. There will be no significant Impact of Mass Media on the family
3. There will be no significant Impact of Religious Adherence on the family

4.2. Minor Hypotheses

1. There will be no significant Impact of the Level of Education on the family
2. There will be no significant Impact of Urban Rural difference on the family
3. There will be no significant Impact of the Levels of Income on the family
4. There will be no significant Impact of Gender Difference on the family

5. Scope of the Study

The study intends to highlight the family system of the Naga society with a focus to reinstate the richness and family heritage preserved over the centuries by means of practices and the legacies handed down to the present generation. The research adopted family therapy approach from pastoral perspective alongside the biblical and theological point of view. This would definitely facilitate the counselors to formulate specific models for helping the Naga families. This study is expected to bring into light the awareness among the churches in Nagaland regarding the way they need to care for the families. Above all, the prime focus is to help the family restore strong family system and healthy relationships to counteract any external and internal conflicts that hinder the smooth functioning of the family.

6. Limitations of the Study

The research work is a study on the impact of the selected correlates on the family system of the Naga families; however, to study the entire Naga society would be beyond the scope of this research work; therefore, Naga families living in the States of Manipur, Assam, Arunachal and other parts of the country and Myanmar are not included in this research work. Rather selected families from 16 major tribes living in the State of Nagaland were considered in this research.

Furthermore, the researcher acknowledges that this is not a longitudinal study. In longitudinal study an observational research method is employed in which data is gathered for the same subjects repeatedly over a period of time. Longitudinal research projects can extend over years or even decades. In a longitudinal cohort study, the same individuals are observed over the study period. However, in this research the literature related to the seven correlates namely; Family Communication, Mass media, Religious adherence, Educational level, Place of residence, Gender differences and the Levels of Income, that are considered to have direct or indirect impact on the Naga family were reviewed. Remarkable evidences exist with regard to their collective effects on family. In the light of these evidences, ideas were generated from the empirical and theoretical findings on these variables to construct the items for the scale. Further a pilot study was conducted along with validity and reliability test using standardized tool that has been developed in the field, then only scales was finalized.

To study the entire aspects of Naga family system would be an over-ambitious attempt. Therefore, the present study would be limited to the impact of the selected correlates.

7. Methodology in the Family Studies in Brief

7.1. Instruments

The following instruments were used for the present study:

1. Family Rating Scale
2. Media Influence Scale
3. Religious Adherence Scale

7.2. Procedures for Data Collections

The data for the present study was collected after conducting pilot study among hundred subjects. The pilot study was conducted with the help of the above tools. Then the reliability and validity of the tools were checked and finalized with necessary changes. The subjects for the study belonged to two districts (Kohima and Dimapur) of the state of Nagaland, India. The researcher personally interviewed the subjects and they personally filled up the instruments in the presence of the investigator. To some respondents the researcher had to explain the purpose of certain items. The respondents were by and large co-operative. Though the researcher met the respondents along with the church pastors, some of the respondents were bit reluctant to fill up the questionnaire. To such respondents the researcher had to give a detailed explanation about the purpose of the study and the necessity of the data collection. Most of the participants to the questionnaire in this research were interested to learn the reason for which the information was collected to address the family issues.

7.3. Statistical Techniques

This Empirical research was tested through statistical techniques: Analysis of quantitative data was done through different statistical methods. The tools of analysis such as Analysis of Variance (ANOVA), "t" test and Correlation coefficient test were used in this research.

7.3.1. Analysis of Variance

Analysis of Variance is a statistical tool used in the testing of the equality of variables of more than two categories. Since the present study considered six of the independent variables at a time to investigate their combined effects on the dependent variable (family life), this analysis of variance was employed.

7.3.2. 't' Test

't' Test is one of the statistical methods of testing the hypothesis about difference in mean, especially when it involves twine studies. In this research 't' test is used to compare the mean score of gender difference, urban & rural, high and low income group.

7.3.3. Pearson's 'r' Correlation Coefficient

The correlation between two variables reflects the degree to which the variables are related. The most common measure of correlation is the Pearson Product Moment Correlation (called Pearson's correlation in short). The partial correlation co-efficient test measures separately the relation between two variables in such a way that the effect of other related variables are eliminated. In other words, what will be done is a partial correlation analysis in the measuring of relationship between a dependent variable and a particular independent variable. In this study the Pearson's 'r' (correlation coefficient) method was adopted to see the relation between Naga family system and other independent variables.

8. Design and Sampling Procedures

8.1. Design

A quasi-experimental study was adopted in this present research. This design is useful in conducting studies in fixed or real life situations where researcher is not able to assign subjects randomly to experimental conditions or when the experiments cannot be manipulated collectively. This empirical research employed quantitative methods of data collection and its analysis. A structured questionnaire as primary tools was prepared comprising Naga Family System Scale, Media Influence Scale, Religious Adherence Scale, and the Socio-demographic Inventory on Education Level, Place of Residence, Gender Difference, Income Level, which was distributed to the families to collect data. A pilot study was conducted among 100 samples and then the tools were finalized. Reliability Test and Item analysis also was conducted to select the item for the tool.

The design of a study is ideally formulated to best suit the nature of the problem under investigation, objectives of the study, resources available, characteristics of the population, and need for precision and quality. The present study is to identify the specific correlates of Naga Family System. Those are: the correlation of Family Communication with Naga Family System; the Correlation of Media influence with Naga family system; the Correlation of Religious Impact with Naga family system, Along with this aim, certain specific objectives were also framed such as to find out, the difference between urban and rural families in their family system, The difference between the male and female in their attitude to family system, the difference between high and low level of income and their attitude to family and also to find out the difference between the high and low level of education and the opinion about the present family system.

8.2. Locale and Universe of the Study

The Locale of the present investigation is the State of Nagaland. The Universe is the 16 major tribes of Nagaland comprising 512 families from two districts (Kohima the capital of Nagaland and Dimapur the commercial city of the Naga).

8.3. Sample and Sampling Procedure

The researcher collected samples from 16 major Naga tribes from selected districts of Nagaland. A Stratified random sampling method was adopted for the data collection. The sample for the study consists of 512 families, (32 families each from 16 Naga tribes). The researcher also collected socio-demographic details of the Naga-families. Brief information about personal and socio-economic status as well as educational details was gathered to present the level of influence depending on their exposure to various means of media, lived experiences and other observable factors for better information on the families.

The sample consists of 512 Naga families in the two districts of Nagaland: Kohima and Dimapur. (In these two cities all the tribes live for employment, education, business, and other related affairs).

A stratified random sampling technique was adopted drawing a sample of 512 families from the two districts of Nagaland. A detail sampling procedure is presented in chapter four under methodological section.

8.4. Inclusion and Exclusion Criteria

8.4.1. Inclusion Criteria

1. Naga families settled in Nagaland since 1963
2. Naga families in which both the spouses are Nagas by birth
3. Naga families living within the present state of Nagaland
4. Naga Families with at least a child or more
5. Naga families who are Christians

8.4.2. Exclusion Criteria

1. Naga families who settled in Nagaland after 1963
2. Naga families in which either of the spouses are not Naga by birth
3. Naga families who live outside the present Nagaland state
4. Naga Families without issue (child)
5. Naga Families who are not Christians

9. Working Definition

Definitions of the important concepts considered in this study are presented below. The defined terms are: 1. The Naga Family System, 2. Correlates 3. Family Counselling Models, and 4. Pastoral Care and Counselling.

9.1. The Naga Family System: The term 'system' here refers to the structure, classification, or method of forming Naga families. In this research, the Naga family system refers to the close ties and relatedness, sense of belongingness in spite of separation from one's family members by marriage, fellow-feeling, attentiveness to members of the family, clan and the village, sacrificial spirit for the sake of common welfare, "me first" when it comes to work and "you first" when it comes to food or other such privileges and benefits etc., are some of the variables studied in this research.

9.2. Correlates: The etymology of correlate is correlation or correlative (a mutual relation between two or more things/interdependence of variable quantities).[20] In this study correlates refers to the variables that are considered to have direct or indirect impact on the Naga family, that includes the variables such as, Family Communication, Mass media, Religious adherence, Educational level, Place of residence (Urban and rural), Gender differences and the Levels of Income.

9.3. Family Counselling Models: In this study, family counselling models refer to the various models of counselling employed in the family counselling. An attempt has been made to suggest some family counselling models in the context of the challenging times for family life today.

9.4. Pastoral Care and Counselling: Originally the word "care" is derived from Latin *cura* which means to "care," it also includes the notion of healing.[21] Pastoral care is a process of emotional, spiritual and psychological support extended to people in their pain, loss, brokenness, anxiety and also in their triumphs, joys and victories by the trained pastoral counsellors. Pastoral counselling is the practice

---

20 www.finedictionary.com/correlation.hmtl define correlation as a statistic representation how closely two variables co-vary; it can vary from-1 (perfect negative correlation) through 0 (no correlation) to 1 (prefect positive correlation) "what is the correlation between those two variables?"

21 Howard J. Clinebell, *Basic Types of Pastoral Care and Counselling*, (London Press: SCM Press, Limited, 1984), 27.

of helping the individuals, couples, and families to increase their understanding of emotional and religious conflicts and to help, resolve problems using religious and others important resources. Pastoral counsellors are called and entrusted by religious communities to help people to strengthen their faith in God, as they are trained to listen, respond emphatically, make assessments, and provide resources for people who seek their help. In this research pastoral care and counselling refers to the models and support system extended to families and individuals in various needs through pastoral ministry.

10. Structure of the Research

The composition of the present work comprises of eight chapters.

The First Chapter locates the context of the research under consideration. The rationale of the research is highlighted here, elaboration of the research, Importance of the research, methodology implemented by the researcher, and statistical tools along with procedure for data collection and definition of the key terms are presented in this chapter.

Chapter Two presents the theoretical framework of the research. This chapter looks into the varied details of the concept, characteristics and functions of the Naga concept of family system. The biological, psychological sociological and the relational aspects of the Naga family life has been dealt.

Chapter Three discusses the understanding of Marriage and Family life. It explored the various metaphors and expressions of marriage and family from the Biblical and theological perspectives. To make the study scientific and systematic the researcher has incorporated the Family System Theory. Moreover six major approaches to family therapy like: Structure Family Therapy, Strategic Family Therapy, The Behavioural Approach, the Psychodynamics Family Therapy, and the Family System Model have also been dealt in this chapter.

Chapter Four deals with concise review of each of the seven variables chosen for the research. It has been done to intensify the understanding of the subject matter. Variables like Family Environment, Religious Impact on Family, Media Impact on Family, Level of Education, Place of Residence, Level of Income and Gender Difference were selected for assessment. This chapter also reviewed related research to draw insights for the present work. Presents the methodology employed for the research, which include the design of the study, locale of the study and statistical techniques adopted for the analysis of the data.

Chapter Five presents the methodology employed for the research, which includes the design of the research, locale of the research and statistical techniques adopted for the analysis of the data collected from the extensive field research undertaken by the researcher.

Chapter Six is the empirical research. The analysis and interpretation of the data: which includes description of the plan of analysis (the crux of the research work) as this encompasses the details of the empirical studies done in this research.

Chapter Seven presents the summary of the findings. This chapter discusses the correlations between Communication and Family, Exposure to Media and Family, Religious Adherence and Family, Educational Level and Family, Place of Residence and Family, and Gender Difference and Family. A preventive measure for Family and Family Enrichment and basic skills for family counselling has also been identified. The researcher than discusses in details the strategies for counselling introducing relevant schools of Counselling, such as Bowen's Family System Counselling Model, Experiential Family Counselling Model, Strategic Family Counselling Model, and Structural Family Counselling Model. The strength and limitations of each of the school of family counselling is highlighted.

Chapter Eight which is the concluding chapter proposes New Family Counselling Models. The researcher has made an attempt to introduce several new family counselling models in the context, such as Effective Communication Counselling Model, Gender Sensitive Counselling Model, Individual Family Counselling Model, Family Networking Counselling Model, Couple Group Copunselling Model and Media Awareness Counselling Model. This chapter also made recommendations and suggestions for further research in the related field, summary and concluding remark of the research are also presented in this chapter.

Chapter 2

The Characteristics and Functions of the Family

1. Introduction

Family is one of the most important institution without which there is no human existence. It is the social system of primary relationship from which human derives their major sources of physical, psychological, emotional, and spiritual nurture. This chapter presents the theoretical framework of the research. It discusses the understanding of family, types of family, marriage and family counselling, goals of family counselling. It also deals with the characteristics and functions of the Naga family.

2. Definitions of Family

The word "Family" comes from the Latin word "Familia" meaning "Household" or Household servant", and Latin word *Famulus* which means "Servant." In Roman law *famulus* denotes the group of producers and slaves and other servants as well as members connected by common descent or marriage.[22] According to C. N. Shankar, "Family is a group of persons united by ties of marriage, blood or adoption constituting a single household interacting and intercommunicating with each other in their respective social roles as husband and wife, father and mother, son and daughter, brother and sister, creating a common culture."[23] Whereas, McGoldrick defines family as, ''the primary and the most powerful

22 Vidya Bhusan and D. R. Sachdeva, *An Introduction to Sociology* (Allahabad: Kitab Mahal, 2008), 291.

23 Shankar Rao, *Sociology: Principles of Sociology with An Introduction to Social Thought*, First ed, (New Delhi: S. Chand and Company, 2009), 349.

system to which a person ever belongs. In this framework family consist of the entire kinship network of at least three generations, as it currently exist and as it has evolved through time."[24]

Therefore, the family is the most vital and an indispensable of all social groupings, it is the important and chief group in the society, the simplest and the most elementary form of society. It is the first and the most immediate social environment to which a child encounters the world, because it is in the family that the child develops his/her basic attitudes and perceptions. There is no other factor that affects the lives of an individual in the society, touches them so intimately and continuously as family.

3. The Concept of Family

Family without question is the most important of any groups that human experience offers. Family plays a very important role in the holistic development of individuals and through them, transform the society. As a basic unit of the society it enables to realize the potential of the present generation, to nurture the new generation, and to give care and love to the older generation.[25] This involves the process of acquiring better education, keeping mental health, and achieving empowerment for all.[26] As rightly pointed out by Isaac, today's generation need to have a holistic view of family and at the same time need to have a long term vision about family. The clearer the vision one have for the family the better function can be experienced in the family life.

Family is a place where the members should have security, intimacy and freedom to be just themselves. There are lots of challenges and struggles in the external world and the individual has to get along in this complex world and know how to survive.[27] And each member is expected to contribute something that would sustain the family life.

God is the centre of life and everything should revolve around the divine will and plan. Therefore, life has meaning only in relation to God and life will be useful only in relation to one another. This is learned and practiced only in the family. A family that prays together stays together.[28] This view is also accepted by other religious groups other than Christianity. What contributes to the strength

24 Monica McGoldrick and Randy Gerson, *Genograms in Family*: Assessment (New York: W.W. Norton and Company, 1985), 5.

25 L. Sahayaraj, *Marriage and Family in the Plan of God: Reflections of Saint John Paul II,* (New Delhi: Christian World Imprints, 2014.), 178.

26 Isaac Mar Philoxenos, "Forward" in *Christian Family in Transition: Continuity and Discontinuity,* edited by Koshy P. Varughese, (Faridabad: Dharma Jyoti Vidya Peeth, 2012), 7.

27 Cf. Jesudason Jeyaray, *Marriage, Family and Church: Holistic Child Development* vol. 2, (Delhi: ISPCK/Christian Forum for Child Development, 2014), 7.

28 Isaac Mar Philoxenos, *Family God's Design and Destiny,* edited by K. V. Simon, (Hyderabad: Authentic Books 2009), 8.

of the family is the right relationship it holds with God and with one another. It is believed that common prayer shared by family is a fabric that binds them together.[29] The little importance given to spiritual discipline in the family will have a long-lasting impact on the life of everyone. In every religious tradition there is a belief that spiritual discipline and successful family life go hand in hand.

Family is the focus of the social, political, economic, emotional and religious spheres of lives. Families have always been the wellsprings of strength and stability to the society. It is the source of one's deepest joy. It is called by God, in unity, for a definite purpose – to glorify God. When home is ruled according to the Word of God, angels might be asked to stay within the family.[30] But, today many Christian homes have become an outpost of hell rather than a parcel of heaven, contrary to what God expected from Christian families. Family life has been disintegrated.

Never in the history of the church has such concerted efforts been exerted to save the family. In the postmodern society, to define family has become a difficult task.[31] Family has undergone dramatic transition over the centuries.[32] There is also deterioration of family values and human relationships. The individualism generated by the media world has corrosive effect on family life. People seem less willing to invest time, money and energy in keeping the family strong. People have become more individualistic and selfish. Most families face overwhelming ambiguities which create stress and confusion. "The family is the basic building block of the society, if people don't preserve the family, society will crumble."[33] It is important that each member of the family contribute and participate in the functioning of the family. The secret of a good family life is to recognize that family is a divine agenda initiated and instituted by God.[34] Family seeds must be fertilized so that they may flourish and benefit everyone.

"Every human being is in some way connected to another person or persons. This is a necessary social reality, as well as theological truth, for being connected means being human, and being human means being part of a family."[35] Family is the very first cell in the social structure, the very first social bonding. Without

---

29 Paul W. Henshaw and Harold E. Weemhoff, *Worship in Our Family*, (Nashville, Tennessee: The Upper Room. 1981), 27.

30 Simon K. V., *Family God's Design and Destiny*, edited by K. V. Simon, (Hyderabad: Authentic Books 2009), 17.

31 B. Adam, "Families and Family Study in International Perspective," in *Journal of Marriage and Family*, 66: 2004, 1076-1088.

32 J. O. Balswick and J. K. Balswick, *Family in Pain: Working through the Hurts,* (Grand Rapids: Ravell, 1997). 197.

33 Simon K. V., *Family God's Design and Destiny…*, 19.

34 Jorge Maldonado, *Even in the Best of Families: The Family of Jesus and other Biblical Families Like Ours*, (Geneva/Switzerland: WCC Publications, 1997), 145.

35 R. S. Anderson and D. B. Guernsey, *On Being Family*, (Grand Rapid: Eerdmans Publisher, 1985), Preface.

family, there exist no children or human society of this nature. It is said, "As the families are, so be the humankind."[36] All human come from a family and it is the families that shape one's character, fulfills one's dream and needs are met. Family plays a very important role in the holistic development of individuals and through them the transformation of society.

Family provides the initial learning experiences that make one genuinely human, and moulds children into ideal people. Children grow in an atmosphere of security and affection, and material attributes replace true love and concerns of parents.[37] Home is the place where members in the family understand one another.

God has planned the human race with a mysterious chemistry which draws two strangers to each other, the fusion of temperaments and the fascinating biology necessary for building up a ome.[38] There is nothing on earth that can substitute the rich relationship which is nurtured inside the family.

Family is an institution that plays a major role in exerting influence in the attitude, personality and the behaviour of its members. Hence, the responsibility of the family in the context or environment for the growth and development of the members cannot be overlooked.[39] The family is conceptualized as a system of interconnected relationship whereby the quality of relationship between spouses is seen likely to the quality of care parents provides their offspring and vice-versa.[40] Racus Chasie analysis family as "Our existence commence in the family. The family is where life begins and love never ends. Families are the heart and soul of human society."[41] These relationships are special because they both form and express an individual's identity and character.

The family is a universal elements and the basic cell of human society, which represents many different forms according to period and culture.[42] The family is a group of persons united by the ties of marriage, blood or adoption, constituting a single household; interacting and intercommunicating with each other in their respective social positions of husband and wife, mother and father, son and daughter, brother and sister, and creating and maintaining the common culture. It is a group of community living together, sharing and having mutual understanding, love, care, respect, and creating and maintaining common

36 Simon, *Family God's Design and Destiny...*, 21.

37 Beulah Wood, *Building Stronger Families*, (Bangalore: SAIACS, 2005), 97.

38 Simon, *Family God's Design and Destiny...*, 17.

39 Stuart T. Hauser, *Adolescents and Their Families*, (New York: The Free Press, 1991), 17.

40 Deborah B. Jacobvitz, Nell F., Bush, "Reconstruction of Family Relationship: Parent-Child Alliances, Personal Distress, and Self Esteem," in *Development Psychology*, Vol. 32, No. 4. 1996, 732-743.

41 Rocus Chasie, "Significance of Family Catechesis Today," in *Kristu Jyoti: A Pastoral Theological Catechetical Journal*, 31, No. 1&2 (March & June), 1-6.

42 Anne Borrowdale, *Restructuring Family Values*, (London: SPCK, 1994), 27.

culture.[43] There are many types of families in modern society – traditional two-parent families, single-parent families, couples without children, three-generation families, gay family, etc.[44] Therefore, a subject on family studies must include the above mentioned groups of people, since today the concept of family has become very broad.

The family is a social structure, or system. "The term 'organism' connotes the biological core of the family, its qualities of living process and functional unity, and its natural life history. Whatever affects one part of the family organism automatically affects all parts, just as an infected, injured, or well-functioning hand influences the entire body."[45] It is one of the oldest primary social organizations, which keep on changing throughout the changing time and place. The family is the garden of human personality – the primary place where persons are formed, deformed, and transformed. Parents are the architects of family. Thus, a protestant ideal remains:

The family in its essence is the culmination of marriage between man and woman as marked by the birth (or adoption) of a child in covenant love. The bringing of children into the world and their socialization through highly personal love are the main functions of the family, the essential fruit of marriage, the seal of a couple's union, and the opportunity for profound moral growth through motherhood and fatherhood. The interweaving of this ideal form of the family over several generations creates the extended family with grandparents, whose unique teaching should always be valued and must be maintained.[46]

John Bowring said as cited by Chasie "A happy family is but an earlier heaven." Michael J. Fox said as quoted by Chasie "Family is not an important thing, it is everything." And Mother Teresa said, as cited by Chasie "What can you do to promote world peace? Go home and love your family." And it was Albert Einstein who said, as quoted by Chasie "Rejoice with your family in the beautiful land of life."[47] These are people who have a wonderful image of family, as they each visualize family in terms of an ideal family. It is noteworthy that many committed and devoted people continue to strive for preservation of family life against all the adversaries and challenges.

The family, as a social institution, is being challenged by several contemporary crises. All families have their own unique problems. Present day

---

43 B. C. Rai, *Sociological Foundation of Education*, (Lucknow: Prakashan Kendra, 1998), 185.

44 G., Mishra, G, "Reflection on Continuity and Changes in the Indian Family System," *Trends in Social Research,* 2 (1), 1995, 27-30.

45 Marie Mignon, Mascarenhas, *Family Life Education: Value Education*, (Bangalore: Centre for Research Education Service and Training for Family Life Promotion, 1993), 17.

46 Herbert Anderson, Don Browning, et al. eds. *The Family Handbook: The Family, Religion and Culture,* (Louseville, Kentucky: Westminster John Knox Press, 1998), 17.

47 Chasie, "Significance of Family Catechesis Today," in *Kristu Jyoti: A Pastoral Theological Catechetical Journal*...,1-16.

family is going through a period of transition from a conventional way of life to a techno-conscious way of life.[48] There is a trend towards removal from the family of the established functions of work, religious worship, the nursing of the sick, and education. It is necessary that we preserve some of those rich values and good practices, at the same time refine some of the oppressive and detrimental elements within the family functions, so that family environment is strengthened.

It is also observed that there is greater mobility of the family, the tendency to family breakdown, the rise in divorce, the change in sexual morality.[49] The instability of the family is characterized by downgrading of the authority of parents, a trend toward equalitarianism in the relation between male and female, with a relative decrease in the authority of the father; parental uncertainty on roles and responsibilities; decline in the importance of grandparents; and the irresponsibility of children. It seems that people are unsure of what their family stands for - its strivings, standards, and values. Mother, father, and children each perceives differently what the family is or ought to be.[50] Therefore, it is necessary that family should have its collective vision and common interest. So, that the beautiful family life experienced by members within the family and that blessing is shared with people in the neighbourhood and community.

Today family encompasses an increasing number of variants and the complexities in its nature and characteristics. Childless couples; one-parent families (where the parent is widowed, divorced, separated or singled); adoptive or fostered; reconstituted or blended families mixing children of the current and previous unions of the partners; homosexual couples and with children.[51] Therefore, there is an urgent need for pastoral care and counselling for the families in present day context, so that stronger family environment is recreated toward meaningful life.

4. Types of Families

There are many different types of families, each of which is equally viable as a supportive, caring unit.

4.1. Nuclear Family: Also called a conjugal family, this is the parents and their children living in the same residence or sharing the closest bonds. It is in contrast to a single-parent family, to the larger extended family, and to a family with

48 Joseph George, "The Changing Pattern of Family in India. Exploration in Postmodern Age," in *Ripples,* 1/1. (2008): 11.

49 David Searle, *Truth and Love in a Sexually Disordered World,* (Carlisle, Cumbria, UK: Paternoster Publishing, 1997). 97.

50 Jacob P. Thomas, "Stewardship in Family," in *Christian Family in Transition: Continuity and Discontinuity*, edited by Koshy P. Varughese, (Faridabad/Haryana: Dharma Joyti VidyaPeeth, 2012), 9.

51 Mari Davis, *Discovering What Works for Families*, (Melbourne: The Australian Institute of Family Studies, 1987), 151.

more than two parents. Nuclear families typically center on a married couple; the nuclear family may have any number of children. There are differences in definition among observers; some definitions allow only biological children that are full-blood siblings, but others allow for a stepparent and any mix of dependent children including stepchildren and adopted children; as well as the expansion to include same-sex couples.

4.2. Extended Family: This type of family includes all relatives in close proximity, such as grandparents, aunts, uncles, and cousins. In a family household that is extended, these relatives typically live together and all share daily household duties. This type of family is also called a joint family or multigenerational family depending on which members are included.

4.3. Complex Family: This type of extended family has three or more adults plus their children. This type of family may be formed through divorce and remarriage, or it may be formed through polygamy in societies where that practice is acceptable. Some families may be complex even without formal legal bonds between the adults.

4.4. Step Family: This is a family where the adults have divorced and remarried, bringing children from other unions together to form a new nuclear family. The children may come from several different parents or be on one or both sides of the new union.

5. Family as an Institution

The family as an institution is a universal phenomena. Men and women were created by God to become husband and wife and then parents. God in one personality is both paternal and maternal,[52] for he portrays both the fatherly and motherly qualities. It is God's will that man and woman not only to be companion but also to produce Godly children together. God commanded the people to cleave to each other and become one flesh through marital union. The physical resultant of becoming one flesh can correctly be seen in the offspring of this union. And so, family is seen not merely an invention of a society, but an institution founded by God. The family is God's agency for populating the earth with people who love God and be loved by Him.[53] It is to be formed exclusively through a loving and lifelong marriage covenant between a man a woman (Genesis 1:26-28; 2:18, 24). The Bible is filled with teaching on the family and stories that tell of the triumph and tragedy of families. Both the Old Testament and New Testament contain numerous reflections on the role of father and mother and children. God's special relationship with His people is intended to be carried out through families. The scripture is clear on the

52 P. D. Devananda and M. M. Thomas, *The Changing Pattern of Life in India*, (Bangalore: CISRS, 2007), 154-156.

53 Devananda and Thomas, *The Changing Pattern of Life in India*...,156.

message that individuals themselves and their families suffer when lives are not lived according to God's will.[54]

The family as an institution not only permits survivals but prepares children for life. It was not by accident that the book of Genesis starts with the family first and lays the foundation for the character and purpose of family through the families such as that of Adam, Abraham, Isaac, and Jacob.[55]

Through the prophets, the Lord has explained how father, mother, and children should behave and conduct and feel towards one another. Husband, wife and children need to learn what the Lord expects to do in order to fulfill the purpose as a family. God has ordered the family according to the principle of 'headship.' The husband is first and foremost called by God to love his wife.[56] The self-giving love of Christ for the church is the model that husband ought to emulate. The wife is called by God to love, respect, and be faithful to her husband.[57] As a wife and mother she is to be a role model of godliness and do her best to meet the needs of the family. She is to assist her husband in nurturing their children. Both the parents are called by God not only to meet the material and physical needs of their children but also to instruct children in the ways of God.[58] This will necessitate that parents discipline their children.[59]

6. Family Counselling

Family Counselling is an umbrella term for a number of therapeutic approaches all of which treat the family as a whole rather than singling out specific individuals for independent treatment.[60] According to Burke as cited by John Sommers-Flanagan and Rita Sommers-Flanagan "it is an artful application of scientifically derived psychological knowledge and techniques for the purpose of changing human behavior."[61] In simple words, family counselling can be understood as follow:

1. Family counselling is an effective way to help family members understand problems and make positive changes in their lives.

---

54 Devananda and Thomas, *The Changing Pattern of Life in India...*,157.

55 Kenneth Chafin, *Is There a Family in the House* (Minneapolis: World Wide Publications, 1978), 16.

56 Corinthians 11:3, Ephesians 5:25, 28-32, NRSV.

57 Ephesians 5:22-23, Titus 2;4-5 NRSV.

58 Deuteronomy 11: 18-21; Proverbs 22: 6, NRSV.

59 Larry Christenson, *The Christian Family* (Minneapolis: Bethany Fellowship, 1970), 18.

60 E. Beck-Gersheim, *Reinventing the Family: In Search of New Lifestyles,* (Malden, MA: Blackwell, 2002), 105.

61 John Sommers-Flanaga and Rita Sommers-Flanaga, *Counselling and Psychotherapy in Context and Practices: Skills, Strategies and Techniques*, (New York: Cambridge University Press, 2011), 199.

2. In Family counselling the whole family decides to work through their relationships to improve family communication.
3. The Family counselling looks at how to solve a problem or adjust to a new situation.
4. Family counselling also includes marital counselling with married couples according to the law of the land or married with religious ceremonies.
5. It may also include or to be followed by couple's therapy, which treat relationship issues.[62]

Therefore, family counselling takes into account a wide spectrum of couple's relationship, the art and sciences of human relationship and the role and responsibility of people within the parameter of the family.

Through marriage, we enter into family life. Marriage and family counselling are the two sides of a coin. Hence, a reference to family counselling would also address the issues of marriage. Marriage and family counselling includes; couple and family therapy, marriage and family therapy, family systems therapy, which is a branch of psychotherapy that has a comprehensive approach working with families and couples in intimate relationships; to maintain effective communication, resolves differences through open sharing, and foster change and improvement.[63]

Marriage and family counselling involves the entire members of the family with an aim to address the issues that exist within the family. God's purpose and desire for the family toward a healthy functioning family where everyone feels loved, nurtured[64] protected and cared for as the focal point. Norman Wright quoting Barton says, "family is an institution where one experience God's grace and it is the place where people find nurture, healing, and growing as person in their individuality and in their social relations with others and relationship with God."[65] Thus family is where each member shares their dreams and aspirations, their joys and sorrows, their frustrations and accomplishments, and their shame and delight.

Family being such multifaceted in nature, that an attempt to address the issues of family needs a systematic approach. It tends to view change in terms

---

62 P. Airhert and M. Berdroth, *Faith Traditions and the Family*, (Louisville: Westminster John Knox, 1996), 147-149.

63 Moslener, "Family Systems Theory," in *Baker Encyclopedia of Psychology and Counseling,* 144.

64 Adela Mero, "The Naga Home and Youth," *Doing Youth Ministry in a Naga Context*, edited by Soren Oestergaard and Adela Mero, (Dimapur/Nagaland: Project Nehemiah NBYF, 2002), 123.

65 H. Norman Wright, *The Premarital Counseling Handbook*, (Chigaco: Moody Press, 1992), 12, 79-90.

of the system of interaction between family members.[66] It emphasizes family relationships as an important factor in psychological health.

The different schools of family therapy have in common a belief that, regardless of whether the clients consider it an "individual' or "family" issue, involving families in solution often benefits clients. This involvement of families is commonly accomplished by their direct participation in the therapy session.[67] The skills of the family therapist thus include the ability to influence conversations in a way that catalyses the strengths, wisdom, and support of the wider system.

In the fields' early years, many clinicians defined family in a narrow, traditional manner usually including parents and children. As the field has evolved, the concept of the family is more supportive, long-term roles and relationships between people who may or may not be related by blood or marriage. The conceptual frameworks developed by family therapists, especially those of family system theorists, have been applied to a wide range of human behaviour, including organizational dynamics and study of greatness.[68] Consequently, today family studies have become an interdisciplinary approach encompassing a wide range of field.

7. Goals of Family Counselling

Each marriage and family therapist has his/her specific goals and objectives. But they all work toward leading and guiding the family for a healthy functioning and better relationship. Family counselling sessions are mainly for helping family members to work with their intellectual, relational, economic, social, religious, and communication issues that bother them and hamper family wellbeing. In individual family counselling only one member of the couple comes in for counselling, hoping to find healthier ways to cope. Joseph George in the book "A Study Book on Counselling" edited by George Varghese delineates helpful and insightful objectives of family counselling. The specific objectives of family counselling are listed below:

1. To help family members learn and emotionally appreciate the strengths of their family system and encourage them to work with their limitations in order to facilitate family experience.
2. To help family become aware that if one member of the family has problem, these may be the effect of one or more other members in the family whose perceptions, perspectives, expectations, demands, communication, and emotional attachment that have played negative dynamics impacting the person.

66 Chadha Neerja, Girishwar Misra, and Ratra Amiteshwar, eds, *Counselling and Family Therapy: Basic Concepts and Theoretical Perspectives*, (New Delhi: IGNUO, 2011), 8.

67 Misra, Girishwar, Neerja Chadha, and Ratra Amiteshwa, eds, *Counselling and Family Therapy: Applied Aspects*, (New Delhi: IGNUO, 2011), 9.

68 Misra Girishwar, at el., eds, *Counselling and Family Therapy: Applied Aspects,* 11.

3. To provide a context where family members may reach a state of homeostatic balance which leads to further growth and enrichment of each one involved in the process.
4. To create awareness about individual behaviors, particularly those behaviours that disturb family interaction.
5. To create a relational context where family members can engage in mutual interaction where the relational anxiety is in control.
6. To provide where family members may be encouraged to discuss, identify, and to appreciate the positives roles the members play in the family system.
7. To increase sensitivity, empathy and tolerance within the family which helps to decrease emotionally charged reactions with one another.
8. To increase tolerance in the family experience when they encounter loss, failures, unexpected reactions and behaviours.
9. To increase motivation among the family members to encourage support, and enhance self-esteem and confidence in each other, enabling them for authentic life experiences within family and outside.
10. To work out realistic expectations in marriage and family within the framework of roles and responsibilities.
11. To help each one in the family to articulate and to express their anxieties, fears, and concerns, which have a direct or indirect impact on the family system.[69]

The above quoted objectives are important to help each one in the family to discern the need for acting with purpose and meaning, and to sustain everyone in the family for a fulfilling collective experience.

8. Characteristics of the Naga Family

The more the family is viewed as a universal phenomenon, the more general are its characteristics. Yet the Naga families are more highly conscious of certain typical characteristics. Few distinct characteristic features of Naga Families that are worth mentioning are briefly presented below:

8.1. Permanent Relationship between Husband and Wife

Husband and wife relationship in a family has varied degree of permanency in different cultures and different countries. It is the highest degree of permanency in the Naga context. Only under rarest of rare cases marriage is dissolved, but even in such circumstances it is the clan, relatives, or villagers who often intervene and

---

69 Joseph George, "Marriage and Family Counselling," in *A Study Book on Counselling*, edited by George Varghese, (Tiruvilla, Ammancherry, Kottayam: Christian Sahitya Samithi/TMA Institute of Counselling, 2012), 97-99.

patch up the separated couples.[70] So marriage is not easily dissolved among Naga families.

8.2. Attachment of Blood Relationship

Like the Israelites' concepts of blood, Nagas also regard blood relationship as a very serious issue. Attachment with the adopted children is legal where as with real (biological) child it is blood. Emotional attachment within the members of family is an achievement where as a blood relationship is an inheritance and a responsibility.[71] Each member either adopted or natural offspring is given equal status and rights in the family lineage and genealogy. It is due to this concept marriage within blood relatives is forbidden until the completion of the 7th generation.[72] Even after the completion of the seventh generation, blood relatives do not marry each other.

8.3. Financial Provisions

The typical character of Naga family is its economy. The father is generally considered to be responsible for financial support for all the members of family until each becomes self-earning and self sufficient no matter to whatever the age they may grow, unlike in the Western families where the period of dependency is not open ended. Till now in Naga families due to lack of avenues and opportunities for earning, most of the children depend on their parents financially even after graduation.[73] Nevertheless, there has been a concern raised in regard to improving the financial and economic status of the people in the state. As such gradually young people are taking up various jobs in the private sectors and firms in the region and beyond and they are contributing to the economic life of the family.

8.4. Nomenclature

Naga families have their own family name derived either from their ancestor or from the name of the place of ancestor or from the profession of ancestor (for instance warrior family, Kingship etc) or directly from the name of the father. All the members both male and female are identified with the family name.[74]

70 A. Nshonga, *Traditional Naga Village System and Its Transformation,* (New Delhi: Anshah Publishing House. 2009), 105.

71 J.P. Mills, *The Rengma Nagas,* (Guwahati: Spectrum Publications, 1980), 145.

72 Joseph S. Thong, *Head-Hunter Culture: Historic Culture of Nagas,* (Tseminyu, Nagaland: Khinyi Woch, 1997), 112.

73 Joseph S. Thong and Phanenmo Kath, *Glimpses of Naga Legacy and Culture,* (Kottayam: Society for Naga Welfare Society, Kerala, 2012), 171.

74 Thong, *Head-Hunter Culture: Historic Culture of Nagas...*, 117.

8.5. Permanency of Sexual Relationship

The Naga family rests on the permanency of sexual relationship exclusively between husband and wife. Anything other than this the family is at stake. The sex relationship is need based, situationally controlled and mutually respected, yet barred by family ties. It is taboo to ever imagine marrying one's blood relatives. Even same clan is not permitted to marry, because of fear of some misfortune coming to the family of violators.[75] To this day this practice is strictly maintained, as such when couple from same clan marries they are ex-communicated from the village and in most instances they are cut off from the family ties by their families.

8.6. Common Habitation

Whatever the type it may be, the members of the family live under one roof. Members leave the habitat on a purpose temporarily unless it is a split into nuclear family. Members are ever conscious of their original habitat. Every quarter of the habitat is commonly used by all members of the family.[76] But of late especially among the youngsters they prefer to have their own habitat for want of privacy, autonomy, and independent life.

8.7. Adoption of Culture

The Naga family has an inevitable character of culture adoption. When a family is shifted into the locality of new culture, the members very soon adopt the new culture of any number of times or any cultures. Thus the family has a tremendous capacity for cultural adoption.[77] Nevertheless, the first culture or the culture of origin is never forgotten. Especially the most important ones are preserved through oral tradition, telling of tales by older folks, or through narration and singing of folk songs.[78] Till today among the rural communities of the Naga society the older folks continue to narrate their stories and lived experiences of the people, especially those with cultural and moral values.

8.8. Corporate Belongingness

The materialistic possessions and property belong to all members of the family corporately among Naga society. Of course property right differs to the members after their age of maturity. This kind of corporate belongingness is the determinant factor that keeps the family as one unit. The split of family is the split of corporate belongingness of the possessions, either by an individual member's claim or

---

75 Kath, *Traditional Religious System of the Rengma Nagas...*, 91-92.

76 Nshonga, *Traditional Naga Village System and Its Transformation...*, 131-132.

77 Thong and Kath, *Glimpses of Naga Legacy and Culture...*, 188-189.

78 Carbo Richard. et.al. eds., *Retelling Naga Narratives: More Than Thrice-Told Tales*, (Dimapur: Heritage publishing House, 2014), Preface (xiii-viv).

voluntary disposition.[79] Despite of the growing individualism among the Naga society, corporate belongingness in terms of certain unmovable properties like, cultivable land, farm and ancestral house are owned by the clan members and family as a common property. This is done so that clan and family relationship is preserved.

9. The Functions of the Naga Family

Family is basically a functional whole, the relationship between members are constantly manifested in the forms of care and concern, right and responsibilities, love and affection and needs of mutual edification. To truly understand family life of the people, and to meaningfully minister to the family, we need a wholistic approach to family issues encompassing the biological, psychological, economic, religious, sociological, cultural, and recreational life of the people. Nagas are very diverse groups of people, each village and tribe have their own distinct characteristics; however, there are certain common characteristics that are common to most Nagas. Few of such may be categorized as below:

9.1. Biological Perspective

The family as far as resources are available takes care of the biological needs of its members. Naga families always ensure that every member's basic need is well taken care of. For which reason, it is a pride for the Nagas that there are no beggars among the community.[80] Within the clan members and community at large care for one another is an important aspect of the Naga society.

9.1.1. Reproduction

Nagas believe that married man is incomplete unless he has a son as family linage is counted through male child. In almost all societies of the world, a barren woman is the object of scorn and ridicule, though this concept is challenged by most educated people today. Vatsyayan a sociologist says that in some societies marriagibility is attributed only to a woman who gives evidence of her fertility by conceiving a child before marriage. Of course Nagas do not prescribe to such understanding.[81] However, reproduction is an essential function of the Naga family. Therefore, every married couple is expected to have a child. And when married couples are unable to have children, it brings disharmony and discord.

Today, with so many complications in human life, there are couples in the Naga society who do not have the privilege to nurture their biological child. However, they are not look down or mocked because of their plight. Rather those

79 Kath, *Traditional Religious System of the Rengma Nagas…*, 132., cf., Nshonga, *Traditional Naga Village System and Its Transformation,* 137.

80 Thong and Kath, *Glimpses of Naga Legacy and Culture…*, 98.

81 Thong, *Head-Hunter Culture: Historic Culture of Nagas...*, 118.

couples are encouraged and supported by their respective families and friends. Some of those couples also go for adoption.

9.1.2. Basic Needs of the Family

Foods, shelter, and clothing are the indispensible needs of human beings which are the basic responsibilities of the family. Means and methods of meeting these needs may differ from family to family and culture to culture. But lack of any of these is considered a disgrace by Naga society and may result in diffusion of the family. Begging is unknown to Naga society, therefore dignity of labour is always held at highest esteem.[82] However, today, worse than begging is forced taxation by various self interest groups, and this has made Naga society very unstable and unprogressive.

Commenting on the present scenario of the Naga society, Advocate Khekiye K. Sema Rtd. IAS, and the convener of Action Committee Against Unabated Taxation (ACUAT) in his Autobiography 'Encountering Life-Antics of a Govt. Servant,' stated that "Many sentiments will be hurt by the book," while highlighting how he has put out his honesty in the book "almost with vengeance." During his tenure as a government servant, he could not "open my mouth" about the frequent transfer and other practices that make life difficult within the Nagaland State bureaucracy and outside it. He was transferred 24 times in his 36 odd years in government service.[83] Such is the reality for the Naga society today.

9.1.3. Satisfaction of Sexual Needs

The fundamental functions of the family according to another sociologist Reed, is to regulate and gratify sexual needs. One of the four basic aims of Christian home according to the C.S.I. Prayer book is that wife and husband, that God sanctify and direct the natural instincts and affections created by Himself are redeemed in Christ.[84] The Nagas consider sexual relationship as sacred and limited purely within marriage bond. Sex outside marriage is treated with much severity, even termination of membership from the church. As such, husband and wife are expected to satisfy each other's need.[85] This aspect of marital life is given utmost importance, therefore even in a very busy world, after marriage newly married couple are given adequate time to discover each other and spend quality time together. In certain cases they are exempted from community service or other such compulsory responsibilities.

---

82 Thong and Kath, *Glimpses of Naga Legacy and Culture...*, 58.

83 Khekiye K. Sema, *Encountering Life-Antics of a Govt. Servant,* (Dimapur: Heritage Publishing House, 2015). 120.

84 Rao B. D., Prasada, "A Sociological Perspective of Indian Family," *NCCR* Vol. CVIV/01 (1994), 521-533.

85 Kath, *Traditional Religious System of the Rengma Nagas...*, 19-21.

9.2. Psychological Perspective

Contemporary Christian approaches to the study of family are honestly influenced by psychology. The discipline of psychology has established as its agenda the understanding and the growth of the individual as a person.[86] It has, as much as any other discipline, addressed itself to matters related to the family. When it comes to the study of the family from a Christian point of view, most contributors are either practicing psychologists, such a James Dobson 1974 and Bruce Narramore 1972, or they have been primarily influenced by psychology, as seems to be the case of Norman Wright 1982 and Jay Adams 1972. As a result of this influence, their works tend to display the form of psychology that is determinative for each: behaviourism for Dobson, psychoanalysis for Narramore, and reality therapy for both Wright and Adams.[87]

Here a particular concern of the Naga family that looks after the psychological aspects are briefly dealt with in the following points.

9.2.1. Personality Development

The family provides with the individual a special care of affection, sympathy, love, security, motivation, respect, recognition and so on towards the development of wholistic personality of children and towards the mutual satisfaction or conjugal companionship of parents. Naga parents as far as means are available, attend to the needs of the children and children in turn look after their aged parents.[88] This reciprocal care and nurturing of each other was a vital aspect of Naga family life, but today many younger generations do not care much for their aged parents. The youngsters leave the aged parents to a life of struggle and hardship. Many young couple among the Nagas is impatient to take care for their elderly parents and grandparents.

9.2.2. Protection and Care of the Young

The human child is the most helpless and weak being among all other being. Hence the family responsibility is so great that the helpless young child is nurtured and developed into a state of cosmic personality. Every Naga parents give utmost importance in the upbringing of their offspring.[89] Parents whose kids are wayward and errant are looked down by others; therefore, every Naga parents try their

86 S. D. Pearlman and P. R. Abraham, "Sexual Satisfaction among Married and Cohabiting Individual," In *Journal of Marriage and Family*, Vol. 32, 54-67.

87 R. S. Anderson, & D. B. Guernsey, *On Being Family*, (Grand Rapids, MI: Eerdmans, 1985), 4-5.

88 Esther Jish Rengma and Phanenmo Kath, *Fables, Folk Tales, and Folklores: Narrating Indigenous Tales of North East India,* (Mokokchung, Tribal Development and Communication Centre, 2017), 105. cf., Longchar, Imtijungla, Restore Our Family, (Dimapur: S. Wati Aier and Sons, 2006), 122.

89 Mero, "The Naga Home and Youth," *Doing Youth Ministry in a Naga Context,* 2002, 129-130.

utmost in nurturing their kids. Eventually as their children become responsible people, they would in return care for their aged parents.

9.3. Economic Perspective

Family is the center of economic activity. It is the families which utilize the production of society. Sometimes the whole family jointly pursues occupations like agriculture, trade, farming etc. Even otherwise the economic responsibility is equitably distributed among the members and each one of them is responsible for the growth and maintenance of family economy. The issue of women employment has changed. Now among the Naga society economy is a joint venture of all members in the family. Therefore following important principles are invariably part of family economy.

9.3.1. Division of Labour

Division of labour according to the status and role of the members is the main principle for the coordination of the family economy. The roles that the members play may interchange from family to family, yet a well compromised division of labour helps Naga families in many ways in its economy.[90] A sad reality is, this is a past glory, Nagas today are far from this noble practice.

9.3.2. Budgeting the Resources

Budgeting the resources is the second important principle in family economy. Planning and arranging the income from various resources for various needs of the family as a priority basis is an essential function. Budgeting the income, time, abilities, manpower, talents, resources and influences is the quality of a wholistic family. But in this particular issue Nagas are yet to master, as many families still survive on minimum income.[91] Many Naga families both in the rural and urban sector still find it difficult to meet the basic needs of the family, which is a great concern.

9.3.3. Organization and Care of Property

Organization and care of property in terms of up-keeping, maintenance and gearing the possession to income generating position is also one of the important responsibilities of the family. In recent times there is new trend among the Naga youngsters taking the key position of earning while entrusting the maintenance task to the older generation. This is truer in the field of trade. However, the economy of the family among the Naga family is a universal race in the present days of competition.

---

90 Thong, *Head-Hunter Culture: Historic Culture of Nagas…*, 141.

91 Thong, *Head-Hunter Culture: Historic Culture of Nagas…*, 145.

9.4. Sociological Perspective

Social interactionist (communicationist) perspectives on the family examine how family members and intimate couples interrelate and act together on a daily basis and arrive at collective understandings of their situations. Studies grounded in social communication give us a keen understanding of how and why families operate the way they do.

The family has always been a social institution. When it comes to the study of the family and the creation of models by which family can be understood, we believe that social sciences provide appropriate and beneficial tools for the understanding of the family as an institution and hence, an understanding of what the Bible tells us about the family.[92] Consequently, sociological perspectives on family help a person to be more inclusive and learn how to relate with people around him/her.

Naga Society is social and community oriented therefore they take keen interest in the social life of the community. Family is a basic unit of society. Whatever that happens in the society has its roots and effects corporately in all families of it. Few of the Social functions of the Naga family may be discussed here:

9.4.1. Maintenance of the Clan Status

To establish a status in the society the family determines the individual's mode of earning, wealth, education, service, or contribution. In Naga families the social status basically is determined by the clan system unlike other Indian society by caste system.[93] In spite of tremendous changes in the society the clan or tribal status remains indelible in the minds of the people.

9.4.2. Fostering the Socializing Process of the Family Members

The family is a powerful agent to socialize its members in terms of the form, pattern, cultural trends, values, and habits. Family as a whole reacts to any situation of non culture. In this respect the family as a web of relationships is a spirit that fosters the socializing process of the members.[94] Every occasion related to family, all the blood relatives of the family get together and socialize, and such events are very frequent.

9.4.3. Maintenance of the Social Norm

Family exercises another powerful role of social control over the individual. The prevalent moral norms are enforced upon the individual's conduct and thought process so that the order in the society may remain intact. The family is responsible

---

92 Anderson, & Guernsey D. B. *On Being Family...*, 6.

93 Thong and Kath, *Glimpses of Naga Legacy and Culture...*, 58.

94 Nshonga, *Traditional Naga Village System and Its Transformation...*, 145.

to check the primary stage of antisocial tendencies of individuals. Naga family in order to maintain its family legacy and heritage will make sure that every member behaves according to social norms.

9.4.4. Transmission of Social Heritage

It is family that accumulates and transmits the social heritage. As a result, the tradition, customs, beliefs, traits, ideals, and even negative aspects of superstition, social rigidity and so on are transmitted gradually and constantly from one generation to the next.[95] But, elders of the family always act as custodians of the family and pass on the family values to generations.

9.4.5. Choosing Life Partner

The family renders assistance to an individual in choosing a life partner. Although in the present day context, people have started preferring personal choice of life partner, the Naga family situation has yet to go a long way to facilitate this kind of personal bent.[96] Family always interferes and helps even though it might have started as a love marriage. Ultimately, it is the family that often gives the final decision.

9.5. Religious Perspective

The Naga family has predominantly a Christian culture, though till recent past almost all the Naga tribes were practicing primal religion. They were very religious by nature; this was manifested by series of rituals and rites. For instance, before clearing the jungle for their jhum cultivations, they minutely observe certain genna and rituals and only when there are good signs, then they go ahead with their cultivation. Today approximately 90% percent of Nagas professed Christianity.[97] The members of the family inherit the religion from generation to generation. The religion influences all the family functions. Family is the prime and the best teacher who teaches the religious values, importance of religious applications to life and an optimistic faith for a hopeful future of its members. In the traditional religion, it is the father who acts as family priest, similar to Israelites' practice. Every member is expected to participate in the family ritual as religious functions are considered utmost priority.

9.6. Cultural Perspective

Most literature dealing with the family at popular level is culturally encapsulated. As an institution, the family is the cradle of any culture. Thus, one's bias is established primarily through the influence of own family, which socializes its

95 Mero, "The Naga Home and Youth," *Doing Youth Ministry in a Naga Context*..., 19-21.

96 Kath, *Traditional Religious System of the Rengma Nagas*..., 187.

97 Takuyaba, "Witnessing the Truth in The Society" in V. K. Nuh ed. *Crusade on Naga Morality*, (Kohima: Research wing, CNBC, 1996), 34.

members into the specifics of its culture. This is particularly true with regard to the roles within the family, relationships and their nature, and the rules for those relationships.[98]

Family keeps the culture of society alive. It moulds its members according to social culture of the place. The children are educated in various aspects of socio-cultural norms from their infancy.[99] The family creates such an environment for them that they learn to live and behave in-accordance with the cultural traits, values systems, beliefs and traditions, which continue to influence one's perspective of life.

9.7. Recreational Perspective on Family

The family is the primary source for the recreation of its members. Round the year the Nagas observe various recreational activities for its members. The kinships, friends, neighbours are the primary groups which provides the atmosphere of recreation. The family gatherings, functions, guests, playmates, the halting utterances of children, preaching and scolding of elders and all such occasions and incident compound the family recreation. Since Naga community is comprised of many tribes and sub-tribes, Nagaland is also known as the land of festivals, from January till December one of the tribes or the other is engaged in recreational functions as part of celebrating their festival.[100] The grand recreational function is held every year in December hosted by the Government of Nagaland which is called the festival of Festivals or Hornbill festival, a weeklong celebration.

Thus, the Naga family is a functional whole involved in various moods of actions. These basic functions are common to almost all families irrespective of culture, community and even nation. The functions of the family may show different characters only when it differs in its form, and the seriousness of how each of those aspects are observed and practiced.

10. Conclusion

The fast changing trends in the social, cultural, economic, and psychological scenario pose a growing threat to the institution of family in India. Hence, there is an urgent need to strengthen families in India through equipping its members with right attitude, beliefs, and understanding regarding the significance of family life. This process has been termed family life enrichment. Family life enrichment aims at promoting quality life through responsible decision-making, and an improved understanding of family role, responsibilities dynamics and relationships. This way family life could be enhanced and be able to set family goals and improve family interactions in order to enhance the quality of family life.

---

98 Anderson, & Guernsey, *On Being Family...*, 7-8.

99 Thong, *Head-Hunter Culture: Historic Culture of Nagas...*, 151-152.

100 Thong and Kath, *Glimpses of Naga Legacy and Culture...*, 187.

The discussion in the chapter brought out an account of theoretical framework and background information of family and family environment. This will help to deal with the topic with all its inferences. The families in context has been comprehensively looked into and every details has been outlined so that the readers grasp

Chapter 3

Theological Understanding of Marriage and Family and Major Approaches to Family Therapy

1. Introduction

The family has always been a social institution. When it comes to the study of the family and creation of models by which the family can be understood, we believe that social sciences provide appropriate and beneficial tools for the understanding of the family as an institution and hence, an understanding of what the Bible tells us about the family. In this chapter an attempt has been made to explore the theological understanding of marriage and family. The author acknowledged the growing popularity of the field of psychology in the systematic study of marriage and family life. And since family is perceived as a social institution, it is worth exploring the family systems theory and the major approaches to family therapy. This chapter also highlights the challenges for family research and counselling in order to strengthen the quality of family.

2. Theology of Marriage and Family

Theological considerations play a major role in Christian understanding of family even though the institution of family is not intrinsically Christians and its presence throughout time and space has been recognized quite apart from any theological considerations.[101] The Bible has a very clear-eyed view of family. It presents that family as the basic institution of society, and yet at the same time it understands the problems of this very complex institution, as it encompasses every details of

101 J. O. Balswick and J. K. Balswick, "A Theological Basis for Family Relationships," in *Journal of Psychology and Christianity*, 6:3, 1987, 37-49.

human life. The stories of family life in the Bible highlight issues and questions that continue to concern us today.

The family in a nutshell can be viewed from four foundational perspectives, they are: The *physical* emphasizes the family as the ordained framework for the primarily procreative sexual intercourse (within the sacredness of husband–wife relationships). The *social* emphasizes the propagation and raising or nurturing of children and the mutual relations of the family members. The *spiritual* emphasizes the covenantal, sacramental, or providential characters of the family. The *personal* perspective emphasizes individual experience within institutional forms and the qualitative enrichment of that experience over time.[102]

Theological understanding of marriage and family life are distinguishable by the relative primary given one or more of these foundations. Such understanding cut across denominational and confessional line. It is not possible to highlight all the important theological foundations because the subject on family and marriage is very complex and vast. The following aspects delineate the theological foundations for marriage and family.

3. Biblical Reasons for Marriage and Family

Marriage is not human's idea, neither was it initiated by human. It was God himself who realized human's need for a companion and addressed it. To understand why God instituted marriage, we need to go to the Bible for the answers, as the Bible recorded details of God's people and their experience as families and society. Following are some of the reasons for marriage and family.

3.1. Completeness

God designed Eve to complete that which was lacking in Adam's life. Then the man [Adam] said, "This at last is bone of my bone and flesh of my flesh; this one shall be called Woman, for out of Man, this one was taken" (Genesis 2:23 NRSV). Through marriage the incompleteness was made complete, as man and women joined together as one.[103] The sense of completeness is seen in the very words of Adam.[104] As Adam and Eve complete each other, man and woman are to complete each other by joining together through marriage.[105] God saw the man He created was lonely and created another human (woman) to be his constant companion and partner.

---

102 Mathew Richard, *Study on Family Structure*, (Nashville: Abington Press, 1994), 408.

103 Jean Stapleton and Richard Bright, *Equal Marriage* (Philadelphia: Westminster Press, 1979), 186.

104 Bernard Gunther, *What to do Till the Messiah Comes* (New York: Collier Books, 1971), 114.

105 Robert L. Lessor, *Love, and Marriage and Trading Stamps*, (Chicago: Argus Communication, 1971), 198.

3.2. To be a Helper or Collaborator

I will make him a helper as his partner (Genesis 2:18b, NRSV). Ways the woman can help the man- by counsel, encouragement, comfort, by showing hospitality, by helping financially, socially, emotionally and intellectually.[106] The term helper here is to be understood in much deeper sense, more as complimentary to each other. Helper is someone who is in a position to help the one seeking for help.[107] Women are to play the role of regaining their husbands whenever he is in need of her help and guidance.

3.3. Companionship

The affection, love, and true companionship which grow out of oneness of spirit as each partner models Christ's unconditional love.[108] (Amos). Now concerning the matters about which you wrote. It is well for a man not to touch a woman and vice versa (other than one's married partner).[109] But because of temptation to immorality, each man should have his own wife and each woman her husband (1 Corinthians 7:1-2, NRSV). Paul advised that each man and women should marry so that sexual purity is maintained and people do not yield to the temptation of immorality.[110] True companionship as a result of marriage is to be shared between husband and wife, and this has biblical sanction.

3.4. To Have and to Raise Godly Children

And God blessed them, and God said to them, "Be fruitful and multiply, and fill the earth and subdue it..." (Genesis 1:28, NRSV). God's blessing for humanity is to increase in number and multiply.[111] More importantly God completely entrusted the human race to take responsibility of caring for the earth when he commanded human to subdue the earth.[112] So, that human race as they multiple and increases in number, they would continue to care for the earth.

---

106 Lana Packer, *Women Making a Difference in Marriage* (Nashville: Tennessee: Life way Press, 2003), 13-20 cf. David Searle, ed., *Truth and Love in a Sexually Disordered World,* (Carlisle, Cumbria, UK: Paternoster Publishing, 1997), 6-7, 72-74.

107 Letty M. Russell, *The Future of Partnership* (Philadelphia: Westminster Press, 1999), 115.

108 John Gagon, *Human Sexualities* (New York: Scott, Foresman & Co., 1977), 67.

109 Robert Leslie and Margaret G. Alter, *Sustaining Intimacy* (Nashville: Abington Press, 1999), 10.

110 Alex Comfort, *More Joy: A Companion to Joy of Sex* (New York: Crown, 1974), 37.

111 William H. Masters and Virginia A. Johnson, *The Pleasure Bond: A New Look at Sexuality and Commitment* (Boston: Little, Brown & Co., 1975), 110.

112 Herbert A. Otto, ed. *Marriage and Family Enrichment: New Perspective and Programs* (Nashville: Abington, Press), 113.

3.5. Enjoyment

The physical relationship is a reflection of the loyalty and affection shared among marriage partners who have become "one flesh" (Hebrews 13:4).[113] The principle behind enjoyment is self-control. "Marriage is honorable [precious] in all, and the bed [should be kept] undefiled: but whoremongers and adulterers God will judge."[114] Husband and wife are to satisfy each other and full sexual union is advised so that they can avoid sexual temptation outside of marriage.

3.6. Protection

A husband is to protect his wife by laying down his life for her. (See Ephesians 5:25.) A wife is to protect the interests of her home. (See Titus 2:4–5.) Parents are to protect their children to raise up a Godly seed. There is no better refuge and place of safety than that of home. Every members of the family feels completely safe and secure.

4. The Family as Institution and Relationship

The family is a social institution and a special relationship. As an institution it locates individuals in a network of responsibility and gives them a role in the transmission of culture. As a special relationship it is part of an individual's identity and character, which it both forms and expresses for the good or for bad.

The family as a social institution regulates lines of descent, property, and inheritance. It helps in the division of labour for daily living and supports the economic roles of its members.[115] It is heavily involved with the socialization of the next generation, a task it shares in an uneasy balance with other social institutions.

Family membership constitutes a special relationship unlike others formed in the public sphere, though it shares certain characteristics with friendship and commitment to a profession, belief, or cause.[116] These relationships are special because they both form and express an individual's identity and character.[117] It is in the family where true love is experienced as each member has the freedom and privileges to relate, express and communicate freely about their wishes and desires.

113 Masters and Johnson, *The Pleasure Bond: A New Look at Sexuality and Commitment...*, 112.

114 Robert F. Stahmann and William J. Heibert, eds. *Klemer's Counseling in Marital and Sexual Problems.* 2nd eds. (Baltimore: William and Wilkins, 2007), 16. Cf. Berl and Noam Chernick, *In Touch: Putting Sex Back Into Love and Marriage* (Toronto: Macmillan of Canada, 1977), 78.

115 J. S. Augustine, and Murmi, *The Indian Family in Transition*, (New Delhi: Vikas Publications, 1982), 116.

116 Michael Sadgrove, "Theological Images of Marriage" in *Rethinking Marriage: Public and Private Perspective*, edited by Christopher Clulow, (London: KARNAC BOOKS, 1993), 6.

117 Kenneth Chafin, *Is There a Family in the House* (Minneapolis: World Wide Publication, 1978), 16.

5. Family as Unity between Man and Woman

The Biblical stories of humanity's creation see the nuclear family as part of the very definition of humanity. In the first chapter of Genesis, when God creates humanity, "male and female God created them." (Gen 1:27). The essential, almost ontological nature of the male-female pair-bond is emphasized even more in the story of humanity in Genesis 2. Adam, the earthling, is created a single being from the clay of the earth. When God decides to create a companion for Adam, God creates additional creatures from the earth's clay. But, none of these turns out to be a suitable companion, and so God "splits the Adam," building a new creature.[118] When God brings her to Adam, he acknowledges her immediately as part of his very flesh. The narrator interrupts with an aside to the audience, to hammer home the message: "Therefore a man leaves his father and his mother and clings to his wife, and they become one flesh" (Gen 2:24, NRSV). There is no human life without family.

5.1. Family as Contract and Natural Union

This understanding depicts chiefly on the physical and social foundations for the family. It views the family as a social institution entered into by a private contract which may be blessed by the church.[119] It focuses on the establishment and dissolution of marriage bonds rather than on daily family life and it tends to use economic, legal, or socio-psychological language to articulate its perspectives.[120] In Christian theological perspective, family relationship particularly husband-wife union is considered as legal union which cannot be easily dissolved, unless it is separated by the death of one of the spouses God forbids the breaking of the contract.

5.2. Family and Marriage as a Covenant Relationship

The union between man and woman within the entirely new situations is inaugurated by the new covenant sealed in the name of Christ. It is also a covenantal union based on mutual trust and respect. In the Old Testament (Deut, 10:20; 11:22, Josh 22:5 etc), denoting the affection and loyalty with which the Israelites are to cleave to God, which signifies an exclusive relationship of the covenant partner (John, 2011, 55).[121] In the same manner the covenant of marriage and family relationship is also entered only by those ready to

118 James Casey, *The History of the Family*, (Oxford: Basil Blackwell, 1989), 100-101.

119 William J. Lederer and Don D. Jackson, *The Mirage and Marriages* (New York: W.W. Norton, 1968), 19.

120 Wayne E. Oates and Kirk H. Neeley, *Where to Go For Help*, (Philadelphia: Westminster Press, 1978), 98.

121 S. Barton, "Biblical Hermeneutics and the Family," in *The Family in Theological Perspectives*, S. Barton ed, (Edinburgh: T&T Clark, 1996), 3.

pledge their permanent fidelity to one another and to God as well.[122] From a covenant perspective, membership in the community is more communal than individualistic.

5.3. Family and Marriage Relationship as Sacramental

According to Catholics and Orthodox churches, marriage is the seventh sacrament and for the Christian couples the marriage union becomes a sacramental state.[123] Couples, who enter into marriage union, set out not only to become one flesh, but they consecrate themselves at the same time to fulfill as married couples. It is a very special and important mission of the church. So, the married Christian couples have to uphold and promote the values, by the manner of their lives and co-operation with other members of the church.

God in a unique way is the one who instituted marriage. God therefore primarily rules marriage; as such His authority over it is supreme. Marriage is a path to be travelled together. The truly married couple loves each other and belongs to each other as much as they belong to God and together obey His voice.[124] Marriage is a sacrament precisely because it is a sacred sign which brings grace and which is the image of the mystical union of Christ with the church.[125] Christian marriage is therefore a state of life, divinely established, with the express purpose of enabling those who embraces it to grow in holiness. It also offers countless of opportunities for the exercise of virtue in fulfilling God's purpose in human's life.

5.4. Family and Marriage Relationship as Mutual Sacrifice

Marriage and family relationship is a mutual sacrifice and self-giving love. The couple's relationship with Jesus Christ is reflected and actualized in their most intimate and profound relationship with one another. They are under the authority of one another, for in their own self-renunciation to the Lord, they both find their true centre not in their own self but in the other. That is possible only in and through their participation in the costly sacrifice of Jesus Christ who loved and gave his life for humanity.[126] If human relationship is strong and sacrificial, it only reflects the sacrifices made by someone who sacrificed even the last drop of His blood for the sake of humanity.

---

122 J. O. Balswick and J. K. Balswick, *A Model for Marriage: Covenant, Grace, Empowering, and Intimacy*, (Downers Grove, IL: InterVarsity, 2006), 17.

123 Santhosh, John, *Spirituality of Marriage*, (Delhi: ISCPK, 2011), 54.

124 Jessie Bernard, *The Future of Marriage*, (New York: Bantam Books, 2002), 89.

125 John, *Spirituality of Marriage...*, 55-56.

126 John, *Spirituality of Marriage...*, 56.

5.5. Family and Marriage Relationship as Lifelong Commitment

When two people marry they enter into an estate of marriage, which God has established. In Family marital relationship there is an essence of a divine joining together, which requires obedience to God and that the union remains life-long pledge.[127] When a man and woman come together in the union of marriage there should be undivided loyalty which constitutes the mutual commitment required of them by God. It is a commitment of life-long reciprocal faithfulness.

6. Families in Early Christianity

The lasting contributions of early Christianity to the Christian tradition of family have been significant and wide-reaching. A current understanding of family would conclude that not all of them have been helpful. Yet, the Bible and the legacy of early Christianity have provided the framework upon which the Christian's ideal of family have been constructed. The lasting contributions can be summarized in five points: Relativization of the demands of family of origin with regard to the demands of the gospel; Encouragement to harmony within the family through relationships of submission; Justification of the patriarchal ideal of family structure by the fatherhood of God; Imaging of family relationships after the analogy of theological relationships, thus enhancing the dignity of the family; and display of the variety and flexibility of family structures.[128]

First, One strong image of family that arises from the New Testament, in particular from Synoptic Gospels, is that the family of origin cannot be trusted to support one's call to discipleship, and in some cases can be definite obstacle. This attitude takes its cue from the attitude of Jesus himself in these Gospels, more strongly in Mark than in the others. Early in Mark, members of Jesus' family's answers rejects the exclusive claims of blood ties in favor of a widened understanding of family based on discipleship: "whoever does the will of God is my brother and sister and mother" (Mark 3:33-35; Matt. 12:46-50; Luke 8:19-21) though the remark is toned down some in Luke. Later sayings of Jesus about family include rejection of candidates for discipleship who do not love Jesus more than family members.[129]

The picture does not look promising for the family of disciples. But, the fact is that for the synoptic Jesus, many of his miracles restore family members to each other. At the same time there is solemn warning that all social ties, even the

---

127 Boab O. J., 'Marriage', *The Interpreter's Dictionary*, (New York: Abington Press, 1962), 283-285.

128 Casey, *The History of the Family*, 118-119. cf, Browning, Don, Bonnie Miller-Mclemore at, el., *From Culture Wars to Common Ground: Religion and the American Family Debate*, (Louisville: Westminster John Knox Press, 1997), 115-117.

129 Witte John Jr, *From Sacrament to Contract: Marriage, Religion and Law in the Western Tradition*, (Louisville: Westminster John Knox Press, 1997), 293. cf, James K., Farge, *Marriage, Family and Law in Medieval Europe*, Toronto/Buffalo: University of Toronto Press, 2010, 987.

most intimate ones, must be revitalised in the light of the demands of the gospel. A process begins here that will continue through the early tradition in different ways: family of origin though very important, takes second place to the family of the church. Family bonds are not abolished, but they are reshaped and widened.

Second, a somewhat different picture is presented by some other NT literature, and this is the second lasting contribution. The so called "household codes" of Colossians, Ephesians, and Peter encourage the kind of subordinate relationship that were a common features of Greco-Roman and Jewish family ideals: wives to husband, (adult) children to parents, and slaves to masters. The patriarch male husband, master, and father is idealized as a source of earthly authority in the name of God, just as he is representative of the power of the state in the conservative social philosophy of the time, in spite of ample evidence of women heads of households, women slaves owners, and adult children operating independently of their fathers.[130]

What is seldom realized by readers of those texts today is that in their own context, they also take a significant progressive step forward. Instead of addressing only the male authority figure as do other discussions of household management, the NT household code address both sides of the relationship, and the subordinate member first: wives, then husband; children, then parents, slaves, then masters (Eph. 5:22-6:9; Col. 3:18-41).[131] In doing so, they acknowledge both sides to uphold the quality of family life.

The third contribution, one that is being critically assessed today, is the pervasive symbolization of social under the image of fatherhood. Not only the NT household codes but the entire theological structure of Christian revelation casts the fatherhood of God as source of Trinity, creation, and our understanding of the role of Jesus. Especially the Gospel of John, with its strong casting of the God-Jesus relationship as Father-Son-and the later Trinitarian formulas based on it have made it next to impossible for Christian piety to imagine God any other way.[132]

The fixing of normative God-image had had its effects on the family. Mathew 23:9 ("Call no one on earth father because you have one Father in heaven") has been forgotten in favour of Ephesians 3:14-15 "I bent my knees before the Father after whom all family in heaven and on earth is named." The relativity of earthly patriarchal social structure intended by Mathew was soon displaced or perhaps never taken seriously in the first place, by a reinforcement of patriarchal authority in the name of the fatherhood of God. Yet while affirming

130 David Balch, *Let Wives Be Submissive: Domestic Code of 1 Peter,* (Atlanta: Scholars Press, 1983), 118. cf, James Casey, *The History of the Family,* (Oxford: Basil Blackwell, 1989), 121-122.

131 Balch, *Let Wives Be Submissive: Domestic Code of 1 Peter,* 117, cf, K. R. Bradley, *Discovering the Roman Family,* (New York: Oxford University Press, 1991), 178-180.

132 Ann Douglas, *The Feminization of American Culture,* (New York: Alfred A. Knopf, 1997), 212.

the legitimate rights and authority of fathers[133] we must cast a critical eye on human-divine analogy as it is used in this context as well as on the temptation to abuse power in God's name.

A fourth contribution is closely related to the previous one. While discussing the above contention, less helpful result of human-divine image, one must also acknowledge the helpful aspects of this kind of theological reflection. The imaging of family life and relationships after heavenly realities has also in many ways helped to enhance the dignity of family life and the dignity of human persons. The imaging of the fatherhood of God has served as a sobering reminder to human fathers of their solemn responsibility to mirror divine qualities.[134] The frequent casting of believers as children of God fosters not so much an unhealthy dependency as a loving trust and another reminder that the family is the domestic church, the microcosm and mirror of the whole church.

Finally, earthly Christianity witnesses to the many forms that family can take. While the popular image is the nuclear family, the ancient Christian family more often included a much larger group of people. "Family" normally meant not the nuclear blood family, though they may have lived together as a unit, but extended intergenerational network of relationships, as well as all those who shared one roof, whether related by blood or legal ties, as in the case of slaves, freedmen, and freedwomen. In other words, family was a fluid concept that embraced all kinds of living arrangements in many different kinds of household.[135] Soon in Christian thinking, because of some of the factors discussed above, family also took new meaning: the church assembly.

7. Families in New Testament (Living Real Life, and Experiencing Real Faith)

The Bible is replete with the images of family life. A few of the New Testament narratives carry details about family, but the majority of references to family, family members, and family life are just mere snippets. Mathew begins his gospel with extra ordinary account of the birth of Jesus to the family of Joseph and Mary.[136] Luke interweaves the account of the story of Mary with that of the priest Zachariah and his wife Elizabeth to whom John the Baptist was born.[137] Besides

---

133 Beryl Rawson, ed, *The Family in Ancient Rome: New Perspective*, (Ithaca/New York: Cornell University Press, 1986), 227. cf, James Casey, *The History of the Family*, (Oxford: Basil Blackwell, 1989), 125-126.

134 Suzanne Dixon, *The Roman Family*, (Baltimore: John Hopkins University Press, 1992), 120-121. cf., cf, James Casey, *The History of the Family*, (Oxford: Basil Blackwell, 1989), 127.

135 Margaret Bendroth, *Fundamentalism and Gender: 1875 to the Present*, (New Haven: Yale University Press, 1994), 295. cf., Dixon, *The Roman Family*, (Baltimore: John Hopkins University Press, 1992), 230-233.

136 Mathew 1-2, NRSV.

137 Luke 1-2, NRSV.

the two extensive accounts, other references are just fleeting clips of family. There is the account of Salome, the assertive and forceful mother of James and John, who wanted her two sons to be given the delight of place in the Kingdom of God.[138] This is the story of the father who came to Jesus with great anxiety to seek the help

Thus, the early Christianity shows us the many ways in which family was understood and lived. It teaches that the forms and concepts often considered essential by one age are really historically relative and that family will continue to evolve into new forms as the awareness of human needs and ability develops. Better understanding of the family life, forms, structures and functions of both Old Testament and New Testament, could thus enlighten the people, as to how to manage the family in the present context.

8. Family Systems Theory

There were various factors that influence the development of family system theory. However, in the late 1940s and early 1950s, there were three noticeable influences. First Bertalanffy,[139] a prominent biologist, applied laws pertaining to biological organisms, to many areas from human mind to the ecosphere in what he called general system theory. This theory concerned itself with understanding the structural and functional rules considered valid for describing all systems.[140] Although he had no protracted contact with the pioneers of family therapy, he anticipated many conceptual issues that later shaped family system and therapy.

Norbert Weiner, who recognized family interaction and self-regulation through communication and indispensable for the operation of systems made a significant second influence.[141] This process by which results of past performances are reinstated into the system, using self-corrective feedback to influence future behaviour, he labeled cybernetics. Bertanlanffy distinguished cybernetic from systems theory in that he considered it only one way to meet the needs of general system theory.[142] An anthropologist Gregory Bateson[143] had contact

138 Mathew 20:20-22.

139 Karl Ludwig von Bertalanffy, (September 1901-June 1972) was an Austrian Canadian biologist known as one of the founders of general systems theory.

140 R. W. Moslener, "Family Systems Theory," in *Baker Encyclopedia of Psychology and Counseling,* Second Edition. Edited by David G. Benner and Peter C. Hill, (Grand Rapid, Michigan: Baker Books, 1999), 442-444.

141 Mark Rivett, and Eddy, Street. *Family Therapy in Focus*, London/Thousand Oaks/New Delhi: SAGE Publications, 2003, 3. cf. Moslener, "Family Systems Theory," *Baker Encyclopedia of Psychology and Counseling.* 1999.

142 L. V. Bartanlanffy, *General System Theory*, (New York: Braziller, 1968), 102.

143 Gregory Batesone (9 May 1904-4 July 1980) was an English anthropologist, social scientist; linguist, visual anthropologist, semiotician, and cyberneticist who work intersected that of many other fields. In the 1940, he helped extend systems theory and cybernetics to the social and behavioral sciences. He spent the last decade of his life developing a "meta-science".

with cybernetics thinking during the 1960s and saw relevance in applying both general system theory and cybernetics to human interaction to better understand communication. He was attracted to the idea that one could account for both uniformity and variability of human behaviour by assuming they were rule-governed systems.[144] Bateson began a paradigm shift that moved away from focusing on the content of a relationship system to that pattern, process, and communication that explain and elucidated it.

The Polo Alto group was founded by Bateson to focus communication process. Joining him were Jay Haley[145] who continued his own study of communication in families,[146] and John Weakland, another anthropologist. The group noted that study could be divided between verbal and non verbal types. To understand the dynamics beyond internal and linear motivation, the team realized the communication in a family was part of a context or relational system.[147] Through group's work, the cybernetic concept of self-governance system became part of family system thinking.

The family system perspective hence helps each member to see in relation to the other. Ultimately a family system is the parts of the whole family plus the way members interact, process being the way the family system functions. The process in families or transactional patterns, are seen as central to shaping individual behaviour and personality. Family rules organize interaction and function to maintain a stable system by allowing and limiting member's behaviours.[148] These relationship rules provide expectations about roles, behaving, and consequences of family life.

9. Interconnected System Concepts

Family thinkers envision the family as an open system that functions in a broader socio-cultural context over life cycle. Components of family functioning include systemic patterns, communication and problem solving, lifecycle development, and belief system.

---

of epistemology to bring together the various early forms of systems theory developing in different fields of science. His writings include Steps to an Ecology of Mind (1972) and Mind and Nature (1979). Angel Fears (Published posthumously in 1987) was co-authored by his daughter Mary Catherine Bateson.

144 Rivett, and, Street. *Family Therapy in Focus…*, 3.

145 Jay Douglas Haley (July 19, 1923- February 13, 2007) was one of the founding figures of brief and family Therapy in general of the strategies model of psychotherapy, and he was one of the more accomplished teachers clinical supervisor and authors in these disciplines. www.jay-haley-on-therapy.com>html.

146 Rivett, and, Street. *Family Therapy in Focus…*, 4.

147 Moslener, "Family Systems Theory," in *Baker Encyclopedia of Psychology and Counseling,* 442.

148 Moslener, "Family Systems Theory," in *Baker Encyclopedia of Psychology and Counseling,* 442., cf. Anderson, R. S. & Guernsey, D. B., *On Being Family,* Grand Rapids, MI: Eerdmans, 1985.

Family is being viewed as a whole being greater than the sum of its part. Members are connected in such a way that a change in one person affects change in others, impacting the whole system so that causality is seen as circular rather than linear. Cause and affects do not provide adequate understanding of a system. Ongoing reciprocity in relationship develops into predictable and observable patterns. These patterns are influenced from within, where homeostasis (the balance of system) is maintained, as well as influenced from outside the system.[149] The family is required to be open to allow inputs from its environment and other ecosystem. Entropy is the lack of information or energy in family systems. In that a family must be open and closed at various times, it must have feedback to survive. Negative feedback loops are messages (verbal, nonverbal, and contextual) that the output by another has reached pre-determined levels and indicates needs to cut off or reduce inputs.[150] Positive feedback loops signal to allow more inputs into the system.

The ultimate goal of the family system is to maintain homeostasis over time requiring stability (morphostasis) and flexibility (morphogenesis). Systems thinker realize the family must maintain its own value and consistent behaviour while adapting to the family lifecycle developmental tasks; newly married, new born, school age, young adult , midlife, aging.[151] A system model of human development places the individual lifecycle in the context of human family and culture.

10. Major Approaches to Family Therapy

Even though various schools of family therapy have a theoretical commitment to working with the process of family interaction, they are distinguished by conceptual positions. The approaches can be divided problem-solving (structural, strategic, systematic, behavioural, solution-focused, psycho-educational or intergenerational approaches (Psychodynamics, Bowenian, experiential), which are more exploratory or growth oriented.[152] The following models are reviewed and recommended as they are found to be in concurrence and related to the problems indentified in the present study. It is expected that these family counselling models would be useful in guiding the families.

---

149 Steinglass P., "The Conceptualization of Marriage from a Systems Theory Perspetive," J. Paolino and B. S. McCrady, eds., in *Marriage and Family Therapy,* (1978), 97-99.

150 Allen E Ivey, Michael D' Andrea, et al., 5th ed, *Theories of Counseling and Psychotherapy: A Multicultural Perspective, (*Boston, MA: Allen & Bacon, A Pearson Education Company, 2002), 239.

151 John D. Antony, *Psychotheraphies in Counselling,* (Dindagul: Anugraha Insitute for Counselling, (2003) 2005), 17-18. cf, Moslener, "Family Systems Theory," in *Baker Encyclopedia of Psychology and Counseling,* 443.

152 Moslener, "Family Systems Theory," in *Baker Encyclopedia of Psychology and Counseling,* 442., cf. Michael P, Nichols, *The Essentials of Family Therapy,* 4th Edition, (Pearson Education: Boston, New York, San Francisco, 2009).

10.1. Structural Family Therapy: In 1974, Salvador Minuchin and his colleagues developed structural family therapy, at Philadelphia Child Guidance, emphasizes family organization for the functioning of the family system and the well being of its members. Problems are seen as imbalance in the family organization, especially in nuclear parent and child subsystem boundaries. The Symptoms commonly are found in dysfunctional patterns of transactions. The Goal of therapy is to recognize the family structure with more clear and flexible subsystem and boundaries and provide more adaptive coping so the symptom, which is often the presenting problem is, no longer needed.[153] This particular model is recommended in this research because it emphasizes better family organization for the functioning of the family system and the well being of its members with efficient adaptive coping mechanism in addressing problem confronting the family.

10.2. The Strategic Approach was developed by Haley and Madnese, while the Milan team Selvni-Palazzoli and others in 1978 developed the systemic model. The focus for both is the immediate social situation of the identified patient, and the therapy is limited to resolving the particular problem presented. The symptom is considered a communicative theory; the strategic therapist uses indirect influences, interruption of sequence and a more remote style that is highly intellectual. The Milan team utilizes circular questioning of members to tease out the problem, reframe it, and change the sequence of interaction. The most recent development in problem-solving is the solution-focused therapy by de-shaper in 1988; O'Hanlon and Weiner-Davis in 1989, in which the symptoms are ignored and treatment moves toward solution by focusing on exceptions times when the problem was not present and utilizing strengths of family members. Since one of the variables selected for investigation is on the quality of communication, this model would be effective in helping family members to be more effective in their communication; as a result it is expected to resolve family problems.

10.3. The Behavioural Approach resulted from behavioural modification and social learning theory in clinical psychology. It emphasizes family rules and communication process. Symptoms in this model are reinforced by the family, causing failures in relationships.[154] The therapist analyses communication process, both content and relational components, and build skills in negotiation and problem solving. In today context, there are certain elements of behaviour that need to be modified. Even in small family people are composed of various

---

153 Gerald Gorey, *Theory and Practice of Counselling and Psychotherapy*, (Singapore: Brooks/Cole, 1996), 292-392, cf. Michael P. Nichols, and Richard C. Shwartz, *Family Therapy Concepts and Methods*, (New Jersey: Allyn and Bacon, 1995), 257-260.

154 Weiss P. L., "The Conceptualization of Marriage from a Behavioural Perspective," in T. J. Paolino and B. S. McCrady, eds., *Marriage and Family Therapy,* (Louisville: Westminster John Knox Press, 1978), 172.

behaviours, therefore this particular model would be helpful in behavioural modification.

10.4. The Psycho-educational Model has been the most prominent family systems approach to chronic mental illness. Behavioural and structural family therapy elements are utilized while focusing on family education about the illness, offering concrete guidelines for crisis management, problem solving, and stress reduction.[155] The participating family members are involved as teammate in the healing process.

10.5. Psychodynamic Family Therapist relates symptoms to share family projections arising from past unresolved conflicts or losses in the family of origin. A symptomatic member may be a scapegoat as a result. Extended family members may be invited to sessions, or individuals may work at changing relationships outside the sessions. Resolution results in eliminating projection, relationship reconstruction and reunion, and individual and family growth.

10.6. The Family Systems Model was created by Murray Bowen. He believed impaired functional results from poorly differentiated patterns among family members who carry high anxiety and emotional reactivity.[156] The goal of treatment is a process whereby clients are coached to change relationships within their family of origin in order to achieve a higher level of differentiated (increased freedom from emotional family reactivity) and reduced anxiety within the family.[157] Since the present study is on the Naga family system, it is expected that Bowen's family systems model which aimed at changing the relationship within the family would bring positive changes.

10.6.1. The Strength and Limitation

What make the Bowen's theory useful is that it describes and explains the emotional forces within people and how one relate to others. The single greatest impediment to understanding one another is ones tendency to become emotionally reactive and respond defensively instead of listening each other. Like all things about relationships, this emotionality is a two-way street. Some speakers express themselves with such emotional pressure that listeners inevitably react to that pressure rather than hearing what speaker is trying to say. Bowenian theory describe this reactivity, locate its origins in the lack of differentiation of self, and explains how to reduce emotionalism and move toward mature self control-by

155 Moslener, "Family Systems Theory," in *Baker Encyclopedia of Psychology and Counseling...*, 443.

156 Johnson S, and J. Lebow, "The cultural context model: Therapy for couples with approach to single-system evaluation," in *Marital and Family Therapy*, Vol. 26, No. 1, (2000), 23-38.

157 Edward Beal, *Expanding the Horizons for Bowen Family Systems Theory*, (New York: Print. Well, 1996), 197. cf. Nichols P. Michael and Richard C. Schwartz, Family Therapy: Concepts and Methods, (New Jersey: Allyn and Bacon, 1995), 144.

cultivating relationship widely in the family and learn to listen without becoming defensive to one's own beliefs.

The major shortcoming of the Bowenian approach is that in concentrating on individual and their extended family relationship, it neglects the power of working directly with the nuclear family. In many cases the most direct way to resolve family problems in to bring.

10.7. Experiential Family Therapy was developed by Virginia Satir, Carl Whitaker Neill and Knisken. Satir combined communication theory with a humanistic frame of reference, while Whitaker called his model symbolic-experiential family therapy. For both, current problems are viewed as a natural result of life experiences. The general goal of treatment is to achieve a fuller awareness and appreciation of self as family members are guided to communicate feelings and differences. Treatment, therefore, focuses on the here and now, and spontaneity is encouraged. This particular therapy is recommended in this research because this model emphasis on the life experiences of the members in the family and encourages them for better communication, which is a vital factor in family relationship. Moreover, the concept of the guiding the person from their frame of reference which is a major focus of this model would be an important tool in guiding the family.

Family system theory has sought to understand each individual in the context of family as much as it is concerned with family as a whole. It is concerned not only with the identity of an individual but also with how one belongs within the family system. This belonging has been understood both from a system perspective and also theological perspective. Anderson and Guernsey have combined both perspective, utilizing a systems orientation and the concept of covenant. Belonging is not simply a matter of choice but a God-given assumption that is affirmed to members in a family over time. The rational system of family members is the subject of both family systems and theology.[158] As much as biblical concept of covenant explains why we belong in families, a family systems approach provides the framework through which we better understand how we belong to the beautiful concept of family.

10.8. Challenges for Family Research and Counselling to Strengthen Family Life

The rise in the number of single parent household, break-down of traditional joint family system, increase in cases of divorce, individual male migration to cities for work, erosion of authority of patriarch, the attrition of traditional family values, increase in the number of working mothers in cities and single parents, rise in domestic violence and practices of dowry, neglect of children and elderly,

158 Moslener, "Family Systems Theory," in *Baker Encyclopedia of Psychology and Counseling,* 444. Cf., Michael, P Nichols, *Inside Family Therapy, (Boston: Allyn and Bacon,* 1999), 120.

and poor regard for family laws,[159] are enough indications of the danger that the family and ultimately society are increasingly facing in India today.

To combat the continuing erosion of values and the institution of family, there is urgency in setting a systematic school of family therapy and family research, and consistent policies to strengthen the Indian family system. Otherwise, India would be left with no choice, but to face the same problems which are generally faced by many families of developed countries now.[160] To be more specific, the family needs such as: an increased support in the areas of child care, systematic family counselling, social services, income assistance and health services are felt much more than ever before.

It is however recognized that the formulation of a comprehensive single policy given the large size and heterogeneity of society like that of India is quite difficult and burdensome task. At the same time it is also recognized that the formulation of new norms for a desired type of family system based on modern values is perhaps loaded with serious problems of various kinds.[161] The state may not have the required political will to do so for some political expediency or mileage, however, various organizations could collectively address it.

In India laws are not strictly enforced, law does not always prove to be so effective and hence, it may be difficult to regulate the Indian family system through a formal public policy. Increasing state intervention in an informal organization like family may be disgusting to many and it could be counterproductive as well.[162] It is nevertheless, not argued that the development of a national family policy would be an exercise in futility.

In fact, in view of problems of various kinds and possible challenges of future there is a need of Family Policy Council, added with Family research and family therapy system, in each state of India to conduct policy analysis, promote intergenerational solidarity, facilitate strategic leadership involvement and influence public opinion. It should be an autonomous entity but having link to various likeminded institution and organization for an effective result in keeping Indian family; helping family in responsible parenthood, serving as a voice for the

---

159 J. K. Baral, and A. P. Bishoyee, "Family in Transition: Some Theoretical and Methodological Questions," in J. K. Baral and A. Chowdhury (eds), *Family in Transition: Power and Development*, (New Delhi: Northern Book Centre, 1999), 21-25.

160 Jacob Cherian, "Marital Relationship in the Context of Family of Origin Issues," in *Christian Family in Transition: Continuity and Discontinuity*, edited by Koshy P. Varughese, (Faridabad/Haryana: Dharma JoytiVidya Peeth, 2012), 56-74.

161 Aparajita Chowdhury, David K. Carson et. al, eds., *Family Life Education in India: Perspective, Challenges, and Applications*, Edited by Chowdhury Aparajita, David K. Carson et. al, (Jiapur/New Delhi/Bangalore/Mumbai: Rawat Publications, 2006), 54.

162 S. Bharat, "Family Socialization of the India Child," in *Trends in Social Science Research*, Vol.4, No.1, June, (1991), 106-110.

family and assisting advocates for family ideals who aim to recapture the moral and intellectual high ground in the public arena.[163]

It is recognized that under the prevailing circumstances, the institutions, church and civil society can play a vital and effective role. In any case, because of rising individualism, competiveness and openness in society and ever-increasing aspirations for higher attainments in life coupled with greater autonomy of individuals in society, an ideal family life may be a distant dream. Wittingly or unwittingly the people should by and large remain prepared to pay the likely prices of modern or post-modern way of life. Traditionalism is no answer, either.[164] In such a context it has become an imperative to seriously consider a family research and family therapy, to provide a lasting impact on the life of the Indian family.

As stated by Jacob Cherian "The need for developing indigenous, culturally appropriate measures should be a concern..., as Indian church has entered into new millennium, the scientific and theologically oriented family researches and model of interventions addressing the family issues are vital. Further we are to have a gospel critique of Indian family,"[165] to address the crucial problems related to social issues such as poverty, dowry, domestic violence, and various kinds of abuse in the context of the family.

11. Conclusion

This chapter encapsulates the theological foundation of marriage and family. Various expressions and perception about marriage and family life has been explored and discussed here. The chapter also highlighted the major approaches in family therapy. A comprehensive outlook and understanding of family life is expected in order the help the families to function smoothly.

163 Chowdhury, David K. Carson et. al, eds., *Family Life Education in India: Perspective, Challenges, and Applications...*, 55.

164 Kenilo Kath, *Traditional Religious System of the Rengma Nagas,* (Kolkata: Anshah Publications, 2005), 13-37.

165 Cherian, "Marital Relationship in the Context of Family of Origin Issues," in *Christian Family in Transition: Continuity and Discontinuity*, 56-61.

Chapter 4

Impact of Select Collelates on Naga Families

1. Introduction

Though there has been extensive research on family related issues in the west as well as in the Asian context, there has not been much research undertaken on the impact of certain correlates on family. As such this chapter aims to review the available literature related to the concept of family studies in relations to, a) Naga family system b) Family Environment, c) Media Impact, d) Religious Adherence, and e) socio-demographic variables (Educational level, Place of residence, Gender differences and the Levels of Income on the family life. This is to ascertain the impact of the select correlates on the family life, in order to establish the magnitude of their impact on family life.

2. Naga Family System

The term 'system' here refers to the structure, classification, or method of forming Naga families. In this section an attempt is made to present the Naga family structure or system that is followed in Naga society. The foundation of family is the oldest human institution and the most fundamental, and without hesitation the first social unit. Thong and Kath asserts that, Among the Naga tribes it has been observed that the unit in the family tie is an important integration factor. In the past, the Nagas unlike some other tribes do not migrate from one place to another, other than the call of duty, job or other such responsibilities.[166]

166 Joseph S. Thong, and Phanenmo Kath, *Glimpses of Naga Legacy and Culture*, (Kottayam: Society for Naga Welfare Society, Kerala, 2012), 171.

Thong and Kath commenting on the Naga preference for settlement, inheritance, marriage, responsibilities in the social, and religious life, claimed that:

The Nagas are, in fact, known to love permanent dwelling and one wonders as to the way in which they lived in the days gone by. Unfortunately there are not many written chronicles on the Naga ways of living and yet there are enough reasons to believe that, tremendous change has undergone with regard to family system, values, ethos, and practices. The traditional Naga family system followed nuclear and exogamous. It is composed of father, mother, and little children living in the same house. The grown up sons and daughters sleep in the clan/khel bachelors' dormitory or the girls' dormitory but share the same food, meat and rice-beer with the parents in the morning and evening. Such practices are almost forgotten, nonetheless, in the form of community feast or feast of merit which is till today practiced among the several tribes like Rengmas, Sumis, Angamis, Puchurys, etc. Still in many villages young people prefer to sleep with their age group, peers and friend rather than parental homes.[167]

However, in the recent years, young Nagas have started to migrate to various cities of India and other countries in search of jobs and other better earning avenues. Today, in most theological seminaries under the Senate affiliated colleges and other private colleges; Nagas have starting to teach and have taken up other administrative roles.

Nagas do not prescribe joint family, as such it is practiced rarely and only when there is no alternative, i.e., because of poverty, physical handicap, or even if jointly stays for temporary only. The general practice is that as soon as a son marries and becomes the head of family he goes and set up a home of his own. The Nagas follow patriarchal, patrilocal and patrilineal family, where the husband is the head, owner and administrator; the wife goes and lives in the house of the husband, and the descendants are traced through the father's ancestors. As the head of the family, father is expected to provide for, look after and maintain the position of the family.

An intelligent, brave and eloquent head of family is respected even outside the home environment and these very qualities may entitle him to an important position in the clan, village and tribe. He is also the family priest and performs his duties during festivals and other ceremonies. He must portion out family lands between his male children and make a will in the customary form to provide for his wife in the event of his death. Besides performing the above duties within the family he represents his family in the clan meetings and in all court related affairs.

The eldest son in the family prepares himself to shoulder much of the responsibilities after the death of his father. The eldest son may be dint of his personality and intelligence, inherit the village office held by his father even though that office may not be hereditary. He is also expected to look after his aged

167 Thong, and Kath. *Glimpses of Naga Legacy and Culture*, 2012...,151-152. Cf. Pikato Sema, *British Policy and Administration in Nagaland*, 1992.

parents when the daughters are married and the sons after marriage have moved out, especially his old mother if she survives his father.

Ever since God created human beings, they started to live in families. Thus the family is the most primitive institution of human history. The development of its norms, characteristics and functions is always a subject of debate because of the reasons like conflicting message found in the writings on the subject, complexity of the influence of radical socio-cultural change on family structures and function, ideological conflict over the meaning of family, lack of attention to the critical view of the economics with regard to the family functions,[168] dynamic nature of theological interpretations of family in different backgrounds of theology, and so on. Three correlates of family are reviewed in this section, i.e. a) Family Environment, b) Religious Adherence and, c) Media Impact on Family.

3. Family Environment

The home of family is an institution that plays a major role in exerting influence in their attitude and behaviour. Hence, the role of family context or environment for the growth and development of member cannot be overlooked or neglected. Hausar states that family is very significant in the life of members because, "it is the arena in which they forge their earliest attainment, first experience separation and loss, discover the world of sibling and begins their life-long learning of social and physical"[169]

According to Structural Family System therapist like Minuchin, the family is conceptualized as a system of interconnected relationship whereby the quality of relationship between spouses is observed by to the quality of care parents provide their offspring and vice-versa.[170]

Numerous researches has been done by Indian scholars as well as foreign writers on the impact of select correlates on family system, and the study results indicate that there are certain factors that effects family harmony. Anungla Aier in her article "Ministry to Naga Families" edited by Soren Oestergaard and Adela Mero, lamented that there is a sea change in Naga family especially the value system. Family environment with regard to family interaction, family prayers, respect for elders, fellow-feeling etc has been greatly challenged with the advancement of mass media and globalization process. Aier, cautioned that unless an immediate redressal steps are initiated, Naga society is bond to social

168 S. C. Paulraj, "Social Change and Family: A Post-modern Concern," *AETEI*, 04/02 (1991), 10-21.

169 Stuart T. Hauser, *Adolescents and their Families*, (New York: The Free Press, 1991), 17.

170 Deborah B. Jacobvitz, and Nell F. Bush, "Reconstruction of Family Relationships: Parent-Child Alliances, Personal Distress, and Self Esteem," *Developmental Psychology*, Vol. 32, No. 4, 1996, 732-743.

catastrophe and anarchy.[171] The decline in family values and the lost of ethos in the society is really felt.

According to Boholi Z. Sema in her book "Parent-Children Relationship among the Naga Society Toward Family Enrichment" stated that transition is taking place in the structure of Naga families, the value system, the individualistic feelings, a growing consumerist life style, lack of communication among family members, and exposure to the outside world; they have multiplied like a virus to become a basic family problem in Naga society.[172] Family environment as a whole is fast losing its value system as people in the family has become more individualistic than a decade ago. This demands a systematic research on the impact of correlates on Naga families for healthy family functioning.

Imtijungla, Longchar in her book "Restore our Family" observed that there is fast decline of family values and family ethos among the present day Naga family. The reason has been that various factors contributed to this invasion of family values. With the impact of mass media, rampant usage of modern gadgets, and the process of mono culture, family sharing and interaction has completely lost. "We are on the verge of completely losing rich family heritage, sharing, needing and caring."[173] Most families hardly come together for prayers needless to say even couples find it difficult to spend quality time together.

Wood in her case study on Indian families, and published in her book "Families in the Plan of God: A Theology from South Asia" reveals that families are changing rapidly. In a bid to prevent an onslaught against the institution of family, many Christian advocate "getting back to traditional family values." However, undercurrents that undermine families has existed long back-problems such as urbanization, media influence, gender difference/female infanticide, multiple discrimination against the girl child, religious adherence to one particular religion, manipulation of family members, etc. Returning to "traditional family values" cannot serve us well in all respects.[174] However, families in India revolve around maintaining social relationship. Family links are strong, and families have much to treasure and keep, while surrounded by gradual remodeling that is taking place. Indian families often have values that other cultures might covet, values that resonate with Christian principles Christian workers in India could keep and encourage these in the present time.

---

171 Soren Oestergaard, and Adela Mero, eds. *Doing Youth Ministry in a Naga Context*, Dimapur, (Nagaland: Project Nehemiah NBYF, 2002). 165.

172 Boholi Z. Sema, *Parent-Children Relationship among the Naga Society Towards Family Enrichment*, (Dimapur: Shikhu Scholastic Press, 2012), 143.

173 Imtijungla Longchar, *Restore Our Family*, (Dimapur: S. Wati Aier and Sons, 2006), 45.

174 Beulah Wood, *Families in the Plan of God: A Theology from South Asia*, (Bangalore: SAIACS Press, 2010), 24-27.

Fast changing trends in the technological advancement coupled with rampant bombardment of media are threatening the sanctity of our families. In such a scenario Joseph Mar Thoma, the Metropolitan, suggest that:

In a fast changing society, families need to be equipped to face the realities of today and tomorrow, in which churches as an institution realizes its ministry to the family as one of its cardinal responsibilities in its intimate engagement with the family. Systematically planned researches and studies intended at analyzing the challenges faced by the families and suggesting some pointers for the responses to such challenges is a need of the time and God given vocation, in which the Church and pastoral care-giver needs to carry out with utmost care.[175]

As a minister of the word of God and a practicing family counsellor, the researcher has also experienced and felt the enormous need to systematize programmes and researches that addresses the various need of the of the families.

Chowdhury and Carson in their study on the challenges to contemporary Indian family environment lament that today's "Indian family is in a fluid, transitional state and is experiencing ambiguities in family role, relationships, responsibilities, and models for emulation."[176]

The emotional support structure is weakening and external entities (e,g., school, religious institutions) are taking part of the socializing roles earlier played by the families. Such a scenario has far-reaching implications for the emotional and psychological well-being of individuals, as seen for example in the children and adults. In extreme situations, individual pathology and relationship difficulties are resulting in higher incidences of family disintegration. There are various contributory factors such as media impact, religious adherence, gender role differences etc. In books, and on radio and television, these men and other evangelical family champions worry over a fairly consistent list of concerns. They decry movies, music and television programmes that frighten children and expose them to explicit sex and violence. They abhor the spread of the gay rights movement and the rise of feminism. It's not as if the family never had troubles before. But scant decades ago, most westerners agreed that lifelong monogamy was ideal, that mothers should stay home with children, that premarital sex was to be discouraged, that heterosexuality was the unquestioned norm and that popular culture should not corrupt children.[177] Today not a single one of these expectations is uncontroversial.

---

175 Joseph. Mar Thoma, "Forward," in *Christian Family in Transition: Continuity and Discontinuity*, edited by Koshy P. Varughese, (Faridabad, Haryana: Dharma JyotiVidya Peeth, 2012), 5.

176 Aparajita Chowdhury, David K. Carson et. al, eds., *Family Life Education in India: Perspective, Challenges, and Applications*, edited by Chowdhury Aparajita, David K. Carson et. al, (Jiapur/ New Delhi/Bangalore/Mumbai: Rawat Publications, 2006), 250.

177 Rodney Clapp, *Families at the Crossroad: Beyond Traditional and Modern Options*, (Downers Grove, Illinois, USA/ Leicester, England: InterVarsity Press, 1993), 10-15.

Amato and Booth in the Book "A Generation at Risk: Growing Up in an Era of Family Upheaval" reveals that during the last three decades, remarkable transformations have occurred in the American family, including changes in economic well-being, gender roles, family relationship and family structure. Changing expectations about gender role within the family mean that husbands and wives today must negotiate rights and responsibilities that previous generations look for granted, thus increasing the potential for marital tension.[178] Along with these changes, the divorce rate has increased to an all-time high.

Brigitte and Berger in the study on "The War over Family: Capturing the Middle Ground" found out that there is the view that the family and its values are in steep decline. This decline is variously interpreted in terms of its causes broad social trends or specific ideological movements or changes in religion and morality on one hand, and impact of media and mono culture popularized by globalization process on the other hand.[179] But, most of those holding this view agree that the alleged decline of the family is harmful both to the individual and the society. The studies on Naga families, and families in general suggest that there is an urgent need to present a relevant family counselling models and family enrichment programmes in order to cope with the present crisis and also to facilitate further understanding of meaningful family life in this challenging society.

4. Religious Impact on Family

Religious influence on the family has received much attention in the past several years. A variety of studies have been undertaken to determine different aspects of religious influence on various areas of family life. Shafranske in her article "Religion and the Clinical Practice of Psychology" published by American Psychological Association, stated that religion is part of the human belief system and survey studies reveal that 90% percent of the world's population identifies itself with a religion.[180] So, according to this finding there are only 10% of the world population who are inclined to any religion.

One intuitive meaning of "religious" is spiritual, in the sense of being other-worldly, indifferent to material necessities,[181] increased respect for the inner, contemplative practice of traditional religious systems and the defence of patterns of beliefs and values. One of the functions of a religious belief system

178 Paul R. Amanto, and Alan Booth. *A Generation at Risk: Growing Up in An Era of Family Upheaval,* (Cambridge/London: Harvard University Press, 2000), 51-60.

179 Brigitte Berger, and Peter L. Berger, *The War Over the Family: Capturing the Middle Ground,* (New York: Anchor City, 1993), 105-107.

180 E. P. Sharfanske, (ed). *Religion and the Clinical Practice of Psychology,* (Washington D.C: American Psychological Association, 1996), 15-20.

181 Beit-Hallahimi, and Argyle M, *The Psychology of Religious Belief, Behavior and Experiences,* (London: Routledge, 1997), 118.

and a religious world view is to provide an ultimate vision of what people should strive for in their lives[182] and the strategies to reach those goals[183] such as religious commitment and rituals, devotion and self-sacrifice. Religion plays a positive role in the development and maintenance of moral behaviour and altruistic motivations such as helpfulness, tolerance, patience, honesty and obedience to God; hence, it is claimed that religiousness is associated with being a "better person" in numerous way, including maintaining healthy family relationship.[184]

Tezenlo Thong a scholar from Nagaland in his Ph. D research "Religion and Theological Studies" submitted to the University of Denver and Iliff School of Theology, stress the intrinsic connection between religion and family life.[185]

Kenilo Kath, in his book "Traditional religious system of the Rengma Nagas" stated that there is close association between religious adherence and family relationship. The author asserts that one's religiosity tend to impact family life, those inclined towards religion and religious activity seem to be more devoted and caring towards family life and its affairs.[186]

Kevin J. Coldwell, in "The Impact of Religion on Family Life" a study conducted at the University of Wisconsin, Madison, examines the effects of religion on family functioning levels. A survey of 87 university students was conducted to collect data on several aspects of religious participation and on family types and functions using the FACES II instrument. These data were then correlated. The results mirror previous findings as several religious factors play at least a small role in family functioning. Attendance at other religious activities and family prayer showed the greatest effects on levels of family functioning, while inter-religious support was negatively related to family functioning.[187] Overall, a "rationing of religion" interpretation seems to explain the results as families which were neither over, nor under religious influence seem to have higher levels of family functioning.

Rostosky, Sharon in her book "Why Religion Matters Even More: The Impact of Religious Practice on Social Stability", published by the University of Wisconsin, found correlation between religious shared beliefs in marriage and

---

182 K. I. Pargament, and Park, C. L. Merely, A Defence? The Variety of Religious Means and Ends, *Journal of Sociology*, Issue 51 (1995), 95-107.

183 Robert A. Emmons, and Raymond F. Paloutzian, *Psychology of Religion*. California: Department of Psychology, University of California, 2003, 121.

184 C. Batson, and Raynor-Prince, L., "Religious Orientation and Complexity of Thought about Existential Concerns," in *Journal for the Study of Religion and Family*, 22/1 (1983): 38-50. Cf., R. W. Hood, Spilka Hunsberger B, H. I. Gorsuch,. *The Psychology of Religion: An Empirical Approach*. New York: Guilford, 1996, 131.

185 Tezenlo Thong,

186 Kenilo Kath, *Traditional Religious System of the Rengma Nagas, (*Kolkata: Anshah Publications, 2005), 87.

187 Kevin J. Coldwell, "Impact of Religion in Family Life," In *Survey Conducted at the University of Wisconsin*, Madison, (2012): 115-125.

marital satisfaction, although the nature of the relationship is not certain. For example, some researchers have found that marital satisfaction tends to increase religiosity while other studies of long-term marriages have indicated that similarity in religious orientation, religious faith, and religious beliefs were frequently mentioned as key factors in marital success. The married parents in the present study sample similarly emphasized the importance of shared beliefs. A Jewish father testified that "Our values are always very, very close, which is why we're so close.... It has positively affected our marriage."[188]

Vaughn R. A. Call and Tim B. Heaton in their article "Impact of Religion on Family Life" in *the Journal for the Scientific Study of Religion* postulate a strong relationship between religiosity and marital stability. They incorporate a multidimensional specification of religiosity into event-history models of the religion-marital stability relationship. Results are based on panel data from the National Survey of Families and Households (N = 4,587 married couples). While no single dimension of religiosity adequately describes the effect of religious experience on marital stability, the frequency of religious attendance has the greatest positive impact on marital stability. When both spouses attend church regularly, the couple has the lowest risk of divorce. Spouse differences in church attendance increase the risk of dissolution. All significant religious affiliation influences disappear once demographic characteristics are controlled.[189] The wife's religious beliefs concerning marital commitment and non-marital sex are more important to the stability of the marriage than the husband's beliefs.

Meier, Johnson in his book "Study of Religion and Family" published by Orbis books, observed the correlation between religion and family life. He asserts that religion can have a very positive impact on family values, and it can just as easily have a negative impact on family values.[190] The basic fact is that every religion has its very good and rounding points and it has its share of flaws, regardless of which religion you encounter. Religion can teach discipline, honour, a sense of pride, a sense of right and wrong, and introduce children to a very strong and honoring commitment like no other, in the process a person is shaped into a better person loving, caring and sharing thus contributes positive to family values.[191]

Mc Cree, Millers in his article "Religion and family" in *Journal of Comparative Family Studies* asserts that religion teaches people wonderful things. And it can be

---

188 Sharon Rostosky, *Why Religion Matters Even More: The Impact of Religious Practice on Social Stability*, (Wisconsin: University of Wisconsin Press, 2004), 119.

189 Vaughn R. A. Call and Tim B. Heaton, "Impact of Religion of Family Life," in *Journal for the Scientific Study of Religion*, Vol. 112/04 (1997): 19-27.

190 Meier Johnson, *Study of Religion and Family*, (Maryknoll/New York: Orbis Books, 2003), 115-117.

191 Jay Newman, *Biblical Religion and Family Values: A Person in the Philosophy of Religion,* (New York: Ballantine Press, 2001), 105.

said with certainty that religion can stimulate family values. The way one views religion and religious tolerance shapes the views children have and how they will religiously interact with the world.[192] It is a parent's job to introduce their children to the value of diversity and to avoid undermining other religious views in the world while teaching them the splendor of their own religious views.

Jay Newman, in his book "Biblical Religion and Family Values: A Person in the Philosophy of Religion" published by Ballatine Press, delves into issues concerning Biblical religion, culture, sociology, and family values. He maintains that recent media debates about the Bible and family values have obscured the complex relationship between the family and religion.[193] This research has been supported by many other similar researches.

A study on Religion and family stability found out the beneficial effects of religious worship on family stability. Professors Darwin L. Thomas and Gwendolyn C. Henry of Brigham Young University's Department of Sociology sum up earlier research on the quest by young people for intrinsic relationship between religion and family stability and concluded that: "family and religious institutions need to be studied simultaneously in our efforts to understand the human condition better and for healthy family relationship."[194]

"With striking consistency, the most religious among Americans place a greater importance on the full range of family and friendship activities," concluded a Connecticut Mutual Life report in 1982. A group of Kansas State University professors reached the same conclusion: "family commitment is indeed a high priority in many American families and it is frequently accompanied by a concomitant factor of religious commitment." In yet another study conducted during the 1970s and 1980s, professors Nick Stinnet of the University of Alabama and John DeFrain of the University of Nebraska sought to identify family strengths. From their nationwide surveys of strong families, they found that 84% percent identified religion as an important contributor to the strength of their families.[195] It should be noted that the same pattern appears to hold for African-American families: Parents who attended church frequently cited the significance of religion in rearing their children and in providing moral guidelines. Regular church attendance is the critical factor in marital stability across denominations and overrides effects of doctrinal teaching on divorce. For instance, black Protestants and white Catholics, who share similarly high church attendance rates, have been shown to have similarly low

192 Millers Mc cree, "Religion and Family," in *Journal of Comparative Family Studies*, 42/04 (2003): 293.

193 Newman, *Biblical Religion and Family Values: A Person in the Philosophy of Religion,* 113.

194 Darwin L. Thomas, and Gwendolyn C. Henry, *Religion and Family Studies*, (Brigham: Young University's Department of Sociology, 2009), 55-57.

195 Stinnet Nick, and John DeFrain, *Family Strength and Adolescent Wellness*, (Montgomery: The International Family Life Institute, Inc. 1980), 113, 117.

divorce rates.[196] Furthermore, when marital separation occurs, reconciliation rates are higher among regular church attendees and highest when both spouses have the same high level of church attendance. Findings on the other end of the marital spectrum reinforce the point: A 1993 national survey of 3,300 men aged 20-39 found that those who switch partners most are those with no religious convictions.

Significantly, cohabitation before marriage poses a high risk to later marital stability, and premarital cohabitation is much less common among religious Americans. "The cohabitation rate is seven times higher among persons who seldom or never attend religious services compared to persons who frequently attend," writes David Larson of the National Institute of Healthcare Research. "Women who attended religious services once a week were only one-third as likely to cohabit as those who attended church services less than once a month."[197] Furthermore, "If the mother frequently attended religious services, both sons and daughters were only 50% percent as likely to cohabit as adult children whose mothers were not actively religious." Rockford Institute President Allan Carlson summarizes the pattern: "Social scientists are discovering the continuing power of religion to protect the family from the forces that would tear it down."[198] Examining the general life-style of female and male, Mark D. Regnerus of the University of Texas at Austin finds a big difference between those who attend and never attend church, with those attending the church regularly found to be tolerant, family oriented and trustworthy.[199]

Religion and Religious faith is the salient and inextricable thread and fabric in the quilt of family life for the families, and they cannot be adequately understood independent of their faith. It is anticipated that through this glimpse into the above researches and findings that it will help better understand those of various faiths and that many will learn from these faithful parents who taught their children. Perhaps, the above statements would illuminate our desire for stronger and healthy family relationship and thus further prompt us to seek a sacred connection and communion with a real and relational God.

5. Impact of Media on Family

How do media influence the family? The degree of influence depends on the availability and pervasiveness of media. All of the traditional mass media still have great influence over our lives. Books once were supremely influential because

196 Nick and Defrain, *Family Strength and Adolescent Wellness*, 118.

197 Larson David, *Religious Survey of American Family*, (Minneapolis: National Institute of Healthcare Research/Fortress Press, 1996), 110-114.

198 Chandy Resnick, & Blum, *Religious Survey of American Family*, (Minneapolis: Fortress Press, 1996), 120-125.

199 Mark D Regnerus, "Research on Religion and Family," Research conducted at the University of Texas at Austin, 2007, 31-38.

they came first before newspapers, magazines, radio or television. Newspapers and magazines became great influences after they were developed. Sound recordings and films were and still are influential. Radio and then television were very influential. As the 20th century closed, TV exposed us to untold numbers of images of advertising and marketing, suffering and relief, sexuality and violence, celebrity, and much more.

Reports on the media and family life tend to generate familiar headlines: tales of teenagers glued to facebook and mobiles; a generational divide packed with anxious questions over what the modern media are "doing" to families. New study, *Changing Media, Changing Families*, published on 17th November 2010, takes a different approach. Families, one argues, have a dynamic relationship with the media.[200] So one must ask not only what effects media have on families, but also how the changes in modern family life are changing media itself.

The quantity of media consumed by families in the last decade has grown vastly. About half of the average teenager's waking hours are now spent consuming it in some form a trend that is becoming true of the wider population. And this means the media have shifted from being an incidental part of the private and cultural lives to an increasingly indispensable infrastructure that dominates social relationships, daily timetables, leisure, and family life in particular reveals the study conducted on impact of media on family.[201]

Magazine on Focus on Family has gathered a collection of resources designed to help protect family from unwanted influences. Bob Waliszewski in his recent study found that although movies, music and magazines can inspire, the power of today's media can negatively sway human behaviour and have adverse impact on family life.[202]

Sheila Lopez in her research on the Influence of Media on the Family found that media has all round impact on family. Statistics show that in the year 2009, 54% of U.S. homes had 3 or more television sets, 82% had more than 1 television set and 88% had a DVD player. With the majority of families having access to media in their home and thinking about the kind of programmes or channels available for public viewing it is important that parents and care-givers need strict vigilance. Research has shown that 63% of families watches TV while eating dinner, 53% have no rules about TV use and 51% have the TV on most of the time. Going through these statistics one wonders what is really going on within the family in regards to media. It seems that media (especially TV) has become a part of the family unit. It is a part of most families' everyday life, both collectively

---

200 Pam Morries, David Luries and Racha Jain, *Changing Media, Changing Families*, (Minneapolis: Fortress, Press, 2010), 142-146.

201 Rosenfeld Kanuga, *A Study on Today Media*, (New York: Guilford Press, 2004), 172.

202 Bob Waliszewski, "Impact of Media of Family," *Focus on Family*, 105/05 (2013), 110-119.

and as individual members.[203] This finding can be true even to the others family in the extreme corners of the world.

Programmes available on television today allow more people than ever before the opportunity to experience great music, drama, and art and to be exposed to the thoughts and lives of great men and women. Unfortunately, too few families take advantage of these superb presentations. One reason we may miss them is that less worthy programmes, extraordinarily promoted, often attract more attention.[204] And that is the problem. Television producers overwhelm people with so much fabrication that is based on unworthy of higher natures, which it is impossible for those who do not manage their television viewing to escape the violence and other inappropriate behaviors portrayed on TV.

David Clarke, who has decades of experience on family and media, recently visited with the Parenting Press staff, and expressed his concern about the impact of media on children, even the very young. A generation or two ago, a family's values were often influenced primarily by parents, church, and school. Today, however, the entertainment media especially electronic media of all kinds and the marketing industry often have far more significant impact on what parents and kids believe.[205] Many young people these days do not follow the traditional way of greeting their elders because they assume that the traditional style of giving greeting is out of place.[206] Their dress sense is even nothing to write about reiterated that 'most of the foreign soap operas promote values that are alien to Nigerian culture.

Television influence on family is not only on children alone. Most parents get addicted to particular programmes and by so doing neglect their family and duties. A football fanatic will definitely have problems with his partner in terms of attention and all the rest. Women who love watching 'African Magic' a channel on DStv (Nigerian TV channel owned by multi-choice Pvt. Limited) that broadcast Nigerian made films, will easily be influenced by what they watch. These addictions could be corrected when it involves parents but the basic issue is when kids get addicted to programs that influence their sense of reasoning and the way they relate with people. What this means is, children also learn by imitation, when they see that their parents are addicted to some programs, they will start nursing the idea that being addicted to some basic programs is accepted and morally justifiable. The negative side of this addiction when what

203 Shiela Lopez, "Impact of Television of Family," *Journal of Comparative Family Studies*, (2010): 141-145.

204 Arland Thornton, and Donald Camburn, *The Negative Impact of Media*, (Nashville: Abington Press, 2010), 187-190.

205 David Clarke, *The Impact of Social Media on Children, Adolescent, and Family*, (Washington D.C.: Routledge, 2007), 109.

206 Alabi Soji, *The Influence of Television on Family Institution in Nigeria*, (Nairobi: Print Well Publishing House, 2010), 31-33.

they are addicted to have some negative impacts. This has raised a lot of concerns because the society is being faced with violent crimes, cultism, truancy and early pregnancy among secondary school girls. Values parents teach these days are being contradicted by what children see on television programmes. Children learn by observation and tend to put aside the conventions they grew up with.[207] This has basically become a big problem to parents, guardians, school authorities and the Government.

Indian middle class family reported to spending 2-3 hours per day watching TV with 75% of families reporting that they spent their evenings in television viewing.[208] Young adolescents report that they watch TV for entertainment and not for intellectual stimulation;[209] they prefer watching adult-oriented programming such as movies, film song sequences, soap operas and dislike educational programmes.[210]

L'Engle, Brown and Kenneavey found that more exposure to violence in media that conveys an approval of harassment within family was related to higher levels of family violence and a greater amount of violent behaviour in general. This effect persisted even after controlling for other contextual factors including education, level of income, and religious influences.[211]

Families are often influenced by what the media portray, programmes that portray women as the head of the house could definitely affect the perception a family holds about family institution in the society. Toyin Falola says that 'Nigeria is one of the largest and most important countries in Africa; it is rich in traditions and customs, both indigenous and modern.[212] Yet ever since television culture was popularized things are never the same, it is claimed.

With television playing a major role in today, the society is undoubtedly faced with cultural conquest. Graeme Burton says that the concern about what media do has pushed people to adopt particular lifestyles or pattern of behaviour. These portrayals reflect and reinforce views about the nature of the family in

---

207 Ekhayeme Godwin, *Media and the Changing Trends in Socio-cultural Life*, (Nairobi: Print Well Publishing House, 2012), 197.

208 Usha Abrol, Thapar Vandana Khan, and Srinivastava Paul, *Television Viewing Among Children of Delhi School*, (New Delhi: National Institute of Public Corporation and Child Development, 1991), 105.

209 A. J. Wadkar Gerbner et al. *The Impact of Television on its Viewer and the Family Environment*, (Pune: Pustak Publications, 1998), 51.

210 K. P. Saji Kumar, *Sexual Behaviour in Adolescent: A Study on the Ecological Correlates*, Ph.D. Thesis submitted to M.G. University, Kottayam, Kerala, 2013, 182.

211 L'Engle Brown, and Kenneavey, *Multi-dimensional Effects of Media on Family*, (Grand Rapids, Michigan: Baker Books, 2006), 11-20.

212 Toyin Falola, *Media and African Culture*, (Nairobi: Oxford Publishing House, 2000), 197-198.

society.[213] Changing social norms and television portrayals mean that assessing the impact of portrayals must be an ongoing effort.

James B. Weaver III & Stephanie Lee Sargent in their study on Media effects and Family interaction proved that communication is an essential, indispensable element for the formation and maintenance of families. Indeed, social interaction is the vehicle through which family members establish, maintain, and dissolve their intimate relationships. Within this unique social system, the mass media have become an integral, if not routine part of family life. This entry examines some aspects of how the mass media impact interactions within families, focusing on parents, children, and adolescents. The typical American family home is permeated with media technologies, including multiple television and radio sets, media players, and computers systems, and often, the children are the most keen media consumers.[214] As a result this has adversely effected family interaction, which also resulted to broken families in some cases.

Based on an extensive literature review regarding the influences of media on family, Malamuth Impett stated that individual personality factors may also be important, as research suggests that the type of media people select and find gratifying is predictably related to their personalities and other individual differences that they exhibit in their family life.[215] Using social media web sites is among the most common activity of today's children and adolescent. Any web site that allows social interaction is considered a social media site, including social networking site such as face book, my space, and twitter, gaming sites and virtual words such as club penguin, social life, and the Sims; Video sites such as YouTube; and blogs. Such sites offer today's youth a portal for entertainment and communication and have grown exponentially in recent years. For this reason, it is important that parents become aware of the nature of social media sites, given that not all of them are healthy environment for family.[216] Paediatrics are in a unique position to help families understand these sites and to encourage healthy use and urge parents to monitor for potential problems with cyber bullying, face-book depression, sex and exposure to inappropriate content.

Despite data showing that frequent media users and consumers of numerous unhealthy media messages, mass media influences are rarely included in ecological models and are rarely considered as important contexts for family socialization. Survey studies, which avoided the artificiality of laboratory

213 Graeme Burton, *Media and Behavioral Change*, (Louisville: Westminster John Knox Press, 2005), 109.

214 James B Weaver, and Stephanie Lee Sargent, *Study on Media Effects and Family Interaction*, (Louisville, Ky.: Westminster John Knox Press, 2005), 211-215.

215 Malamuth Impett, *Media and its Impact on Personality*, (Nashville: Oxford University Press, 2001), 110.

216 Gwenn Schurgin O'keeffe, and Kathleen Clarke, *The Impact of Social Media on Children, Adolescent and Family*, (Paediatrics Vol. 127 N0, 4 April 1 (2011), 800-804.

experiments, have not produced uniform results. Many survey studies have found various degrees of association between media exposure and family relationship e.g., McLeod *et al.,* Atkin *et al.,*[217] but some studies either did not find a significant association, e.g., Pfuhl,[218] or were not certain about the presence of a significant association.

6. Socio-Demographic Variables and Family

This section attempts to review the related research on the correlation between family life satisfaction and the socio-demographic variables such as level of education, place of residence, level of income and gender difference. It is presumed by the researcher that the above variables have a combined impact or correlation with family life satisfaction.

6.1. Level of Education and Family

It is not surprising that level of education has significant correlation with family life satisfaction. A study conducted by Harriett K. Light, and Doris, Hertsgaard, among 760 families randomly selected from resident of upper Midwest state to determine perceived family life satisfaction according to education level, by using 20 item Family Life Satisfaction Index. Analysis revealed significant correlation between education level and family life satisfaction. Generally as education level increased,[219] family life satisfaction also increased, presumably due to better earning capacity and higher position in social life.

A research was conducted by Honge Gong, Rebecca Cassells and Marcia Keegan among 9000 samples in Australia on the correlation between family life satisfaction and education level. Better income, wealth and health outcomes have been predicted by human capital theory for better educated people, increasingly international and Australian empirical evidence has found a negative correlation between higher education and family life satisfaction among the older adult.[220] However, this is not the case among the younger age group, where family life satisfaction, especially with respect to finance, health and safety, increases with education.

---

217 C. K. Atkin, J. A. Anderson et al. "Research Evidence of Mass Mediated Health Communication Campaign," in *Communication Year Book* (ed.) D. Nimo. Newbury Park, CA: Sage Publications, 1979, 179.

218 Reimer Pfuhl, "Cultivate Viewers and Readers: A life-style Perspective," in Signorielli and M. Morgan (eds.), *Cultivation Analysis: New Direction in Media Effects Research*, (Newbury Park: CA. Sage, 1990), 151-160.

219 Light Harriett K. and Doris Hertsgaard, "Education: Significant Factor in Family Life Satisfaction" *Research in Rural Education*, Vol. 3/1 (2010), 7-15.

220 Honge Gong, Rebecca Cassells, and Marcia Keegan, "*Understanding Life Satisfaction and the Education in Australia: A Profile from HILDA Wave 9*" National Centre for Social and Economic Modelling, 2011, 115-120.

An Empirical research conducted by Tony Vinson and Mathew Ericson, among 1400 respondents found there is statistically significant correlation between education and life satisfaction (r =.083, p = 002). The researcher found that both the correlation and significance increased (to r =. 101, p = <.000). One explanation for this may be because of the statistically significant variance in the life satisfaction and education variables People with higher education tend to be happier as they are more successful in the professional life.[221]

6.2. Place of Residence and Family

Choi, Byoung Mohk Department of Social Welfare, far East University and Lee, Jang-Young Department of Sociology Kookmin University in their research on Comparison of Life Satisfaction between Urban and Rural Residence using regression multiple analysis to measure the relative influence of five independent variables (Income, education, family communication, husband wife relationship, and other family relationship) affect to the dependent variable, subjective life satisfaction. In urban five independent variables affect the life satisfaction. However, in rural the four variables of income, education, family communication, and other family relationship except husband-wife relationship affect to the life satisfaction.[222] The importance of income for the life satisfaction from the many previous works is reaffirmed by this study.

A comparison of urban and rural differences in relation to family life satisfaction was conducted through an empirical test. Data were drawn from nationality representative sample of married adult from the USA.[223] The Multivariate analysis revealed a reciprocal relationship between family life satisfaction and urban-rural difference.

A population-based study to examine the association between life satisfaction and rural-urban residence in six region of Italy including gender and education was pressed into the investigation. The sample comprised of 4999 people drawn from various age group. The result revealed that there is a strong correlation between urbanization and loss of traditional cultural values; as a result it slowly affects family life. Whereas people in the rural setting with pro-traditional mind-set to preserve traditional values without considering

---

221 Tony Vinson, and Mathew Ericson, *Life Satisfaction and Happiness,* (Richmond, Australia: Jesuit Social Service, 2012), 26-28.

222 Jang-Young Lee, Byoung Mohk Choi, "Life Satisfaction Comparison between Urban and Rural People in Korea," Paper presented *at XII World Congress of Rural Sociology of the International Rural Sociology Association*, July, 6-11 (2008), Goyang, Korea.

223 John F. Toth, Ralph B. Brown and Xiaohe Xu, "A Comparison of Rural-Urban Difference in Relation to Family Life Satisfaction," *Work, Community, and Family*. Vol. 5. Issue 2. (2010), 181-202.

the changing trends also create harmful tension among the people in the community.[224]

The above empirical studies result clearly indicates that there are strong correlation between family life and place of resident. People in the rural resident are found to be more culturally and socially conscious and contributes to its preservation, whereas as people move toward in the urban, they slowly neglect cultural and traditional ethos.

6.3. Level of Income and Family

In a survey conducted among large sample (208,016 respondents) from 90 countries (Western Europe, Eastern Europe, Middle East, North Africa, Sub-Saharan African, and Asia) by Department of Sociology, University of Western Ontario, Social Science Centre, London, Ontario, January, 2012, found that level of income has significant correlation with family life satisfaction. Income is important for explaining variation in life satisfaction, but is most important in poor regions and is least important in regions with high GDP/capita. Household resources explain less than one percent of variation in life satisfaction in Western European countries, but six to seven percent in Asia and sub-Saharan Africa. It may be that the welfare state guarantees a lower bound on income and a level of basic needs in the richest regions and income is most important for life satisfaction in areas where absolute poverty is most common.[225] The results indicate that people with higher income enjoys higher family life satisfaction than vice versa.

A quantitative research conducted by the Institute for Research on Household Economics to investigate the correlation between income level and family life satisfaction among large sample in Japan. Findings indicate that higher level of income results to higher level of family life satisfaction.[226] A large volume of previous research and here as well has also focus on other factors that are important such as personal relationship with family, neighbours and community members, factors that are considered in the present research as well.

A large scale analysis by Gallup World Survey in 2006, which includes opinion on Family Life satisfaction with various aspects of life including Income level was conducted in 130 countries. Although a very solid relationship was found between satisfaction and income, raising doubts regarding the well-known Easterlin Paradox, a new paradox arises: "Unhappy growth," where faster growth

224 Carta M. G. Koveas, V. Hardy MC., et al "Life Satisfaction: Urban-Rural Difference," in *Clinical Practice Epistemology*. Vol. 8. No. 2 (2012), 102-109.

225 Rachel Margolis, and Mikko Myrskyla. *Income: Regional Difference in the Determinants of Family Life Satisfaction*. London: Department of Sociology, University of Western Ontario, Social Sciences Center/Max Planck Institute for Demographic Research, 2012.

226 Akihito Toda, "Satisfaction Levels (Qualitative Data): Family Life Satisfaction" *Japan Labour Review* Vol.10. No. 4, (2013), 1-41.

rates are accompanied by lower levels of satisfaction.[227] The losses of satisfaction associated with growth are more pronounced in the material domains of life and are greater in richer and more urban societies.[228] At the individual level, although higher income tends to be reflected in greater satisfaction, an increase in the income of the social group to which an individual belong has the opposite effect.

6.4. Gender and Family

Study was conducted among 3,277 Japanese adults (1,679 men and 1,598 women) using ordered logic models with a rich set of explanatory variables to investigate gender differences in relation to family life satisfaction. The study found that men are less satisfied with life when living without their spouse; women are less satisfied with life when they live and/or have close relations with their parent-in-laws, a large number of people and social activities enhance life satisfaction for women but not for men. Men are more sensitive to overall family relations than women, while the relative importance of social relations is higher for women.[229] The results confirmed gender difference in associations of family life satisfaction.

Kate, Levin, Dallago, Lorenzo, and Currie Candace examined gender-difference in connection to family life satisfaction among 5,126 samples in Scotland using multilevel linear regression analyses. The study found that there is significant correlation between gender-difference and family life satisfaction.[230] Besides gender-difference family communication and personal relationship also play an important role in family life satisfaction, similar variables are considered in the present study.

Stephen Humpert from University of Lueneburg, (Germany) Institute of economics in his research on Gender Differences and Life satisfaction found that society that is open to both genders in term of role, privileges and responsibilities gains higher family life satisfaction than those societies that is reserved, traditional and patriarchal inclined.[231] The result from the above empirical studies shows a close relationship between gender and family life satisfaction. Family that are open to both man and woman in terms of their role, privileges and rights are likely to experience higher family life satisfaction.

---

227 wwwhttps://ourworldindata.org-survey on family life satisfaction and income: evidences from around the world. Accessed on 07/04/2018.

228 Eduardo Lora, and Juan Camilo Chaparro, *The Conflictive Relationship between Family Life Satisfaction and Income Level*, (New York Avenue/Washington, D.C.: Inter-American Development bank, 2008), 3-15.

229 Takashi Oshio, "Gender Differences in the Association with Family Life Satisfaction," *Journal of Cross-Cultural Gerontology* vol. 27 No. 3 (2012): 259-274.

230 Levin Kate, Dallago Lorenzo and Currie Candace. "The Association between Gender-Difference and Family Life Satisfaction," *Social Indicators Research* April 2012, vol. 106, No. 2 (2012): 287.

231 Humbert Stephen, "Gender Difference and Life Satisfaction," *Journal of Happiness Studies.* Vol. 1 No. 1 (2013): 1-22.

7. Conclusion

A comprehensive review of the related research has been done in this chapter. The above review of related researches has highlighted ample scope for the study of the correlates (a, Naga family system b) Family Environment, c) Media Impact, d) Religious Adherence, and e) socio-demographic variables (Educational level, Place of residence, Gender differences and the Levels of Income on the family life) chosen for this particular study. Since extensive studies have been done, as indicated in the review of the related research on the impact of select correlates on families it is expected that a study in the Indian context is viable and feasible.

Chapter 5

Methodological Matters in Family Studies

1. Introduction

The present chapter exclusively deals with the methodology employed in this study. It includes the design of the study, the locale of the study, the sample and sampling procedure, socio-demographic details, inclusion and exclusion criteria, method of study, the description of the tools administration of the tests, scoring and processing of the data, and outline of the statistical techniques adopted are explained. The rationale for presenting the methodological details is to highlight how each of the dependent variables has been chosen, it also give an idea how they has been tested through standardized tools.

The researcher acknowledges that this is not a longitudinal study. In longitudinal study an observational research method is employed in which data is gathered for the same subjects repeatedly over a period of time. Longitudinal research projects can extend over years or even decades. In a longitudinal cohort study, the same individuals are observed over the study period. However, in this research the literature related to the seven correlates namely; Family Communication, Mass media, Religious adherence, Educational level, Place of residence, Gender differences and the Levels of Income), that are considered to have direct or indirect impact on the Naga family, were reviewed. Remarkable evidences exist with regard to their collective effect on family. In the light of these evidences, ideas were generated from the empirical and theoretical findings on these variables to construct the items for the scale. Further a pilot study was conducted along with validity and reliability test using standardized tool that has been developed in the field, then only scales was finalized.

2. Design of the Study

The design of a study is ideally formulated to best suit the nature of the problem under investigation, objectives of the study, resources available, characteristics of the population, and need for precision and quality. The purpose of the present study is to identify the specific correlates of Naga Family System. Those are: the correlation of Family Communication with Naga Family System; the Correlation of Media influence with Naga family system; the Correlation of Religious Impact with Naga family system, Along with this aim, certain specific objectives were also framed such as to find out, the difference between urban and rural families in their family system, The difference between the male and female in their attitude to family system, the difference between high and low level of income and their attitude to family and also to find out the difference between the high and low level of education and the opinion about the present family system. The details of the methodology adopted for the study is presented in the following subsections.

3. Locale and Universe of the Study

The locale of the present investigation is the State of Nagaland. The Universe is the 16 major Naga tribes who had settled in Nagaland prior to 1963 (the year Nagaland got its Statehood). The sample for the study comprises of 512 Christian families from two districts, Kohima the capital of Nagaland and Dimapur the commercial city of the Naga.

4. Sample and Sampling Procedure

The sample for the study consists of 16 Major Naga tribes from two Districts of Nagaland. A Stratified random sampling method was adopted for the data collection. The sample for the study consists of 512 families, (32 families each from 16 Naga tribes). The researcher also collected socio-demographic details of the Naga-families. Brief information on the personal and socio-economic status, as well as educational details were also gathered to present the level of influence depending on their exposure to various means of media, their religious adherence, level of income, place of residence, and gender difference factors for better information on the families.

4.1. Inclusion Criteria

4.1.1. Naga families settled in Nagaland since 1963
4.1.2. Naga families in which both the spouses are Nagas by birth
4.1.3. Naga families living within the present state of Nagaland
4.1.4. Naga Families with a least a child or more
4.1.5. Naga families who are Christians

4.2. Exclusion Criteria

4.2.1. Naga families who settled in Nagaland after 1963

4.2.2. Naga families in which either of the spouses are not Naga by birth
4.2.3. Naga families who live outside the present Nagaland state
4.2.4. Naga Families without issue (child)
4.2.5. Naga Families who are not a practicing Christians

4.3. Sampling Procedure

The sample consists of 512 Naga families in the two districts of Nagaland: Kohima, the capital city and Dimapur the commercial town of Nagaland. (In this two cities all the tribes lives for employment, education, business, and other related affairs). A multistage random sampling technique was adopted drawing a sample of 512 families from the two districts of Nagaland. The following figure shows the procedure adopted for the sampling:

Table 1.0. Distribution of Sample According to Tribe, Education, Income, Residence and Gender

Sl. No.	Tribe Wise	Educational Level		Income Level		Place of Residence		Gender
		High	Low	High	Low	Urban	Rural	
1.	**Angami**	10	6	7	9	11	5	Male
		9	7	5	11	6	10	Female
2.	**Ao**	6	10	11	5	9	7	Male
		8	8	9	7	5	11	Female
3.	**Chakhesang**	5	11	8	8	6	10	Male
		7	9	12	4	5	11	Female
4.	**Chang**	8	8	7	9	10	6	Male
		5	11	6	10	9	7	Female
5.	**Lotha**	4	12	10	6	7	9	Male
		8	8	5	11	9	7	Female
6.	**Mao**	10	6	8	8	5	11	Male
		9	7	6	10	7	9	Female
7.	**Khiammingam**	4	12	5	11	10	6	Male
		9	7	6	10	11	5	Female
8.	**Konyak**	8	8	7	9	10	6	Male
		5	11	12	4	9	7	Female
9.	**Phom**	5	11	8	8	6	10	Male
		7	9	5	11	7	9	Female
10.	**Pochury**	8	8	4	12	7	9	Male
		6	10	9	7	5	11	Female
11.	**Poumai**	10	6	5	11	9	7	Male

		5	11	8	8	10	6	Female
12.	**Rengma**	10	6	7	9	8	8	Male
		8	8	5	11	7	9	Female
13.	**Sangtam**	12	4	7	9	6	10	Male
		5	11	10	6	7	9	Female
14.	**Sema**	8	8	5	11	6	10	Male
		9	7	10	6	11	5	Female
15.	**Yimchungrii**	9	7	8	8	6	10	Male
		4	12	11	5	9	7	Female
16.	**Zeliang**	8	8	9	7	6	10	Male
		11	5	10	6	8	8	Female

The first stage of sampling was identifying the families in Dimapur and Kohima. After families were identified, a list of Naga tribes recognized by the Government of Nagaland was taken into consideration. There are 17 tribes that are recognized by the government of Nagaland. The tribes are Angami, Ao, Chakhesang, Chang, Kachari, Khiamngam, Konyak, Kuki, Lotha, Pochuri, Phom, Rengma, Rongmai, Sangtam, Sema, Yimchunger, and Zeliang. In the course of the study Rongmai an offshoot of Zeliangrong has been recognized as a distinct tribe (2013) making the latest (17th Schedule Tribe) inclusion in the tribes of Nagaland. However, the data collection was done before the tribe was recognized as a separate tribe. Nonetheless they are included in the zeliangrong tribe as some of the respondents were from the tribe while dealing with the Zeliangrong.

Kachari and Kuki tribes were omitted intentionally, the reason been that, though they are recognized tribe under government of Nagaland their present population in Nagaland is rather small, and in spite of repeated attempts to contact the church leaders of the two tribes, the researcher was unsuccessful to contact them, as they don't have well organized church (infrastructure), in the case of Kacharis, they are predominantly Hindus and practices other tribal religions. For which two other Naga tribes namely Mao and Poumai are included in the purview of the research. The reason being that though these two tribes are yet to get state recognition as a tribe in Nagaland, they have fairly large Christian population settled in Nagaland since 1963 (fulfilling one of the Inclusion Criteria). Moreover, they have large Christian congregation both in rural and urban areas in Kohima and Dimapur districts where empirical research was conducted. Since the research was done among Christian population this two tribes were included in the research.

The second stage of sampling was preparation of the list of families in Kohima and Dimapur. For the purpose, tribal Churches and Association of the selected tribes were contacted. With the help of the church pastors and association (diocese) leaders families list from each tribe was prepared.

The third stage of sampling is the selection of the final sample of families. From the above list using the inclusion and exclusion criteria, a sample consisted of 512 families were selected randomly from sixteen tribes. Thus the sample for the study consisted of 512 families out of which 270 married men and 242 married women represented. 240 were from rural resident and 272 were from urban resident; 270 were with high qualification (Graduate and above) out of which 142 men and 128 women participated, and 122 men and 120 women who were with plus two qualification. Moreover 240 who draw month salaries of more than Rs. 25,000/- represented the high income families and 272 who draw monthly salary of below Rs.24,000/- represented the low income family, respectively.

5. Socio-Demographic Details

This section give details break-up of the samples according to the family status and other socio-demographic variables such as educational level, place of residence, Income level, and gender, are under consideration.

This gives an idea of the procedure for the selection of the sample.

Table 2.0. Distribution of Sample According to Educational Level

Education Level					
		Frequency	Percent	Valid Percent	Cumulative Percent
No of Valid Cases	High (Graduate Plus)	270	52.0	52.0	52.0
	Men	142	30	30	
	Women	128	22	22	
	Low (SSLC or Plus 2)	242	48.0	48.0	100.0
	Men	122	25	25	
	Women	120	23	23	
	Total	512	100.0	100.0	

Table 2.0. Gives an idea of two levels of educational background of the respondents. The low educational level were those with qualification up to SSLC or Plus 2 passed, and those with high educational qualification were graduate and above. Here 142 men were with high level of education and 122 with low education. And 128 women were with high education and 120 with low level of education. People with higher educational qualification exceeded people with lower qualification due to their open participation in the survey conducted; as such there is no other motive.

Table 3.0. Distribution of Sample According to Place of Residence

Place of Residence					
		Frequency	Percent	Valid Percent	Cumulative Percent
No of Valid Cases	Rural	240	46.0	46.0	46.0
	Urban	272	54.0	54.0	100.0
	Total	512	100.0	100.0	

Table 3.0. Indicates the categorization of the sample from two places of residence. 272 respondents represent urban and 240 respondents represent rural resident respectively. This un-equal number of division is done simply because there were more families from urban settings who could easily be assessable than the rural resident.

Table 4.0. Distribution of Sample According Income Level

Income Level					
		Frequency	Percent	Valid Percent	Cumulative Percent
No of Valid Cases	High (Above Rs. 25,000) monthly	240	46.0	46.0	46.0
	Low (below Rs.24,000) monthly	272	54.0	54.0	100.0
	Total	512	100.0	100.0	

Table 4.0 shows the division of the sample according to income level. The sample is classified into two groups. Group 1, indicates those with high level of income earning monthly salary of Rs. 25,000 and above. Group 2, are those with low income drawing monthly salary of less than Rs. 24,000. Here 272 of the respondents are from low income families and 240 of the respondent are from high income family.

Table 5.0. Distribution of Sample According to Gender

Gender+					
		Frequency	Percent	Valid Percent	Cumulative Percent
No of Valid Cases	Male	270	52.0	52.0	52.0
	Female	242	48.0	48.0	100.0
	Total	512	100.0	100.0	

Table 5.0. Shows the classification according to gender. Male samples represented by 270, and female sample by 242. Male respondent surpassed the female respondent because male were more vocal and willing than their female counterpart.

6. The Tools

The researcher used the following tools to bring forth data for the present study. Family Rating Scale, (ii) Media Influence Scale and (iii) Religious Impact Scale. The details about the tools are presented below.

6.1. Description of the Tools

The description of the tool used in the present study is furnished below:

6.1.1. Personal Data

The personal data (Socio-demographic and background information) was gathered using the schedule, which involves items that deal with data on tribe, level of education, location of residence, gender and level of income. This has been presented along with the following scales.

6.2. Family Rating Scale (FRS, Bernice S. and Rudolf H. Moos (2009) Thelma, Debby and Richard, 2011)

The subject matter of the present study deals with impact of select correlates on family environment and functions. In this context, impact of select correlates with the present family function and style assumes a great significance. The tools developed in other contexts may not be relevant for the special situation of Naga families and therefore, it was decided to construct one for the purpose of the present study. The researcher thus standardized the scale for the present study.

6.2.1. Conceptualisation

The literature related to the topic impact of select correlates and its effect on the family functioning in the present context was reviewed with a view to identify the various aspects and dimensions involved in the measurement of the family. Interesting evidences exist with regard to the effect of select correlates upon family. In the light of these evidences, ideas were generated from the empirical and theoretical findings to construct the items for the scale.

The evaluation of the impact of select correlates on family life is the subject matter of the scale. This task has been achieved by the construction of a questionnaire providing indexes of the factors that impact family life. For this purpose, it was necessary to define the construct and identify its components. The items in the scale depict the patterns of present day families that have been impacted by various factors. The following factors were taken into consideration.

a. Family Relationship
b. Fellow Feeling, Learned Values,
c. Attentiveness to Kins, clan and Village,
d. Respect for Elders and accepting Advice,
e. Sacrifices for Common good/welfare.

6.2.2. Item Generation

Accordingly, items were constructed relating to family environment and family functioning styles. The responses of the subjects towards the items were recorded using a 5-point format representing the extent to which they agree with a given statement. A total of 20 items were initially generated to serve as the item pool from which representative items could be selected. A thorough scrutiny of the item pool, which examined the objectivity, clarity, representation, etc., of the item resulted in the selection of 15 items to be included in the draft scale.

6.2.3. Tryout

The draft tool was pilot-tested on a sample of people who were married. The sample included 46 married women and 54 married men drawn from the survey, who participated in the pilot study of the present work. The responses to the scale were made according to the instructions printed along with the test items.

6.2.4. Item Selection

The final selection of the items from the draft scale was made using the same procedure as in the case of other test described earlier. As mentioned earlier, the selection process involved a way of determining the internal consistency among the set of items used to measure the variable. The item analysis was done to identify those items that form an internally consistent scale and eliminate those that do not. The data obtained from 100 married people who participated in the pilot survey were rank ordered. From this list, the upper and lower extreme groups of 33 married people were selected to form the high and low subgroups. As the next step, the t-values of items (based on mean scores obtained by the high group and low group on the item) were computed and ranked. Thus, at the end of the screening process, the first 15 items with t-values ranging from -3.236 to -5.471 were retained for the final scale. When the item analysis was completed, 15 items were retained in the final version. Instructions to the respondents were printed at the beginning of the test. Both the instructions and the items were prepared, which made it easy for its self- administration. A copy of the final scale is given in Appendix III.

6.2.5. Reliability

To ensure the inclusion of only the best items in the final scale, Cronbach's Alpha method was utilised. The purpose of analysis was to identify those items that form an internally consistent scale and eliminate those that do not. The table which shows the reliability is given in the Appendix IV:

6.2.6. Validity

The test has been developed following a systematic method which involved construction of an item pool based on review of relevant literature, item scrutiny, and item analysis. Extensive discussions with the experts in the field ensured the face validity of the scale. Examination of the items contained in the scale may testify to its content validity.

6.3. Media Influence Scale (MIS, Dohnt and Tiggermann (2006) Saji and Lucita, 2011)

The subject matter of the present study relates to correlates of media influence on Naga family. In this context, correlation of family life with exposure to media assumes a great significance. The tools developed in other context may not be relevant for the special study of Nagaland and therefore, it was decided to construct one for the purpose of the present study.

6.3.1. Conceptualization

The literature related to the topic of media Influence of Family was reviewed with a view to identify the various aspects and dimensions involved in the measurement of the media influence. Remarkable evidences exist with regard to the effect of media on family. In the light of these evidences, ideas were generated from the empirical and theoretical findings to construct the items for the scale.

The evaluation of the exposure to media is the subject matter of the scale. This task has been achieved by the construction of a questionnaire providing indices of the contact of married people with mass media. For this purpose, it was necessary to define the construct and identify its components. The items in the scale portray the pattern of families exposing themselves to the influence of media. Mass Media includes the television, movies, music, internet social networking, and printed media. The test items focus on both within and outside of home environment. The following factors were taken into consideration.

i. Mass Media Impact on Family
ii. Television Impact on Family
iii. Movies Impact on Family
iv. Music, Mobile and Internet Impact on Family
v. News Paper, Magazine and Radio Impact on Family

The procedure followed for the development and standardization of the test was similar to that followed for the earlier tests.

6.3.2. Item Generation

The task of generating items for evaluating the media influence was to be done carefully as it must cover all the significant areas of media influence. The stem of the items consisted of statements intended to measure the exposure to movies, television, internet, audio, printed media etc. Each item was designed with special care and effort. Modifications in the item content were made after consultation with experts and a team of married people, and couples who were approached at the initial phase (pilot study) of the study. A list of 20 items was prepared, which was subjected to critique by experts. After meticulous evaluation and revision of the items, 15 were selected in the final draft scale.

6.3.3. Tryout

The draft scale was administered to a representative sample of 100 married people as per the method mentioned earlier. The subjects were to give responses as directed in the test. For each positive statement, integral values of 5, 4, 3, 2, and 1 were given to each of five response choices respectively. For the negative statements, the weighing scheme was reversed so that higher scores always indicated favourable attitude positions. The total score for each subject was obtained by summing up the weights of component items. A response sheet was not scored if there were more than three omitted items.

6.3.4. Item Selection

The final selection of the items from the draft scale was made using the same procedure as in the case of other tests described earlier. As mentioned earlier, the selection process involved a way of determining the internal consistency among the set of items used to measure the variable.

The item analysis was done to identify those items that form an internally consistent scale and eliminate those that do not. The data obtained from 100 married couples who participated in the pilot survey were rank ordered. From this list, the upper and lower extreme groups of 33 married men and women were selected to form the high and low sub-groups. As the next step, the *t*-values of items (based on mean scores obtained by the high group and low group on the item) were computed and ranked. Thus, at the end of the screening process, and after the discussion with the expert the first 15 items with t-values ranging from -3.270 to -6.402 were retained in the final version. The scale contained 15 statements. The *t*-values of the selected items are given in appendix VI.

6.3.5. Reliability

To ensure the inclusion of only the best items in the final scale, Cronbach's Alpha method was utilised. The purpose of analysis was to identify those items that form an internally consistent scale and eliminate those that do not. The table which shows the reliability is given below: Instructions to the respondents were printed at the beginning of the test. Both the instructions and the items were prepared, which made it easy for its self- administration. A copy of the final scale is given in Appendix VII.

6.3.6. Validity

Examination of the items contained in the scale may testify to its face validity and content validity. Seeking expert opinion tested the face validity of the scale. The construct was defined and the items were framed on the basis of insights gained from review of related literature. Further, the systematic procedures followed for item analyses and item selection also helped to ensure validity of the tool.

6.4. Religious Adherence Scale (RAS, Pfiefer and Waettly (1995), Saji and Lucita, 2011)

The RIS was developed on the basis of the conceptual framework provided by an extensive review of related literature. It is often recognized that religion has great influence on individual as well as community life. Another important correlate of the family is religious impact on family life. Therefore, it became imperative to construct a tool to measure the impact of religion on family. Generally the culture in Nagaland is very much religious oriented. Review of literature revealed that the religion has a great role in the family life and its relationship. Religious adherence and its components are very unique and different in Indian situation when it is compared to western countries. This prevented the adoption of available western tools for assessing the religious impact on family. Hence, it was decided to construct a tool for assessing the impact of religion in connection with the present study.

6.4.1. Conceptualisation

The present tool is intended to assess the religious devotion of the Naga families. The items of the test consisted of the specific areas of religiosity. The major domain of this variable is the extent of active involvement and interest in religion and its activities. The following factors were taken into consideration.

i. Importance of Prayer
ii. Religious Perception and belief
iii. Religious experience and ritual
iv. Zeal and Passion to Witness
v. Giving importance to Religious function and Respect for Religious Leaders

6.4.2. Item Generation

In the present tool, the domains include the interest towards reading scriptures, participating in rituals and practices and the interest for personal meditation and attendance in the religious places. Suggestions and opinions were sought from a small group of religious representatives and also from the married people and married couples.

A total of 20 items were initially generated to construct the item pool from which the most suitable and representative ones could be selected. From the initial pool of 20 items, 15 were selected for inclusion in the final draft scale after rigorous scrutiny and screening process.

The response format for the items was based on the nature of the responses to be made to each of the specific items. The subjects were asked to tick on a 5-point scale based on the choices presented. These response categories represented the extent of agreement with a statement.

6.4.3. Tryout

The draft scale was tried out on a married people. The sample included 46 female and 54 male drawn from the survey, who participated in the pilot study of the present work. The responses obtained were scored as explained below.

For each positive statement, integral values of 5, 4, 3, 2, and 1 were given to each of five response choices respectively. For the negative statements, the weighing scheme was reversed so that higher scores always indicated favourable attitude positions. The total score for each subject was obtained by summing up the weights of component items.

6.4.4. Item Selection

The final selection of the items from the draft scale was made using the same procedure as in the case of other tests described earlier. As mentioned earlier, the selection process involved a way of determining the internal consistency among the set of items used to measure the variable.

The item analysis was done to identify those items that form an internally consistent scale and eliminate those that do not. The data obtained from 100 married men and women who participated in the pilot survey were rank ordered. From this list, the upper and lower extreme groups of 33 married people were selected to form the high and low subgroups. As the next step, the *t*-values of items (based on mean scores obtained by the high group and low group on the item) were computed and ranked. Thus, at the end of the screening process, and after the discussion with the expert the first 15 items with t-values ranging from -3.066 to -5.692 were retained for the final scale. The *t*-values of the selected items are given in the appendix IX.

6.4.5. Reliability

To ensure the inclusion of only the best items in the final scale, Cronbach's Alpha method was utilised. The purpose of analysis was to identify those items that form an internally consistent scale and eliminate those that do not. The table which shows the reliability is given below:

When the item analysis was completed, 15 items were retained in the final version. Instructions to the respondents were printed at the beginning of the test. Both the instructions and the items were prepared in English, which made it easy for its self-administration. A copy of the final scale is given in Appendix X.

6.4.6. Validity

The test has been developed following a systematic method which involved construction of an item pool based on review of relevant literature, item scrutiny, and item analysis. Extensive discussions with the experts in the field ensured the face validity of the scale. Examination of the items contained in the scale may testify to its content validity.

7. Statistical Techniques

SPSS (Statistical Package for the Social Science) a computer application that provide statistical analysis of data was used for analysis and testing hypotheses. Analysis of quantitative data is done through different statistical methods. The tools of analysis such as Percentage Analysis, Analysis of Variance-test (ANOVA), "t" test, Correlation coefficient test, Chi-Square test, and Factor Analysis were used in this research.

7.1. **Percentage Analysis** is the Method to represent raw streams of data as a percentage (a part in 100 – percent) for better understanding of collected data.

7.2. Anova

Analysis of variance is a statistical tool used to test the quantity of variance of more than two categories. Since the present study is considering seven independent variables at a time to investigate their combined effects on the dependent variable (family system), this analysis of variance was used.

7.3. 't' Test

't' Test is one of the statistical methods of testing the hypothesis about difference in mean especially when it involves twine studies. In this research, 't' test is used to compare the mean score male and female, urban and rural, low and high income group, low and high level of education.

7.4. Correlation Coefficient

This refers to the relationship between any two or more variables. In this study the correlation coefficient method is used to see the relation between family life and other seven independent variables.

7.5. Chi Square

Chi- Square test of independence is a non-parametric test of statistic significance for bivariate tabular analysis. It is used to examine the association between two categorical variables. In this research Chi-Square was applied to identify the association between family life environment and other seven variables.

7.6. Factor Analysis

Factor Analysis is a statistical technique that can uncover relationship patterns underlying hundreds of interesting phenomenon such as changes in family system, changes in interest rate (economic studies), changes in relationship pattern etc. Factor analysis is used to analyze large number of dependent variables to detect certain aspects of the independent variable (called factors) affecting those dependent variables. In this study factor analysis is used to determine how the seven independent variables affect the dependent variables i,e., family system.

8. Conclusion

For an empirical research a detail presentation of the methodology employed for the analysis of the collected data is imperative, so that how each variable has been tested could be ascertained. Therefore, the detailed description of methodology of the present study is presented in this chapter. It provides a clear picture for analysis of the data prepared for the present investigation. The subsequent chapter elucidates the data analysis, discussion and its relevant interpretation.

Chapter 6

Analysis of the Field Research and Interpretation

1. Introduction

This chapter deals with the analysis of the data and its interpretation with discussion. The plan of analysis is given at the beginning explaining the mode of analysis. The conclusions elucidated from the analysis are provided at the end of this chapter.

2. Plan of Analysis

A universal data design of analysis at the onset of the chapter will help the reader in understanding the facts easily. As stated earlier, the present study was designed to determine the specific select correlates and its impact on the Naga family life in order to suggest relevant family counselling models. The variables considered in the study could be classified as following: (i) the socio-demographic parameters which include, educational, place of Residence, income and gender difference (ii) correlation of Family environment and family life, (iii) correlation of exposure to media and family life and (iv) correlation of religious adherence and family life.

3. Analysis of the Socio Demographic Parameters

As stated clearly in the opening chapter, an extensive survey was conducted among the population of Naga families in order to identify the socio demographic parameters and determinants of the family life. The socio demographic parameters included the tribe of the respondent, gender, place of residence, level of education, and the level of income. Data from 512 respondents (270 men and 242 women) were obtained in the survey, which was conducted using a stratified sampling technique.

"t"-test, chi-square, and analysis of variance, were chosen as the main tools of analysis. "t"-test is utilized to check the relationship between family system and its independent variables.

The results obtained are presented in the following section.

4. Results and Discussions

To systematically present the analysis, results and discussion, this chapter is organized into the following main sections:

1. Correlation of Communication and Family
2. Correlation of Exposure to Media and Family
3. Correlation of Religious Adherence and Family
4. Correlation of Education and Family
5. Correlation of Place of Residence and Family
6. Correlation of Income and Family
7. Correlation of Gender and Family

4.1. Correlation of Communication and Family

In this section an attempt is made to examine the correlation between communication and family satisfaction. It was explored by using a Chi-square test, Factor Analysis and Multi Regression Test. This was done to examine whether there is any significant correlation between communication and family satisfaction among the married couples. The results are presented in the following Tables.

Table 6.0. Chi-square Test: Crosstab (Communication and Family Life Satisfaction)

Crosstab					
Count					
		Satisfaction			
		Low	Medium	High	Total
Family communication	Low	4	0	0	4
	Medium	144	194	0	338
	High	0	130	40	170
	Total	148	324	40	512

Table 7.0. Chi-square Test: Association between Communication and Family Life

Chi-Square Tests			
Association between Communication and Family	Value	df	Asymp. Sig. (2-sided)
Pearson Chi-Square	167.597[a]	4	.000
Likelihood Ratio	221.191	4	.000
Linear-by-Linear Association	160.678	1	.000
No of Valid Cases	512		

*Highly significant (p value .000 <0.05)

Table 7.0 reveals there is significant association between family communication and family, since the significant value is less than 0.05, as the communication level increases family also increases and when level of communication among the members of the family diminishes level of satisfaction among the members of the family also decreases.

Communication is the best means to maintain healthy relationship, without proper communication life in the family would be very difficult and level of satisfaction would be affected.

Table 8.0. One way ANOVA Test: Correlation between Communication and Family

ANOVA						
		Sum of Sqaures	df	Mean Square	F	Sig. level
F1	Between Groups	556.112	33	16.852	8.658	.000
	Within Groups	930.386	478	1.946		
	Total	1486.498	511			
F2	Between Groups	839.852	33	25.450	14.445	.000
	Within Groups	842.148	478	1.762		
	Total	1682.000	511			
F3	Between Groups	612.397	33	18.557	14.110	.000
	Within Groups	628.664	478	1.315		
	Total	1241.061	511			
F4	Between Groups	2118.294	33	64.191	30.108	.000
	Within Groups	1019.111	478	2.132		
	Total	3137.404	511			
F5	Between Groups	1432.892	33	43.421	19.053	.000
	Within Groups	1089.327	478	2.279		
	Total	2522.219	511			

**Highly significant (significant level .000 <0.05)

Significance value is less than 0.05, prove that there is significant correlation between the dependent variable (family satisfaction) and the independent variables such as: Family Relationship (F1), Fellow Feeling, Learned values (F2), Attentiveness to Kins, Clans and one's Village (F3), Respect for Elders and Accepting Advice (F4), and Sacrifices for common good or welfare (F5). These are the five variables taken into consideration in testing their impact on family.

It is obvious that Family satisfaction would be high and it is correlated with strong family relationship, fellow feeling and learned values, attentiveness to kins, clans and one's village, respect for elders and accepting their advice and where there is sacrifices for common good or welfare.

Table 9.0. Correlation-Coefficient Test: Between Communication and Family

Co-efficients[a]						
Model B		Unstandardized Coefficients		Standardized Coefficients		
		Std. Error	Beta	T	Sig.	
1	(Constant)	-1.547E-15	.000		.000	1.000
	F1	1.080	.000	.261	1.186E9	.000
	F2	1.090	.000	.278	1.179E9	.000
	F3	1.060	.000	.239	1.043E9	.000
	F4	1.070	.000	.379	1.588E9	.000
	F5	1.050	.000	.340	1.473E9	.000
a. Dependent Variable: Family						

The model is Family (X) = constant+1.08 F_1+1.09 F_2+1.06 F_3+1.07 F_4+1.05 F_5

All the five variables (Family Relationship (F1), Fellow Feeling, Learned values (F2), Attentiveness to Kins, Clans and one's Village (F3), Respect for Elders and Accepting Advice (F4), and Sacrifices for common good or welfare (F5), positively affect family, of these five, Family is highly associated with F_2, because high value of the beta coefficient is 1.090.

F2 which is represented by variables like, attentiveness to one's kins, clan, and village is the most crucial and important factor for smooth family function. Tribal society has strong communal foundation. Sharing, giving and supporting. Therefore, no single family is left alone both in time of happiness and trouble. It is the kins, clan and villagers who always stood by the family in every circumstances of family life. Thus the result with high beta coefficient 1.090 is accurate reading of this factor.

Table 10.0. Factor Analysis: High component Score Test among the scale on Family

Component Score Coefficient Matrix					
	Component				
	1	2	3	4	5
A1	-.228	.207	.101	.014	.483
A3	.180	.194	.156	-.212	-.220
A5	-.066	.372	-.048	.142	.068
A6	.015	.140	.171	.263	-.410
A7	-.061	.406	.009	-.177	.017
A9	.076	-.141	.532	-.133	.043
A10	-.078	-.047	.438	.084	.021
A12	.154	-.154	.010	.337	.064
A13	-.095	-.026	-.020	.644	-.045
A14	.062	-.097	.061	.050	.520
A16	.220	.046	-.114	.207	.006
A17	.209	.120	-.148	-.174	.283
A18	.349	-.157	.108	-.125	-.095
A19	.287	-.025	.074	-.042	-.090
A20	.201	.430	-.394	.005	-.106
Extraction Method: Principal Component Analysis. Rotation Method: Varimax with Kaiser Normalization.					

High Component Score is for A14, Out of these 15 variables considered, A14 is most prominent one.

A 14, is a statement that stated that "Rich and poor families alike enjoy equal status among the Naga classless society" with. 520 score in factor analysis i.e., 67.9% believe that Naga society which was a classless society is no more the same. Today, there is fast changing trend, and rich and poor do not enjoy equal status anymore as it was some decades ago.

This trend needs to be addressed with all seriousness. There is clear indication that Naga society which till recently enjoys classless society is in a transition period. Many social critiques from Nagaland have started rising concern on this issue. It is therefore necessary to tackle this issue once and for all for the betterment of the society.

4.2. Correlation of Exposure to Media and Family

In this division an attempt is made to examine the correlation between Exposure to media and family life. It was explored by using a Chi-square test, Factor Analysis and Multi Regression Test. This was done to examine whether there is any significant correlation between Mass media and family among the married couples. The results are presented in the tables below:

Table 11.0. Chi-square Test: Crosstab (Media and Family)

Crosstab					
Count					
		Media Scale			
		Low	Medium	High	Total
Family Scale	Low	0	4	0	4
	Medium	6	328	4	338
	High	4	158	8	170
	Total	10	490	12	512

Table 12.0. Chi-square Test: Correlation between Mass Medias and Family

Chi-Square Tests			
	Value	df	Asymp. Sig. (2-sided)
Pearson Chi-Square	46.561[a]	4	.0361
Likelihood Ratio	46.237	4	.0382
Linear-by-Linear Association	42.172	1	.041
No of Valid Cases	512		

*significant (p value .0361 <0.05)

There is significant correlation between Media and family, since the significant value is less than 0.05. Mass media if used for right purpose is rather very essential and necessary, however in this study we are dealing with the negatively impact of media. Family in which there is unrestraint and excessive use of media, like television, internet, mobile, movies etc. becomes a threat and hazardous for family life.

This result is obvious, as per literature review and related studies, it is found that families have been tremendously confronted and challenged by mass media. Naga families who were considered to have strong believed in traditional family values and uphold the family ethos and close ties are in transition period. As a matter of fact, various mass media has impacted family life so much so that many family value which were traditionally considered as the inheritance and heritage or the trade mark of the Nagas are been challenged by today's Mass media.

In the recent past only radio and newspapers along with hardly two-three national television channels were accessible by both rural and urban families in Nagaland. But today, hardly any village is without connection of cable (satellite) TV, latest magazines, internet connection, smart mobile phone etc., which promote individualism and personalized lifestyle. As such even within the same family people don't have sufficient time to share their happiness or sorrow, which in turn affects the family fabric and ties.

The researcher is not all together rejecting the use of modern means of communication; rather it is highly recommended that these modern means of communication should be use for right purposes, also there should be strict monitoring by the parent on the usage of media especially by today's generation.

Table 13.0. ANOVA Test: Relationship between Mass Media and Family

ANOVA						
		Sum of Squares	df	Mean Square	F	Sig.
M1	Between Groups	1657.395	26	63.746	20.044	.000
	Within Groups	1536.088	483	3.180		
	Total	3193.482	509			
M2	Between Groups	1061.767	26	40.837	12.344	.000
	Within Groups	1597.937	483	3.308		
	Total	2659.704	509			
M3	Between Groups	487.176	26	18.738	12.870	.000
	Within Groups	703.187	483	1.456		
	Total	1190.363	509			
M4	Between Groups	329.028	26	12.655	10.039	.000
	Within Groups	608.846	483	1.261		
	Total	937.875	509			
M5	Between Groups	362.303	26	13.935	11.161	.000
	Within Groups	603.048	483	1.249		

**Highly significant (significant level .000 <0.05)

Significance value is less than 0.05, means that there is significant correlation between the dependent variable family life and the independent variables M1, M2, M3, M4, M5.

M1-represents Mass Media Impact on Family, M2-Television Impact on Family, M3-Movies Impact on Family, M4-Music, Mobile and Internet Impact on Family, and M5-represents News Paper, Magazine and Radio Impact on family.

Mass media play a crucial role in today's context. The impact of mass media on the life of family is enormous. The research result shows that there is high significant correlation between family and mass media, the lesser exposure to media and balance use of media has positive impact on family, where as random and uncontrolled usage of media has adverse impact on family well-being and family functioning.

Table 14.0. Coefficient–Correlation Test: Between Mass Media and Family Life

Coefficients[a]						
Model B		Unstandardized Coefficients		Standardized Coefficients		
		Std. Error	Beta	t	Sig.	
1	(Constant)	1.312	.276		4.757	.000
	M1	.979	.013	.476	75.513	.000
	M2	.943	.014	.418	67.583	.000
	M3	1.101	.021	.327	51.496	.000
	M4	1.107	.024	.292	46.738	.000
	M5	1.014	.024	.271	42.277	.000
a. Dependent Variable: Family Life						

The model is Family (X)=constant+0.979 M_1+0.943 M_2+1.101 M_3+1.107 M_4+1.014 M_5

All the five variables positively affect Family, of these five, Family is highly associated with M_4, because high value of the beta coefficient 1.107

M4 represents the variable such as; Music, Mobile and internet which has become a menace to family life so much so that most families are not in real peace. Even in the remote villages mass media has great impact on people's life. Especially music, mobile phone and internet usage has replaced family worship, family sharing and family time together.

Table 15.0. Factor Analysis: High component Score Test among the scale on Mass Media

Component Score Coefficient Matrix					
	Component				
	1	2	3	4	5
B1	-.052	.016	-.032	.509	-.211
B2	-.066	.460	-.115	.032	-.209
B3	-.097	.051	-.099	.469	.156
B5	.124	-.073	.160	.305	.106
B6	.274	-.004	.041	-.141	-.263
B9	.030	-.109	.425	-.091	.218
B11	.221	.115	-.171	.185	-.272
B12	.043	-.094	.516	.044	-.111
B13	.090	.080	.380	.068	-.239
B14	-.002	.461	-.130	-.070	.154
B16	-.026	.379	-.009	.032	.122
B17	**.043**	**.068**	**-.065**	**.014**	**.552**
B18	.311	-.088	.166	.203	-.044
B19	.336	.001	.017	-.152	.129
B20	.350	-.063	.041	-.063	.186
Extraction Method: Principal Component Analysis. Rotation Method: Varimax with Kaiser Normalization.					

High Component score is for B17, hence it is the prominent factor.

B 17 refers to statement put forward in the respondent question "Nagas still maintains me first when it comes to work and duties and you first when it comes to food and other such privileges" such was the practice of the Nagas, in the recent past which is missing among the present day generation. People vouched against the statement rather highly: .043, .068, .061, .014, .552, shows that such concept is difficult to be found among the people in this individualistic lifestyle in the present day Naga society.

4.3. Correlation of Religious Adherence and Family Life

Table 16.0. Chi-square Test: Crosstab (Religion and Family Life)

Crosstab					
Count					
		Religious Scale			
		Low	Medium	High	Total
Family Scale	Low	2	2	0	4
	Medium	0	220	118	338
	High	0	56	114	170
	Total	2	278	232	512

Table 17.0. Chi-square Test: Correlation Between *Religious Adherence Family*

Chi-Square Tests			
	Value	Df	Asymp. Sig. (2-sided)
Pearson Chi-Square	43.167[a]	4	.049
Likelihood Ratio	40.703	4	.0401
Linear-by-Linear Association	40.048	1	.051
No of Valid Cases	512		

*significant (p value .049 < 0.05)

There is significant correlation between Religious Adherence and family, since the significant value is less than 0.05. It is assumed and generally accepted view that religious person are more family oriented. People who are religiously inclined tend to focus on family welfare and vice-versa; therefore there is a significant correlation between religion and family life.

Nagaland is a religious state with approximately 95% percent of its population professing Christianity. In fact Christianity is a new religion for the Naga, against their primal religion which was the religion of the Naga tribes till recent past. Both in the traditional Primal religion and Christianity, people are so passionate about their religion. Therefore, Religious adherence would have significant impact on the Naga family system.

Table 18.0. ANOVA Test: Correlation Between Religious Adherence and Family

ANOVA						
		Sum of Squares	df	Mean Square	F	Sig.
R1	Between Groups	738.923	32	23.091	12.175	.000
	Within Groups	908.513	479	1.897		
	Total	1647.436	511			
R2	Between Groups	570.225	32	17.820	10.906	.000
	Within Groups	782.650	479	1.634		
	Total	1352.875	511			
R3	Between Groups	925.387	32	28.918	17.230	.000
	Within Groups	803.924	479	1.678		
	Total	1729.311	511			
R4	Between Groups	1027.886	32	32.121	16.516	.000
	Within Groups	931.606	479	1.945		
	Total	1959.492	511			
R5	Between Groups	1200.782	32	37.524	22.649	.000
	Within Groups	793.585	479	1.657		
**Highly significant (significant level .000 <0.05)						

Significance value is less than 0.05, means that there is high significant correlation between the dependent variable family and the independent variables: R1, R2, R3, R4, R5.

Religious Adherence Scale is represented by; giving importance to prayer (R1), Religious perception and belief (R2), Religious experience and Ritual (R3), Interest and passion to witness Christ (R4), and giving importance to religious functions and respect for religious leaders (R5).

Each of these statements above carries three questions each and minutes details of religious life was explored, the result. 000 shows that there are a strong correlation between religious adherence and family satisfaction.

Table 19.0. Coefficient–Correlation Test: Between Religious Adherence and Family Life

Coefficients[a]						
Model B		Unstandardized Coefficients		Standardized Coefficients		
		Std. Error	Beta	t	Sig.	
1	(Constant)	1.264	.432		2.926	.004
	R1	.965	.030	.266	31.766	.000
	R2	1.160	.034	.290	34.465	.000
	R3	1.019	.034	.288	30.181	.000
	R4	1.007	.032	.303	31.042	.000
	R5	1.120	.030	.340	37.707	.000
a. Dependent Variable: Family						

The model is Family life (X)=constant+0.965 R_1+1.160 R_2+1.019 R_3+1.007 R_4+1.120R_5

All the five variables positively affect family, of these five, family life is highly associated with R_2, because high value of the beta coefficient 1.160.

R2 refers to religious experience and rituals. Nagas been a very religious oriented community has lot of religious activities throughout the year, as such they take religious functions and ritual very seriously, sometime it affects their official and social duties and obligation, which is basically not a healthy sign for Christian testimony. In fact being religious person one should be an example for other to emulate.

Table 20.0. Factor Analysis: High component Score Test among the scale on Religious Adherence

Component Score Coefficient Matrix				
	Component			
	1	2	3	4
C1	.404	-.240	.009	.087
C2	.116	-.142	.348	-.058
C5	.322	-.049	.064	-.131
C6	-.170	.043	.460	.027
C7	.009	.032	.393	-.076
C9	.116	-.059	-.085	.357
C10	-.062	-.110	.010	.387
C11	**-.092**	**-.006**	**-.046**	**.452**
C12	.032	.038	-.080	.351
C14	.261	.064	-.063	.031
C15	.293	.159	-.148	-.028
C16	.074	.340	-.273	.000
C18	-.231	.361	.083	.062
C19	-.060	.378	.034	-.095
C20	.037	.257	.084	-.054

Highest Component score is for C11, hence the most prominent factor is C11.

C11 refers to the statement put forward in the respondent question "Only religious faith and adherence helps us to please God and achieve proximity to God" as in accordance with the Biblical teaching that by faith alone we are drawn close to God and not by our deeds. People seem to have right understanding about maintaining closeness to God.

4.4. Correlation of Education Level and Family

Table 21.0. Chi-square Test: Crosstab

Crosstab					
Count					
		Family Scale			
		Low	Medium	High	Total
Education Level	High	4	167	85	256
	Low	0	171	85	256
	Total	4	338	170	512

Table 22.0. Chi-square Test: Correlation Between Levels of Education and Family

Chi-Square Tests			
	Value	**df**	**Asymp. Sig. (2-sided)**
Pearson Chi-Square	4.047[a]	2	.132
Likelihood Ratio	5.593	2	.061
Linear-by-Linear Association	.133	1	.715
No of Valid Cases	512		

* Significant (p value .0132<0.05)

There is significant correlation between Education Level and Family, since the significant value is than 0.05.

Level of education is a detriment factor for family. People with higher educational qualification know the art of nurturing one's family as such it have a significant relationship with family. People with lesser educational degree lacked the art of maintaining a healthy family life, because they are less read and most of those people lacked motivation for life.

Whereas people with higher education degree, support each other in every aspect of family life. At the same time people who are well qualified will do well in nurturing, caring, and maintaining their family because they are well informed about the success of running a family. In such case people's qualification make much difference between high or low level of education. Consequently there is significant relationship between education levels and family life.

4.5. Correlation of Place of Residence and Family

Table 23.0. Chi-square Test: Crosstab

Crosstab					
Count					
		Family Scale			
		Low	Medium	High	Total
Place of Residence	Rural	2	163	91	256
	Urban	2	175	79	256
	Total	4	338	170	512

Table 24.0. Chi-square Test: Correlation Between Place of Residence and Family

Chi-Square Tests			
	Value	df	Asymp. Sig. (2-sided)
Pearson Chi-Square	1.273[a]	2	.529
Likelihood Ratio	1.274	2	.529
Linear-by-Linear Association	1.196	1	.274
N of Valid Cases	512		

*Not Significant (P value .529>0.05)

There is no significant correlation between Place of Residence and Family, since the significant value is more than 0.05. As a matter of fact people whether resides in urban or rural cannot claim to have higher level of family life satisfaction. Family depends on constant and open sharing, providing each other's needs and aspiration, spending and devoting oneself to the affairs of the family and doing one's responsibility as family member. Therefore, it is safe to conclude that place of residence will have no significant impact on family as proved by the study that p value is >0.05

4.6. Correlation of Income-Level and Family

Table 25.0. Chi-square Test: Crosstab

Crosstab					
Count					
		Family Scale			
		Low	Medium	High	Total
Income Level	High	4	163	89	256
	Low	0	175	81	256
	Total	4	338	170	512

Table 26.0. Chi-square Test: Correlation Between Levels of Income and Family

Chi-Square Tests			
	Value	Df	Asymp. Sig. (2-sided)
Pearson Chi-Square	6.803[a]	2	.041
Likelihood Ratio	6.348	2	.042
Linear-by-Linear Association	.133	1	.715
N of Valid Cases	512		

*Significant (p value .041<0.05)

There is significant correlation between Income Level and Family, since the significant value is less than 0.05. In a materialistic and highly commercialized world people tend to assume that having more money and resources to spend means better and more satisfying life. Well this is the way what commercialized and business world promote. The concept of accumulation of wealth and unhealthy competition of riches is also link with life status.

Having better means of living and more resources is indeed a blessing, if those means are from right sources through proper channel. Since family life satisfaction is linked with higher income and more means to spend, it is imperative that we educate people about dignity of labour, earning through one's own sweat, healthy means of competition. Moreover, one should speak about equal distribution of wealth on the part of the government. Of late there has been so much disparity on the issues of government grants and developmental activities. Because of the present status-quo there is significant correlation between income level and family life satisfaction, for which people need to be told about kingdom values, that riches on earth need not necessarily be riches in heaven.

4.7. Correlation of Gender-Difference and Family

Table 27.0. Chi-square Test: Crosstab

Crosstab					
Count					
		Family Scale			
		Low	Medium	High	Total
Gender	Male	4	163	89	256
	Female	0	175	81	256
	Total	4	338	170	512

Table 28.0. Chi-square Test: Correlation Between Gender Difference and Family

Chi-Square Tests			
	Value	df	Asymp. Sig. (2-sided)
Pearson Chi-Square	6.803[a]	2	.041
Likelihood Ratio	6.348	2	.042
Linear-by-Linear Association	.133	1	.715
N of Valid Cases	512		

*significant (p value .041 < 0.05)

There is significant correlation between Gender and Family life, since the significant value is less than 0.05. By gender difference refers to the role, responsibilities and privileges enjoys by men and women in the society. Naga society been patriarchal in nature, in-spite of many protection and rights sanction for the women, women in Naga society still faces lot of difficulties in implementing these rights in practice. Most of the decisions for the family are taken by their male counterpart. As such men play an upper hand in the affairs of the family. As a result family life is affected with one sided (male oriented) for which gender equality must be taught to the people.

5. Summary of the Results and Tenability of the Hypotheses

Sl. No	Hypothesis	P-Value	Inference/decision
1	There will be no significant Impact of family communication on Naga Family Life	< 0.05	Reject the hypothesis
2	There will be no significant Impact of Mass Media on the Naga Family Life.	<0.05	Reject the hypothesis
3	There will be no significant Impact of Religious Adherence on the Naga Family System.	< 0.05	Reject the hypothesis
4	There will be no significant Impact of the Level of Education on the Naga Family System.	<0.05	Reject the hypothesis
5	There will be no significant Impact of Urban Rural divide on the Naga Family System.	>0.05	Accept the hypothesis
6	There will be no significant Impact of the Levels of Income on the Naga Family System.	< 0.05	Reject the hypothesis
7	There will be no significant Impact of Gender Difference on the Naga Family System.	< 0.05	Reject the hypothesis

6. Conclusion

This chapter dealt with the analysis and interpretation of the family and its correlates. The important among the result is that communication has significant impact on family, Mass media has significant impact on family life, Religious adherence also has strong impact on family, levels of income too has high significant impact on family, further more gender difference has its impact on family life. The following chapter is an attempt to draw out summary of the major findings, implications for family counselling models.

Chapter 7

Summary of the Research Findings Implications for Family Counselling

1. Introduction

This chapter consists of mainly three sections. Section 'A' presents the summary of the findings and tenability of the hypotheses. Section 'B' presents the implications of the present study. It also highlights basic skills of family counselling and strategies for counseling interventions. Four schools of psychotherapy have been dealt in this chapter. 1. Bowen's Family System Counselling Model, 2. Experiential Family Counselling, 3. Strategic Family Counselling Model and 4. Structural Family Counselling Therapy. The relevancy and application of each of these models are also dealt in this section along with its strength and limitations.

2. Section A: Summary and Findings

An attempt is made to suggest family counselling models or techniques. If family is to be fully understood, no single counselling model would be sufficient and effective enough for various cultural settings, social set up, economic background and religious orientation. Therefore, the researcher has taken into consideration some of the models that could be helpful while dealing with families and couples. Before suggesting family counselling models, a quick retrospection of the study is presented.

3. The Study in Retrospect

The present study "the impact of select correlates on Naga family system: Implications for family counselling models is undertaken in the context of the tremendous challenges faced by contemporary families in the functioning of the family life. The global phenomenon of family unrest and pressure in the healthy functioning of the family is clearly visible and a reality in the Asian, Indian and local context as well. In the light of the above scenario, the present study was designed with an aim of investigating the impact of select correlates on Naga family system: Implications for family counselling models.

In view of accomplishing the objectives of the study, the investigator selected the descriptive method. Descriptive research involves collecting data in order to test hypotheses or to answer questions concerning the current status of the subject of the study.[232] A descriptive research is carried with specific objectives and hence it results in definite conclusions. This type of research tries to describe the characteristics of the respondents in relation to a particular product or a practice or culture of importance. The researcher designed a suitable questionnaire to capture data from the respondents to test the hypothesis of the study and come out with conclusions after data analysis. The kinds of conclusions which are derived in such studies are descriptive in nature. Among the different approaches that may be used in descriptive research, the survey method is selected for the present study. A survey is an attempt to collect data from the members of the population with respect to one or more variables. In a sample survey, the researcher infers information about a population of interest based on responses drawn from that population; preferably the sample is either random or stratified random sample.[233]

The sample for the study consisted of married people with two levels of education high and low, urban and rural residence, high and low income, and married male and female. The sample comprised of 512 married people drawn from 16 tribes of Nagaland.

The Family Rating Scale, Media Influence Rating Scale and Religious Adherence Rating Scale were used to test their correlation and level of impact on family. In addition to this a data sheet was used to bring out socio-demographic and background information. The present study had seven independent variables; four of these are socio-demographic variables; namely, level of education, place of residence, gender difference, and level of income. The other independent variable considered were, family communication, mass media, and religious adherence. The study had mainly one dependent variable namely family.

SPSS (Statistical Package for the Social Science) a computer application that provide statistical analysis of data was used for analysis and testing hypothesis. Analysis of quantitative data is done through different statistical methods. The tools of analysis such as Analysis of Variance-test (ANOVA), Correlation coefficient test, Chi-Square test, Stepwise Multiple Regression, Multidimensional Scaling, Percentage Analysis, and Factor Analysis were used in this research.

---

232 L. R., Gay, *Education Research: Competencies for Analysis and Organization (3rd ed.)*, (New York: Merrille Publication Co. 1990), 135, 137.

233 Gay, *Education Research: Competencies for Analysis and Organization,*... 139-140.

Next is an attempt to highlight the summary of the actual research findings and the tenability of the hypotheses proposed for the study.

4. Summary of the Findings

1. Correlation between Communication and Family Life
2. Correlation between Exposure to Media and Family Life
3. Correlation between Religious Adherence and Family Life
4. Correlation between Education Level and Family Life
5. Correlation between Place of Residence and Family Life
6. Correlation between Income-Level and Family Life
7. Correlation between Gender-Difference and Family Life

4.1. Correlation between Communication and Family Life

The results of the study revealed that level of communication has a high significant correlation on family. Couples and family members who experience frank and open communication enjoy higher family life satisfaction. Therefore, the research's main hypothesis that there will be no significant impact of family communication on family life is rejected.

In this highly individualistic age, where even members of the same family hardly have time for sharing, fellowship, and communion, it is imperative on the part of the church to educate its members on the importance of constant family interaction. Both among the couples and family as a unit, most have sufficient time to share, to have fellowship and also go for outing together. Life will only get busier in this challenging and demanding world, but that does not mean that one should neglect family life; rather every member of the family is expected to play their part in sustaining and nurturing the family.

4.2. Correlation between Exposure to Media and Family Life

The study result uncovered that excessive exposure to mass media has a high significant impact on family. With the advancement of mass media, life has been very fast, but at the same time mass media too have lot of negative impacts affecting the healthy family functioning. As a result, the hypothesis that "there will be no significant impact of mass media on family" is nullified.

There is an urgency to educate people about the negative impact of media. The enormous impact that media have on people's life cannot be simply overlooked. Every individual young or old has been impacted by media. For which media awareness programmes should be organized through seminars, lectures, and interactive discussion to enlighten people on the right usage of media.

4.3. Correlation between Religious Adherence and Family Life

The researcher hypothesized that "there will be no significant impact of religious adherence on family" (hypothesis 3). In the analysis the correlation between religious adherence and family life was found to be highly significant. Therefore, the given hypothesis is rejected.

Religion holds a crucial factor in the life of the people. Contrary to the proposed hypothesis, highly significant correlation is found between religion and family life. For which the essence of true religiosity and spirituality need to be cultivated and practice by the people. Nagaland which claimed to have more than 95% Christian population must strengthen their religious belief, as religious person seem to have greater sense of responsibility towards family life and its affairs.[234]

4.4. Correlation between Educational-Level and Family Life

In the analysis the correction between religious adherence and family has significant relation. Contrary to the hypothesis (4) that there is a significant impact of the level of education on family. This is in contrary with the hypothesis; hence the given hypothesis is rejected.

Education is the key factor for enlightenment to success in life. Therefore, in contrary to the proposed hypothesis, there is significant impact of the level of education on family among the Naga society. Which demands a concern for the Naga educated married men and women, to use their acquired knowledge and learning for the good of the society and their own selves. In spite of high literary rate among the Nagas, they still need to be told about the value of education, that through education society progresses and stronger family relationships are developed.

4.5. Correlation between Place of Residence and Family Life

In conformity with our hypothesis 5, it is found that there is no significant correlation between place of residence and family life. Hence our hypothesis, that "there will be no significant impact of rural-urban divide on family" has been upheld, as the analysis result is in conformity to the given hypothesis.

It is rather positive and encouraging result, people either in the rural or urban seems to hold on to learned values and practices. In-spite of migrating to town and cities for job or business related affairs, they still cultivate values system learned and inherited from fore-parents. This trend needs to be encouraged. Certain learned values continue to stay with people that even after migrating to towns and cities they preserve and maintain the values inherited from the elders and parents.

234 Most writing on the percentage of Christianity in Nagaland agreed that Nagas of Nagaland would be approximately around 95%. Cf. Sema, *Parent-Children Relationship among the Naga Society towards Family Enrichment*..., 11.

4.6. Correlation between Income-Level and Family Life

The researcher hypothesized that "there will be no significant relationship between Income level and family." However, the results of the study revealed that there is significant correlation between level of income and family life. For this reason, the given hypothesis (6) is proved wrong.

In a materialistic and commercialized world today, life has been challenged with the concept of happiness for those who have enough means to spend, and Naga Christians are not free from this. Therefore, the concept of true riches and happiness as recorded in the scripture need to be told.

4.7. Correlation between Gender-Difference and Family Life

In the analysis the correlation between gender-difference and family life is found to be highly significant. The study result shows that gender role, status and position in the society determines the level of happiness in the family. Thus, the given hypothesis that there will be no significant impact of gender difference on family is rejected.

Gender inequality is still a big concern among the tribal community. Nagas with predominantly Christian population and patriarchal social set up also faces this issue rather seriously. Therefore, the Christian community needs to be told to practice what it preaches. Large numbers of female undergoing theological training has not really impacted the gender issue to the expected level. At the surface level it may seem like Naga women enjoys better status than most other women in the country. May be to certain extend the Naga women enjoys certain privileges, but there are still in many areas like, leadership role in the society, status in the church, and their position in the family itself; the Naga women need to be really liberated.

5. Section B: Implications for Family Counselling

In order to guide and prepare the Naga families toward better understanding of family values and the importance of family relationship, various Counselling methods has been suggested. However, before intervention methods are introduced, it is important to understand the preventive measures, so as to effectively guide and nurture families towards healthy functioning family.

6. Preventive Measures for Family and Family Enrichment

Most of the problems faced by the families could be prevented if timely help is given by the counsellors and family therapists. There are several preventive measures in caring for the family and family enrichment programmes. Three specific preventive measures suggested by Douglas Anderson, Charles Stewart, and Margaret Sawin are discussed here. They are simple, practicable and easy to follow.

Douglas Anderson illustrates a variety of "Family Growth Groups"- an approach he defines as "a programme involving three to five families who meet regularly for mutual care and support and for the development of family potential."[235] Anderson sees such programmes as having these unique advantages as family-strengthening approaches:

(1) The family growth group goes beyond most traditional family life education programmes by involving the whole family together as a unit in the experience...

(2) The family growth group provides a supportive network of families to strengthen the family unit. In a society that fragments the family and that isolates families from extended kin and other families in the community, there is increasing need for programmes that gives families a sense of community and belonging...

(3) The family growth group facilitates family change and growth by focusing upon development of family potential. Family potential can be understood as those latent resources within every family for changing and growing, loving, and caring, communicating, resolving conflicts, adventuring, creating and experiencing joy. The family growth group provides opportunities for families to increase their awareness of their unique strengths and resources and then to actualize these dormant capacities in family living.[236]

Margaret Sawin has developed as cited by Howard Clinebell a model of family education and nurture called "Family Clusters." Sawin summarizes the preventive measure in caring and strengthening the families in the following statements:

(1) To provide an intergenerational group of family units where children can be relate easily to adults and adults to children;

(2) To provide a group which can grow in support and mutuality for its members;

(3) To help families discover and develop their strengths through increased loving, caring, joy, and creating;

(4) To provide a group wherein there is opportunity for families to model for each other aspects of their family systems in communication, decision making, disciplining, interrelating, problem solving etc.;

(5) To provide a group where parents can gain perspective about their own children through contact with other children and other adult's perception of their children; likewise, where children can gain

235 Douglas Anderson, "The Family Growth Group: Guidance for an Emerging Means of Strengthening Families," *The Family Coordinator*, January. 1974, 7.

236 Anderson, "The Family Growth Group: Guidance for an Emerging Means of Strengthening Families," *The Family Coordinator...*, 7-8.

perspective about their own parents though contact with other parents and other children's perception of their parents;

(6) To provide an opportunity for families to consider experiences seriously related to themselves as individuals, as family members, as group members, and as members of a faith community.

(7) To provide an opportunity for positive intervention into family systems so as to facilitate their living and growing together more productively.[237]

Whereas Charles Stewart suggests three basic dimensions to church's strategy for strengthening families:

(1) The church should develop a network of caring and express its family concerns through visiting the sick, the grief-stricken, and those who are homebound. Intercessory prayer for those undergoing crisis may become a regular part of the church's order of service...the congregation is the primary agent of pastoral care with its pastors serving as enablers and consultants as well as visitors.

(2) The church should develop a family ministry through its educational programme. This ministry may be affected through intergenerational classes...; intergenerational retreats for the entire church membership including single, widowed, and divorced persons-these are ways in which groups may study together and develop the family support bonds which such inclusive study generates.

(3) The church focuses finally on family enrichment and counselling. Most family members can be helped to cope with the developmental passage points and accidental crisis periods through enrichment experiences... Family counselling should be available to those families for whom group interaction and support are not enough to help them through a critical period. The pastor will need to be aware of those who are under stress... and who require more counselling help than an enrichment group can provide.[238]

These models can be supervised by the counsellors and family therapist working with families. They are simple, easy to follow and practicable. The three preventive measures as suggested above when applied in dealing with families would be to a great extend able to address the problems faced by the families and thus help family towards healthy family and better functioning.

Furthermore, counsellors and family therapists engaged in helping the families must acquire certain skills; such as conceptual skills, technical skills and interpersonal skills, as part of preventive measures, so that any interventional

237 Clinebell, *Basic Types of Pastoral Care and Counselling...*, 303-304.

238 Charles Stewart, *The Ministers as Family Counsellor*, (Nashville: Abington Press, 1970), 173-175.

procedures they employed would be successful. Discussed below are some of the fundamental skills required in the prevention and care of the families.

7. Basic Skills for Family Counsellor or Therapist

On the part of the family therapist it is essential that they obtain skills: such as conceptual skills, technical skills and interpersonal skills for dealing with families. They are briefly discussed here.

7.1. Conceptual Skills

A concise presentation of conceptual or theoretical framework of family has been discussed in the second chapter. However, for the clarity of the subject, once again an emphasis is made on the necessity of the conceptual skills to be adopted by the family counsellors and therapist dealing with family's various issues. It is imperative for the family therapist to gain conceptual or theoretical skills to enhance the therapeutic relationship with the client or family that he/she is dealing with. The advantage of having conceptual skills is that counsellor would be able to convince the confidence of the family and couple with whom the he or she is dealing with.

7.2. Technical Skills

Family problem and issues are varied and they need various procedural skills or technical skills. The term technical here refer to the scientific know how of the skills that family therapists can employ in dealing with family issues. As there are diverse family issues and problems, so also there are various technical skills that would be helpful in addressing each of the problems to be handled or resolved.

7.3. Interpersonal Skills

Counselling in true sense is the art of human relationship. The success of any counselling session depends on quality of the interpersonal relationship. The family therapist is expected to know the magnitude of interpersonal skills. Human to human or people to people relationship is indispensible in a therapeutic relationship. Therefore, family therapists and counsellors involved in family counselling should acquire basic interpersonal skills toward meaningful and productive family counselling sessions.

Pastoral Counselling is generally understood in three modes: "The pastoral care in general, which includes all that a pastor does; pastoral counselling that concerns more structured ministry to the specific needs of the individuals; and pastoral psychotherapy."[239]

Just like the three modes, there are also three related but distinct objectives in Pastoral care. The first is known as reactive pastoral care. In this form of care,

239 Ezamo, Murry, *An Introduction to Pastoral Care and Counselling*, (New Delhi: ISPCK, 2011), 141.

care giver responds to the crisis situation of a client. Secondly, Proactive Pastoral Care. The emphasis of this type of care is on prevention rather than cure and thirdly developmental care.[240] This type of care is usually aimed at meeting the developmental challenges in each phase of life. Taking these three modes and objectives, the mission of the church through its ministry of Pastoral Care and Counselling is to train, educate and empower parents and counsellors, so that they function effectively both individually and collectively. "The general view is to call upon the church to help family by education and advice, to cope with the new situations and preserve Christian values of life."[241] Hence, in the light of the significant findings of this research, the need of approaching families with various counselling models is essential for an effective counselling of the family.

Different therapies which are relevant to the families are also discussed in order to facilitate the role of the pastoral care giver for the effective functioning of the families. Various counselling intervention, methods and approaches are being used to achieve this goal, with a focus to bring out helpful insights for presenting the implications for pastoral care and counselling. The aim of family therapy or counselling is to understand the families undergoing various pressures and challenges in their day-to-day family life. Different approaches in family counselling may be used to fulfill this objective.

8. Strategies for Counselling Intervention

Among the professionals who write about family counselling, there exists considerable disagreement about which methods are most effective for producing helpful changes in family functioning. Part of the disagreement is a result of the lack of any general agreed upon core of family theory and result of a diversity of preferences among a number of theories or models of family counselling.

Furthermore, although an increasing numbers of researches have been studying the effectiveness of family counselling, the publications tends to report the use of a global approaches, such as strategic, structural, communicational or conjoint family therapy, instead of systematically investigating the effectiveness of specific intervention strategies. Still, many family counselling models share the use of many specific intervention strategies which they have in common, and in practice, most family counsellors are eclectics and therefore, use a variety of strategies derived from the different models. For these reasons and for the clarity of the family counsellors, the classical schools of family counselling are discussed in brief as a foundational basis. Toward the end, simpler family counselling have been suggested. In certain models similar expression and ideas might be

240 Nalini, Arles, "Restructuring Pastoral Care in India: Shades of the Past in Shaping the Future" *Bangalore Theological Forum* Vol. XXXVII, No.1 (June), 2005: 34-35.

241 Arles, "Restructuring Pastoral Care in India: Shades of the Past in Shaping the Future" *Bangalore Theological Forum*..., 35.

discovered, however, as far as the researcher's knowledge is concern these models slightly differ in their approaches and applications.

8.1. Techniques

The following family counselling models and techniques have been used in working with couples and families to stimulate change or gain greater information about the family system. Each technique should be judiciously applied and viewed not as a cure, but rather as a method to help mobilize the family. The when, where, and how of each intervention always rests with the therapist's personal experience, professional judgment and personal knowledge and skills.

8.1.1. Bowen's Family System Counselling Model

Bowen's family system model is a comprehensive view of human behaviour. It is a theory that suggests that individuals cannot be understood in isolation, but rather as a part of their family. Families are systems of interconnected and interdependent individuals. His theory is understood as the 'transgenerational' or 'intergenerational' family therapy. Since a predictable pattern of interpersonal relationships connects the functioning of the family members across generations, a family can be understood well when we analyze it from at least three-generation perspective. Thus his therapy is family centered and hence called "Family System therapy," Bowen's family system therapy gives emphasis on family as the fundamental unit for understanding the individual's behavior and action. In the study of his therapy, we can conclude that in order to change an individual's behaviour, we need to first gain awareness of how the individual's choices are affected by current and historical family behavior. Also, a significant aspect of this therapy is that, the way to change oneself is to change one's relationship with others.

Bowen's therapy focuses on the balance of two forces. The first is 'togetherness' and the second is 'individuality.'[242] Two much togetherness creates fusion and prevents individuality, or developing one's own sense of self. Too much individuality results in distant and estranged family. Central to his theory, Bowen identified eight key concepts: Among them he focused more on differentiation of the self and triangulation. Some of his major concepts are briefly dealt here.

8.1.1.1. Differentiation of the Self

Differentiation is the ability to separate from thinking, the separateness of emotion and intellect level.[243] If one is not differentiated, one can hardly distinguish thoughts from feeling. Since one's intellect is so flooded with feeling, one is

242 Nichols, *The Essentials of Family Therapy...*, 85.

243 A. L., Napoliello, & Sweet, E. S "Bowen Theory: A Study of Differentiation of Self, Social Anxiety, and Physiological Symptoms," in *Contemporary Family Therapy* June 2002, Vol., 24 Issue 2, 355-369.

almost incapable of objective thinking. On the contrary, the differentiated person is able to balance thinking and feeling, being capable of making rational decisions because they distinguish between their thoughts and feelings. More specifically, differentiation of self can described as the way and individual manages the interplay of the individuality-and togetherness forces within a relationship system.[244] In sum, it is the ability to be an individual while simultaneously functioning as part of a team.

8.1.1.2. Triangulation

Triangulation here refers to three-way relationship. When there is stress in a relationship between two people, they may invite a third party into the relationship to reduce the anxiety and gain stability.[245] This is the essence in triangulation. The emotional tension may seem lessened but the underlying conflict is not resolved or rather it is made worse by the process of triangulation. On the surface, triangulation may apparently be innocent and healthy but it is not so. For instance, a woman experiencing distance from her husband may involve herself too much in caring for her son. This caring act for the child is only a way of reducing the tension she is experiencing on account of the distance from her husband.[246]

8.8.1.3. Multigenerational Transmission Process

This concept describes the transmission from generation to generation.[247] At a time in every generation, a child that is most fused will be the one less differentiated in self while the least involved child moves toward a higher level of differentiation. Usually illness will be transmitted not only beyond the individual to the family, but also beyond the nuclear family to several generations.[248] An identified problem, which in turn was the problem is the result of his/her parent's problem, which in turn as the problem of their parents and so on, for several generation.[249] The actual problem rests with multigenerational sequence in which all family members are actors and reactors.

8.1.1.4. Societal Emotional Process

According to this concept, the emotional system governs behaviour on a societal level, promoting both progressive and regressive periods in a society. The societal emotional processes are like background influence affecting all families. For instance, in a society where there is a great social pressure, the crime rate in

244 Antony, *Psychotherapy in Counselling...*, 22.

245 Nichols, *The Essentials of Family Therapy...*, 87.

246 Gerald, Gorey, *Theory and Practice of Counselling and Psychotherapy*, (Singapore: Brooks/Cole, 1996), 75.

247 Nichols, *The Essentials of Family Therapy...*, 89.

248 Antony, *Psychotherapy in Counselling...*, 31.

249 Antony, *Psychotherapy in Counselling...*, 31.

the same society will be high.[250] This particular concept will be very relevant to understand the emotional influence in the Naga society. There is a high social unrest and pressure in the Naga society. Extortion, corruption, and killing are rampant today; therefore, it has direct influence on members in the Naga families. The treatment Techniques are presented here.

8.1.1.5. The Genogram

The genogram, a technique often used early in family therapy, provides a graphic picture of the family history. The genogram reveals the family's basic structure and demographics.[251] Through symbols, it offers a picture of three generations. Names, dates of marriage, divorce, death, and other relevant facts are included in the genogram. It provides an enormous amount of data and insight for the therapist and family members early in therapy. As an informational and diagnostic tool, the genogram is developed by the therapist in conjunction with the family.

Genogram guide the counsellor to address problem-maintaining issues in either or both families of origin, and to plan realistically regarding long term family change.[252] In recent years Naga families are also going through transition, where children are not able to count more than three generations. Through the genogram techniques families could be reconnected to their roots and ancestral legacies.

8.1.1.6. Relationship Experiments

Its main purpose it to help family members become aware of the systems process and to recognize their own role in the family relationship.[253] Pursuers are encouraged to restrain their pursuit, stop making demands, and decrease pressure for emotional connection, while those who distances themselves are encouraged to move toward the other person and communicate personal thought and feelings. In this age of individualism this technique could be helpful tool in bringing the Naga family that are experiencing isolation and disintegration.

8.1.1.7. Coaching

"Coaching is a technique to counsel the clients directly to work on their family problems. It involves asking process questions designed to help the clients figure out family emotional process and their role in them. It does not imply telling

250 Antony, *Psychotherapy in Counselling...*, 303.

251 M. McGoldrick, J.K. Pearce, and J. Giodana, *Ethnicity and Family Therapy,* (New York: Guilford Press, 1985), 176.

252 D. John Antony, *Family Counselling: The Classical Schools,* (Dindigul: Anugraha Publications, 2005), 44.

253 Nichols, *The Essentials of Family Therapy...*, 97.

family members what to do."[254] It rather act as a sensible coach in assisting the members in the family to make the process smooth and functional.

8.1.1.8. Multiple Family Therapy

"The purpose of this technique is that one couple may learn more about emotional process by observing others.[255]" The aim to keep each family unit a contained triangle along with the counsellor, to work on the emotional communication between families.

What makes Bowen's theory useful is that it describes the emotional forces that regulate how one relates to other people. The single greatest obstruction to understanding one another is people's tendency to become emotionally reactive.[256] This reactivity traces its origins to the lack of differentiation of self, and it explains how to contain emotionalism and move toward self-control- by cultivating relationships widely in the family and learning to listen without becoming defensive or untrue to one's own belief. Research has supported Bowen's notion that differentiation is related to trait anxiety (negatively);[257] psychological and physical health problems (negatively),[258] and marital satisfaction (positively).[259] Finally, consistent with Bowen's belief in the multigenerational transmission process, researchers have found that parents' and children's belief are highly correlated.[260]

8.1.2. Relevance and Application of Bowen's for Family Counselling

Bowen's goal to reduce the anxiety in human lives and find symptoms of relief and to increase the level of differentiation of the self in each member of the family will be effective in helping the Naga families.

In the recent time excessive individualism has been observed among the Naga families. Consequently, this model would be applicable in the context of the Naga families that experiences anxiety, and the need to restructure the extreme individualism. This way the communitarian spirit, which was considered to be the trade mark of the Nagas could be recreated and the family and community

254 Antony, *Family Counselling: The Classical Schools...*, 45.

255 Antony, *Family Counselling: The Classical Schools...*, 44-45.

256 Nichols, *The Essentials of Family Therapy...*, 100.

257 J. M, Griffen and R. A, Apostal, Testing the Effectiveness of Bowen's Concept of Differentiation in Predicting Psychological Distress in Individuals Age 62 Years or Older, in *The Family Journal*, July 1, 2017.

258 Jehad M. Alaedein, "Is Bowen Theory Universal? Differentiation of Self among Jordanian Male and Female College Students and between them and a Sample of American Students through Bowen's Proposition"in *Educational Sciences*, Vol. 35. No. 2. 2008.

259 Parven Karkhaneh at el, "The Study of the Effectiveness of the Bowen Self –Differentiation Counselling on Marital Conflicts on Married Women," in *International Journal of Life Science and Pharma Research*, Vol., 6. Issue 4, October 2016.

260 Nichols, *The Essentials of Family Therapy...*, 102.

life may further be strengthened. Far more important than developing methods and techniques of family therapy, Murray Bowen made profound contribution in the understanding of how to functions as individuals, and how to get along with one's families, and how these are related.

8.1.3. Critiques on the Limitations of Bowen's Theory

Though Bowenian family systems therapy is a popular mode of treatment that both therapists and people in treatment have attested to the effectiveness of the approach, at present there is a limited base of empirical evidence backing the approach.[261] Even though the evidence base is growing, more data—particularly from objective sources—may help confirm its efficacy.

A second criticism of the approach is the seemingly unwavering neutrality of its practitioners. Some mental health experts believe that by remaining neutral, unaffected, or silent at all costs, practitioners of family systems therapy may be giving tacit approval to any harmful behaviours individuals in therapy may be exposing themselves or other people to.[262]

There are major differences between Indian and Western family structure. Rakesh K Chadda and Koushik in their article "Indian Family Systems, Collectivistic Society and Psychotherapy" observed that Indian society is more communitarian that encourages interdependence and co-operation, with the family as central thing of social structure unlike the western society that is individualistic in nature. "Indian families are more involved in caring of its members, and also suffer greater illness burden than their western counterparts. Indian families are more intimate with the patient, and are capable of taking greater therapeutic participation than in the west."[263]

Using Bowen's theory of differentiation to Indian context may not be appropriate always since Indian society still has a collectivistic culture where interdependence and traditional values are given higher importance. Hence, with globalization and affinity towards western lifestyle contributed towards change of family values and understanding of marriage. The rigid hierarchical structure of Indian families poses challenges to therapist who tries to improve communication

---

261 Jenny Brown, "Bowen Family System Theory and Practice: Illustration and Critique," New Zealand Journal of Family Therapy 20, No. 2 (June 1999), Under "The Process," http//www.thefsi.comau/wp-content/uploads/2014/01/Bowen-Family-System-Theory-andPractice-Illustration-and-Crtiques.pdf (Accessed on April 25, 2018).

262 William M. Fleming, "Family Systems Theory-Challenges and Future Derictions," JRak http://family.jrank.org/pages/598/Family-Systems-Theory-Challenges-Future-Direction.html (Accessed on April 30, 2018).

263 Rakesh K. Chadda and Koushik Sinha, "Indian Family Systems, Collectivistic Society and Psychotherapy," in Indian Journal of Psychiatry 55, No. 2 (January 2013) under "Introduction," https://.www.ncbi.nlm.nih.gov/pmc/article/PMC3705700/ (Accessed on June 12, 2018).

pattern of families to communicate feelings and thoughts.[264] This is a reality even in the context of the Naga family.

There are certain crucial understandings from the perspective of postmodern context regarding family therapy that also need to be reflected upon. Postmodern theorists value and emphasize localized experiences and multiple perspectives and they contest on the idea that can describe family in terms of structure or organization or communication. The central theme of postmodern theory is the need to understand particular individuals situated within his/her socio-cultural, political, economic and historical context through client-practitioner discourse.[265]

There are concerns related to the concept of differentiation of self of Bowen, he believed that it is necessary to take an average of functioning of family for many years in order to assess individual's basic level of differentiation. Consequently, the issue is that stress level of family differs over many decades. Moreover, without assessing functioning of an individual's nuclear family it is not possible to assess the functioning at their expense. Hence, the question is on the meaning of taking average of the functioning of a person.[266] There are evidences that members of the family can enhance the functioning of a person and that person's family over many decades. In spite of certain limitations Bowen's theory, is still helpful and applicable. Many family therapists employ and adopt his techniques in helping the families.

8.2. Experiential Family Counselling Model

As its name indicates, experiential therapy involves actions, movements, and activities rather than the more traditional "talk therapy." Experiential therapy is actually a category, rather than one specific type of therapy. Examples of experiential therapy include recreational therapy, expressive art therapy, music therapy, adventure therapy, psychodrama, etc.

One of the many advantages of experiential therapy is that the activities and experiences that form the core of the process provide opportunities for therapist to observe the patient in situations where the patients are not focused on the therapy itself. Experiential family therapists Satir and Whitaker involved in a therapeutic encounter with family members, encouraging mutually open, honest and direct expression of emotions. These therapists aim to create a context of trust and acceptance, a safe place where people will be prepared to take risks in revealing

264 Chadda and Sinha, "Indian Family Systems..., under "Family Oriented Psychotherapy: Process and Issues in Practice." (Accessed on June 13, 2018).

265 Robert R. Green and Robert G. Blundo, "Postmodern Critique of Systems Theory in Social Work with the Aged and their Families," *Journal of Gerontological Social Work* 31, No. 3-4 (1999) 95. http://www.tandfonline.com/doi/abs/10.1300/J083v31no3_06 (Accessed on 13, June 2018).

266 Randall T. Frost, "Challenges of Conducting Bowen Family Systems Research on Differentiation of Self," in *Differentiation of Self: Bowen Family Systems Theory Perspectives*, ed. Peter Titelman (New York: Routledge, 2014), 327.

and sharing their innermost vulnerable feelings which are often masked by more distancing and defensive behaviours. This sharing of 'real' emotions strengthens the emotional bonds in the family. Experiential therapists are active and fascinating yet are careful not to undermine the client's autonomy and self-healing potential, i,e. they are facilitative rather than instructive.[267] These therapists have a strong belief in the innate potential of each human being: "I regard people as miracles and the life within them a sacred.'[268] Experiential therapists encourage learning through action, for instance, family sculpting is a useful technique for exploring and dealing with interpersonal boundary issues.

Among the most recent experiential approaches is the *Emotionally Focused Couples Therapy* of Greenberg and Susan Johnson, which draws on Perls, Satir and the MRI group.[269] Another specialized approach to the inner emotional life of families is Richard Schwartz's *Internal Family Systems Therapy*, [270] in which clients' conflicting inner voices are personified as parts and then reintegrated using a variety of psychodramatic techniques.[271]

8.2.1. Treatment Techniques

In experiential family counselling model, there are actually no strict techniques but only people. Here the restorative power of the counsellor's personality is an important factor. In such a context a counsellor who is alive, aware and fully feeling person will awaken potentials in families. Open and genuine counsellors foster openness and authenticity in their clients too.[272]

8.2.1.1. Family Sculpting

Developed by Duhl, Kantor, and B. S. Duhl. Family sculpting provides for recreation of the family system, representing family member's relationships to one another at a specific period of time. The family therapist can use sculpting at any time in therapy by asking family members to physically arrange the family. Adolescents often make good family sculptors as they are provided with a chance to nonverbally communicate thoughts and feelings about the family.[273] Family

---

267 Virginia Satir, *The Satir Model: Family Therapy and Beyond,* (Palo, Alto, CA: Science and Behavior Book, 1991), 13.

268 Satir, *The Satir Model: Family Therapy and Beyond…*, 40.

269 S. M. Johnson and Leslie Greenberg, Emotionally Focused Couple Therapy, in A. S. Gurman (Ed), *Clinical Handbook of Couple Therapy*, (New York: The Guildford, 2008), 107-137.

270 Richard, Schawartz, *Internal Family Systems Therapy,* (New York/London: The Guilford Press, 1995), 133-140.

271 Greenberg, *Clinical Handbook of Couple Therapy…*, 78-84. Cf. Nichols, *The Essentials of Family Therapy…*, 157.

272 Antony, *Family Counselling: The Classical Schools…*, 54.

273 Tracy D. Baldo and Basilia C Softas-Nall, Family Sculpting in Supervision of Family Therapy, in *The Family Journal* 6 (3), 1998, 231-234.

sculpting is a sound diagnostic tool and provides the opportunity for future therapeutic interventions.

8.2.1.2. Family Reconstruction

Family reconstruction is a type of psychodrama of rebuilding through which clients explore significant events in three generations of family life. This helps members identify the roots of their old learning, formulate a more realistic picture of their parents, and discover their unique personality. Clients could make use of group members for this purpose. Family maps, family life-fact chronology or wheel of influence (a spatial diagram of all the significant people in one's life) or some combination of these three could be used.[274]

The experiential family counsellors also could employ drama, reframing, humour, touch, Gestalt therapy and person centered therapy depending upon the context and situation. Experiential therapy helps family members get beneath the surface of their interactions to explore the feelings that drive them. At its best this approach helps people to drop their defenses and come together with more immediacy and authenticity. Given family therapy's emphasis on behaviour and feeling side of their experience is surely a welcome idea.[275]

Experiential model works from the inside out-strengthening families by encouraging individual self-expression, reversing the usual direction of effect in family therapy. Personal integrity and self-fulfillment are seen as innate human capacities that will emerge spontaneously once defensiveness is overcome. These profound concepts of self expression against defensiveness and personal integrity would be helpful in guiding the Naga families, more-over Satir's statement "I regard people as miracles, and the life within them a sacred"[276] should inspire Nagas to value life, as Nagas who are otherwise affected by communal clashes and fratricide in the name of freedom struggle. Satir's expression of valuing life together with Viktor Frankl concept of the meaning of life should enlighten the present day Nagas to cherish life and value it.

8.2.1.3. Reflection on Experiential Family Therapy

At this stage of learning about family therapy models, the researcher considered using experiential family therapy as the primary model with clients. Uncertain about how good and fit the standard techniques of experiential therapists, such as sculpting, would be, but the researcher intends to remain open minded. Having a belief system very closely aligned with humanistic psychology; the researcher too believes that humans are innately good and inclined to growth, and that it is the systems of interaction and oppression one inherit that hinder that process.

274 Antony, *Family Counselling: The Classical Schools...*, 55.

275 Nichols, *The Essentials of Family Therapy...*, 170-172.

276 Satir, *The Satir Model: Family Therapy and Beyond,...* 40.

Nurtured in a holistic-oriented family of dedicated Christian priest (parents). The researcher internalized the belief systems and modes of communication, enjoyed practice of intimacy, honesty, and emotional fluency and fluidity, the peer-counselling and peer relationships for many years. Having strong conviction that the ability to notice experience as it is and to express it authentically in language, behaviour, and affect, and one's ability to compassionately notice the expression of others' experience is the key to be able to have deep relationships. The researcher is convinced that the depth of one's relationships is a large part of what make lives meaningful, beautiful, and useful.

There is a way that many family therapy models, in their focus on family systems, treat the individuals in those systems with less than full respect, actually lying to clients in some situations, to trick them into improving,[277] short of that, treating them as more or less fortunate cogs, Black Boxes, in their family systems. Something noteworthy about this model is the way Virginia Satir, especially, is not manipulative, except in her compassionate reframing. The way experiential therapists recognize the uniqueness and lovable-ness of each individual is noteworthy, and the way they view that recognition as the means for positive change is a workable model in the context of caring for the Naga families.

8.3. Strategic Family Counselling Model

The prominent proponents in the strategic family counselling model are Jay Haley and Cloe Madanes. Theirs is called 'communication' therapies. In strategic counselling, the counsellor initiates what happens during treatment and designs a particular approach for each problem. In this model the counsellor takes the initiative and responsibility for directly influencing family members, in order to bring beneficial change. The main concern of the counsellor is about the theory and means for inducing change.[278]

The strategic school applied Gregory Bateson's ideas directly to family treatment, resulting in a set of creative ways to generate change, and overcome the resistance, in families seen as cybernetic systems. In the 1970s and 1980s, strategic methods were amply used but later in the 1990s the strategic family method seen as 'therapists-as-expert-manipulator' was rejected in favour of 'therapist-as-collaborator.' All the same this approach contains the elements of sophisticated understanding of family complexities and powerful techniques. [279] They are useful in family counselling.

---

277 R., Fisch, J. H., Weakland, & L. Segal, *The Tactics of Change: Doing Therapy Briefly*, (San Francisco: Josey-Bass, 1982). 107.

278 H. J. Aponte, and J. M. Van Dusen, Structural Family Therapy in A. S. Gurman, and D. P. Kniskern, eds. *The Handbook of Family Therapy: Vol 1.* (New York: Brunner/Mazel, 1981), 310-316.

279 Michael P. Nichols and Richard C. Schwartz, *Family Therapy Concepts and Methods*, (New Jersey: Allyn and Bacon, 1995), 355- 356.

8.3.1. Application of the Strategic Techniques

The strategic family counsellors have a realistic view. They are concerned about techniques that work. Their aim is to eliminate or substantially reduce the symptom. Therefore, they are symptom-focused and behaviour oriented. Their therapeutic tools are tasks and directives. They tend to fortify the generational boundaries and tactically support the various members at certain times.[280]

8.3.1.1. Paradoxical Intervention

Paradoxical Interventions[281] are those which appear absurd because they exhibit an apparently contradictory nature, such as requiring clients to do what in fact they have been doing, rather than requiring that they change, which is what everyone else is demanding. There is a great amount of resistance to change within the family. Added to this, the entry of the counsellor into the family is not welcome. The family members tend to resist the efforts of the counsellor to change. Hence, if the counsellor tells them to do what they are already doing, they are in a therapeutic bind.[282] When they follow the instructions of the counsellor to continue to do the things they have been doing, they are just obeying the counsellor, which means that the members give undue power to the counselor.

8.3.1.2. Reframing

Most family therapists use reframing as a method to both join with the family and offer a different perspective on presenting problems. Specifically, reframing involves taking something out of its logical class and placing it in another category.[283] For example, a father's repeated questioning of his son's behaviour after a date can be seen as genuine caring and concern rather than that of a non-trusting parent. Through reframing, a negative often can be reframed into a positive.

8.3.1.3. The Ordeal Therapy

The ordeal therapy facilitates bonding among family members through practice of apology and forgiveness. Any misconduct on the part of any individual in the family that has seriously affected other members of the family is resolved. Members are asked to apologize and to forgive each other. This way it helps them to restore the family's dignity and once again love, trust and concern for one another is regained.[284]

---

280 Alan S. Gurman, and David P. Kniskern, *Handbook of Family Therapy*, (Richmond, Texas: Routledge, 1981), 374-375.

281 Gurman, and Kniskern, *Handbook of Family Therapy*..., 376-377.

282 Antony, *Family Counselling: The Classical Schools*..., 104.

283 R., Sherman, & N. Fredman, *Handbook of Structural Techniques in Marriage and Family Therapy*, (New York: Brunner/Mazel, 1986), 27.

284 Antony, *Family Counselling: The Classical Schools*..., 107.

Communications family therapy is no mere approach application of individual psychotherapy to families; it is radically new conceptualization that altered the very nature of imagination. What is new is the focus on the form and impact of communication, rather than the content. Communication is described as symptoms. In fact, all behaviour is communicative.

Strategic family counselling model is one of the first and most influential forms of family treatments. "Its theoretical development was based on general systems theory, and the therapy that emerged was a systems approach par excellence." It is expected that this model would help the communication blocked among the Naga families especially among those couples who are not in good communication term with their spouse and also among other family members.

8.4. Structural Family Counselling Model

8.4.1. Important Concepts in Structural Family Therapy

Structural family counselling became the most prominent model in the 1970s. Structural family counselling attempts to offer a clear framework that give meaning to the transaction of the members. Structural Family Therapy is concerned about how families are organized, and the rules that govern their transactions. According to this approach, family problems are maintained by dysfunctional family structures or organization.[285]

Families are organized in subsystems with boundaries regulating the way the members interact with each other. Structural family therapy recognizes that families are competent and capable to solve their own problems.[286] The approach also retains traditional views concerning the importance of power and hierarchy in the family.[287]

Structural model is an approach to understanding the nature of the family, the presenting problem, and the process of change. This change occurs in family members through a new way of their thinking and restructuring of their relationships. The hierarchies, and the clear and even the hidden rules, must be understood before the therapist can help the family to change. This change could result in a better style of parenting and interacting in the family. The three essential concepts in Structural family Therapy are:

- family structure
- family subsystems
- boundaries

---

285 Antony, *Family Counselling: The Classical Schools...*, 65.

286 Jorge Colapinto, *Structural Family Therapy,*(Itasca, Illinois: F. E. Peacock, 1982), 27-31.

287 Jorge Colapinto, Structural Family Therapy. In A. M. Horne & M. M. Ohlsen (Eds.), *Family Counseling and Therapy*, (Illinois: F. E. Peacock Publishers, Inc, 1981), 112-140.

8.4.2. Goals and Techniques of Structural Family Therapy

The primary goal of Structural model is to bring about structural changes within the family system. This is achieved by modifying the family's way of interacting and developing appropriate boundaries. Another goal is to create an effective hierarchical structure where parents are in charge of their children.

The functions of the therapist are to:

- Join the family in a position of leadership so that it is active and involved.
- Map the family's underlying structure (boundaries, hierarchy, and subsystems) and identify its potential for change.
- Plan and implement interventions to transform an ineffective structure to healthy functioning.

8.4.3. Techniques of Structural Family Therapy

8.4.3.1. Joining and Accommodating

Joining is the process of building a therapeutic alliance with every member of the family to get a picture of how the family interacts. From his or her initial greetings and comments, the therapist eases the family members' anxiety and wins them over. For it is important to build alliance with each member of the family.[288]

The therapist conveys respect for the individuals in the family, and for the hierarchical structure.

8.4.3.2. Working with Family Interactions

The therapist gains insight on the problem through observing enactment or the spontaneous behaviour sequences that explain it. Through this exercise, the therapist elicits information about the family structure and could help to:

- Discover if the boundaries are clear, if for example, two people can speak without being interrupted
- Determine who is on the defensive and who attacks
- Identify family members who are central and those who are on the periphery
- Find out if there is enmeshment, for example, parents bringing the children into their discussions.[289]

8.4.3.3. Mapping Underlying Structure

The family structure is revealed when members interact, and mapping captures the interrelationship of the members. The therapist draws a family map to identify

---

288 Salvador, Minuchin S., *Families and Family Therapy,* (Cambridge, MA: Harvard University Press, 1974), 112-114.

289 Nichols and Shwartz. *Family Therapy Concepts and Methods…*, 1995, 137.

rigid, diffuse or clear boundaries, transactional styles, and the structure of the family system, to discover changes that are needed in the system.

8.4.3.4. Enactments

"Family structure is manifest in the family members interaction."[290] The therapist encourages members to role play family conflicts within the session. He or she observes as family members demonstrate how they deal with conflicts. Then the therapist devises interventions to modify their interactions, and creates structural changes in the family.[291]

8.4.3.5. Boundary Making (Restructuring)

Boundary making restructures the boundaries and increases either closeness or distance between family systems. For example, in enmeshed families interventions are intended to strengthen boundaries between subsystems and increase independence of individuals.[292]

8.4.3.6. Unbalancing

During unbalancing, the therapist joins and supports, that is, briefly take side with one individual or subsystem as opposed to another. The goal is to use his/her authority to break an impasse in the family system, and change the relationships in a subsystem or between subsystems.[293]

8.5. Application of Structural Family Therapy in the Naga Context

With an emphasis on these key concepts, the primary goal of therapy is to help to bring about structural changes in the family. This change could result in a better style of parenting and interacting in the Naga families. As of now most Naga parents still lack parenting skill. Importantly, structural family therapists focus on modifying the family structure within the immediate therapeutic context. As such, they use techniques including enactments, highlighting and modifying interactions, unbalancing, and boundary making to restructure family dynamics. Minuchin's structural theory is one of the most widely used conceptual models in the field of family counselling. The reason structural theory is so popular is that it is simple, inclusive, and practical. The basic concepts-boundaries, subsystems, alignments, and complimentary-are easily grasped and applied. It takes into account the individual, family, and social context, and they provide a clear organizing framework for understanding and treating families. It is anticipated that this concept could be useful for counsellors practicing family counselling with the Naga families.

---

290 Nichols, *The Essentials of Family Therapy...*, 144.

291 Nichols, *The Essentials of Family Therapy...*, 144.

292 Nichols, *The Essentials of Family Therapy...*, 145

293 Nichols, *The Essentials of Family Therapy...*, 146.

8.6. How Gender and Diversity/Culture Can Be Incorporated Into the Theory

Since Salvador Minuchin began work on his therapeutic model of structural family therapy times have changed. More awareness has since been given to understanding diversity, culture and gender issues. It is apparent that Minuchin has been very aware of the impact of socio-economic and cultural environment on family and individual functioning. It is important for structural therapists to understand and consider that not all family structures will look the same. Some families may have single parent. Therefore, the power in the hierarchy may look different from a traditional two parent family. Different ethnic groups may appear to have a closeness that is very normal for that group or culture, but could appear to be enmeshed from the perspective of a therapist who was raised in a more individualistic society. It is imperative that the therapist understands his or her own cultural constructs about what a family structure should look like and be careful while planning to apply this method to clients of other cultural backgrounds.

The structural model offers the conceptual framework and the vocabulary for addressing organizational patterns, boundaries, and subsystems. It has yet to apply the framework to the "dimension of gender-either to the gender-based on arrangements in the construction of marital/parental subsystem"[294] or to the gendered coalitions across generations amongst sister or brothers. According to Goldner, the generational distinction is a major focus of attention without notice taken of the distinction between genders. Husbands and wives have been conceptualized as a marital or parental unit, with the most salient distinguishing feature between them ignored, perhaps to avoid falling back into an individualistic view in noting sex differences. In fact, structural family therapy diagrams, until recently, made no gender distinctions.[295]

It is important for structural family therapists to be constantly aware and sensitive to different diversity, cultural, and gender issues that may relate to clients when doing therapy. People come from different backgrounds and receive information differently. After summarizing structural therapy, the researcher is now able to understand the different subsystems and boundaries from a structural point of view. Considering Minuchin's structural therapy when working with diverse relationships can be a useful framework when working with today's Naga families.

294 https://www.ukessays.com/essays/sociology/key-concepts-of-structural-family-therapy-sociology-essay.php (Accessed on June 12, 2018).

295 Essays, UK. (November 2013). Key concepts of structural family therapy. Retrieved from https://www.ukessays.com/essays/sociology/key-concepts-of-structural-family-therapy-sociology-essay.php?vref=1(Accessed on June 12, 2018).

8.7. A Critique of Structural Family Therapy

Structural family therapy is a type of therapy that is ideal for short-term therapy situations. Structural family therapy is still one of the most frequently taught models among family therapists. This model is ideally suited to the practice of family therapy due to its focus on the entire family rather than individuals. It remains true today that one need to look at "man in his social context."[296] As Breunlin, pointed out almost every family therapist today uses some elements of structural family therapy in his or her practice.[297]

Following these events, Minuchin devoted more time to teaching his model of family therapy which has been used successfully in the field of family therapy since the 1970s?[298] As stated above, structural family therapy has had, and continues to have an important effect on the field of family therapy. Lebow find that structural family therapy provides a foundation for "helping and allows the family to change while still retaining its autonomy."[299]

Structural family therapy is an approach with much strength. For instance, it is a favorable model because of its "relative simplicity, concreteness and directness."[300] For these reasons, it is a model that forms a good basis for the practitioner of family therapy. Lebow states that structural family therapy is a very teachable model in that it takes something as abstract as the family and organizes it using concepts like boundaries and hierarchy. Structural family therapy tries to retain a focus on the strengths of the family as well.[301] Further, this approach is versatile, and to this end it has been successful in the treatment of families experiencing various difficulties.

The structural family therapy model appears to be an effective model for a variety of client issues. Nevertheless, there are a few qualifications to these findings.[302] Firstly, as Gladding points out, most of the studies on this model have been based on children and adolescents, and there is a scarcity of evidence on the effectiveness of this model with an adult population. Secondly, as stated above,

---

296 Minuchin, *Families and Family Therapy...*, 4.

297 Breunlin, D., Schwartz, R., & MacKune-Karrer, B. *Meta Frameworks for Psychotherapy: Transcending the Models of Family Therapy*, (San Francisco: Jossey Bass, 1992), 105.

298 M., Nichols, and R. Schwartz, *Family Therapy Concepts and Methods (4th Ed.)*, (Cambridge, MA: Allyn and Bacon, 1989), 199-203.

299 J. Lebow, What does the Research tell us About Couple and Family Therapies? in *Psychotherapy in Practice, 56*, (2000), 1083-1094.

300 Jacobson, N. S. & Addis, M. E. Research on Couples and Couple Therapy: What do we Know? *Journal of Consulting and Clinical Psychology, 61*, (1993). 85-93.

301 C. R., McAdams, Avadhanam, R., Foster, V. A., Harris, P. N., Javaheri, A., Kim, S., ... & Williams, A. E., The Viability of Structural Family Therapy in the Twenty-first Century: An Analysis of Key Indicators. *Contemporary Family Therapy, 38*(3), (2016), 255-261.

302 S. T. Gladding, *Family therapy: History, Theory, and Practice (6th Ed.)* (San Francisco, CA: Pearson Higher Ed, 2014), 129-135.

many of the remarkable results reported by Minuchin and his colleagues have not been replicated.[303] Lastly, many of the outcome of studies on the effectiveness of structural family therapy are quite out-dated, leaving the reader to question the applicability of these findings today.

8.8. Critiques on the Limitations of Structural Family Therapy

Structural family therapy is a model that has some clear strength and has had an unquestionable impact on the field of family therapy. Nevertheless, this model also has some inherent weaknesses. One shortcoming of structural family therapy is the lack of a feminist analysis. While structural family therapy looks at the family within its social context, there is no such assessment for women.[304] Looking at the structure of the family fails to take into account the significance of gender and the power differentials inherent in it.

The increasingly significant societal demand on women in the home goes unrecognized. Further, concepts such as "enmeshed" and "disengaged" have been frequently applied to women[305] even though these terms are merely constructs and have no absolute reality. McGoldrick provides a feminist analysis of structural family therapy, pointing out the irony of the clear distinction that Minuchin makes between generations but not between genders. She stresses that gender is a "structural relationship variable" and not just an individual characteristic.[306]

One final critique of structural family therapy is that it can be disempowering for clients.[307] The therapist is always in control of the process. It is the therapist who decides if the family structure is dysfunctional and then it is he or she that attempts to restructure the family. The client is not a co-creator in the process. If a therapist is seeing a family in which the parents have little power, it does not seem very helpful if the therapist controls the power and replays the same situation the parents are facing at home.

Structural family therapy offers therapists a model that is active and clearly defined. It is suitable in a variety of cases and it is an approach that focuses on restructuring the family to eliminate dysfunctional interactions. Structural family therapy also makes some assumptions about what constitutes a healthy family, for example clear boundaries and a discernible hierarchy. Although, it is said to focus on strengths, some of the terms used are clearly derogatory and imply very

---

303 A. S., Gurman, and D. P. Kniskern, Eds., *Handbook of family therapy*, (New York, NY: Routledge, 2014), 219-221. cf. Pinsof, W. M. & Wynne, L. C. The efficacy of Marital and Family Therapy: An Empirical Overview, Conclusions, and Recommendations, in *Journal of Marital and Family Therapy, 21*, (1995). 585-613.

304 A. R., Mahoney, & Knudson-Martin, C. Will old gender scripts limit new millennium families' ability to thrive. *Michigan Family Review, 5* (1). (2000), 41-52.

305 Nichols, and R. Schwartz, *Family Therapy Concepts and Methods...*, 141.

306 McGoldrick, Gerson, and Schellenberger, *Genograms in Family Assessment...*, 27.

307 Gladding, *Family Therapy: History, Theory, and Practice...*,138. cf.

little strength. Joseph George observed that "the proactive approach at times could be seen as too intrusive and the process forced upon family... empathy is an important dimension of any therapeutic process and the lack of that experience in therapy could be a major drawback."[308]

Structural family therapy however, is an approach that should be taught to family therapists in order to give them a good foundation in family therapy. While this approach may not espouse a collaborative relationship between client and therapist, the practical nature of this model makes it appealing to many practitioners. As discussed previously, the fact that many therapists continue to use this approach today is evidence of its popularity as a family therapy model.

9. Conclusion

This chapter highlighted the summary of the research findings. The research has necessitate or prompted for the application of basic skills for family counselors as a result four classical schools of family counselling has been dealt. The relevancy and the application of each of the school in the context of family counselling along with the strength and limitations of each model has also been highlighted.

308 Joseph George, "Marriage and Family Counselling," in *A Study Book on Counselling* George Varghese, ed., (Tiruvilla/Ammancherry, Kottayam: TMA Institute of Counselling & Christava Sahitya Samithi, 2014), 129-130.

Chapter 8

Proposing New Family Counselling Models

1. Introduction

As indicated in the earlier chapters, family life has been undergoing a drastic change, and it is expected to go through even more crucial time and more complex situation. Today's families are encountering gigantic and upheaval task in relation to family life and personal relationship.

Therefore, in this chapter an attempt has been made to suggest relevant family counselling models to help and assist the families in the smooth functions of the family life.

2. Proposing New Family Counselling Models

Discussed above are some of the classical schools of family counselling models, which the researcher felt it necessary to recommend in dealing with families in various needs. In this section an attempt has been made to present some of the new family counselling models that could be helpful in addressing the family issues in the context of the Naga families. Some of the proposed models are not absolutely new, because some of the concepts have been used in one way or the other. However, the researcher has suggested them purely in the context of the Naga family, taking into consideration the social, cultural, religious, and ethnic uniqueness of the Naga society. They are briefly discussed below:

2.1. Effective Communication Model

The study reveals there is significant association between family communication and family life satisfaction. At the same time level of communication has drastically changed, with the advancement of modern technology and gadgets. As the communication level increases family life satisfaction also increases and when level of communication among the members of the family diminishes level of satisfaction among the members of the family also decreases.

Communication is the best means to maintain healthy relationship, without proper communication life in the family would be very difficult and level of satisfaction would be affected. When family members effectively love one another, there will be simple, fair, straight-forward communication of each person's needs, feelings, and ideas within the family circle. A goal of family counselling is to increase effective communication where a family has deficits in this regards. Communication of course, involves not only the practice of individual members expressing their needs, feelings, and thought to one another but also the regular practice of listening to one another within the family. Love is expressed when the family members care enough to take the time to listen carefully to one another. Often the family counsellor needs to teach listening skills in communicating thoughts and emotions.

In this highly individualistic age, it is observed that members of the Naga families hardly have time for sharing, fellowship, and close association, it is imperative on the part of the church to educate its members on the importance of family constant interaction and open communication. Both among the couples and family as a unit most have sufficient time to share, to have fellowship and even plan for an outing together. Life will only get busier, but that does not mean that one should neglect family life and compromise with it.

2.1.1. Application of Effective Communication Model

1. The counsellor or family therapist must prepare the family members to spend quality time together sharing their joy and sorrow, excitements and disappointments together.
2. Members in the family may be asked to openly and frankly share their deepest feeling and desires, hiding nothing from each other (in the presence of the therapist), this way healthy family life could be experienced.
3. True and genuine love is expressed when family members care enough to take time to listen carefully to one another. Pastoral counsellors working with families may engage the families in caring for one another, and ask them to effectively communicate to each other so that the warmth of family life could be experienced.

2.2. Gender Sensitive Model

The study result indicates that there is significant correlation between Gender and Family life satisfaction. Gender difference refers to the role, responsibilities and privileges enjoys by men and women in the society. Naga society being patriarchal in nature, in-spite of many protection and rights sanctioned for the women, women in Naga society still faces lot of difficulties in implementing these rights in practical life. Most of the decisions for the family are taken by their male counterpart. As such men play an upper hand in the affairs of the family. As a result family life is affected with one sided (male oriented) approach for which gender equality must be taught to the people.

Counselling the family with the lenses of gender equality would be a worth-while attempt in family counselling. Gender equality means the role, responsibilities and privileges enjoys by both men and women in the society.

Addressing the subject from pastoral counselling and biblical perspective, it is safe to vouch that God in all His wisdom and knowledge created male and female with equal dignity, sincerity and respect. So God created humankind in his image, in the image of God he created them, male and female he created them (Genesis 1:27, NRSV).

Studies and researches on family roles and participation of the members revealed that family where both spouses take equal responsibility in decision making, the members live or experience as healthy, functional, and productive family.

When husband and wife are in perfect harmony; respecting each other, valuing the presence of each other, than family life can attain its optimum purpose. Consequently, gender sensitive counselling model could enhance the quality of healthy relationship between the spouse and family at large. This complimentary and active participation of both the spouses and even taking the children into confidence in all of the family matters is suggested.

2.2.1. Application of Gender Sensitive Model

1. Family therapist and counsellor through organising seminar on gender equality in collaboration with the church may address the issues on gender equality.
2. Creating of space for women in the church and society to exercise their gift, talent and potentiality could be an enriching experience for the Naga society; this can be done by engaging the church leaders and key people in the church organizations.
3. Counselling the family with the lenses of gender equality would be a worth-while attempt in family counselling. This way every member of the family would feel respected and valued.

Who is responsible to implement the above cited avowal? It should be the collective responsibility of the church, society and pastoral counsellor or family therapist. Church being the most organised body in Nagaland should initiate to take this cause forward.

2.3. Correcting Excessive Individualism Model

While some families have too much controlling all together, other families are composed of individualistic members who are quite remote from one another. If one could picture enmeshment as two circles right on top of one another, excessive individualism could be pictured as two circles completely apart from one another. The balance to achieve in family life would be overlapping circles which still have some unique space of their own.

Some families maintain a facade of adjustment by avoiding all close contact which could lead to potential conflict. In such a family, the counsellor's goal would be to develop true mutuality. Many Naga families keep up a convincing appearance of unity but lack meaningful relationships. Their unity is based on the avoidance of dealing with the issues and conflicts rather than on a true mutuality of working together and being highly committed to one another.

Following are the steps forward in resolving the excessive individualism by the application of Correcting Excessive Individualism Model among the Naga families.

1. Counsellor using this model can help Naga families to be more inclusive and aware of the need of other members by creating a sense of interdependence and collaboration.
2. Family members can be asked to restrict their personal agenda and encourage being more accommodative, inclusive and working towards mutuality, as it is observed that Naga families has become individualistic, against communitarian spirit.
3. This particular technique can be incorporated together with the effective communication model as suggested above, so that the family counsellor focus on discouraging the excessive individualism and work with the family towards effective communication.
4. It is expected that this could result into desirable and healthy functional family.

2.4. Individual Family Counselling

Any counselling technique is effective and can bring positive outcome only when the issue is address specifically. In this technique the researcher proposed individual family counselling as part of counselling the family.

1. Issues in the family can be tackled when the whole family members are taking into confidence. Some families are not comfortable to discuss their personal problems with others. Especially the Nagas are not comfortable that their problems are discussed in the presence of others. For such families it is better that they are dealt separately by the therapist.

2. Addressing each member in the family would require time and devotion, yet to get positive outcome family counsellor need to focus on each member of the family so that views from every member would be taken into consideration. This way desirable outcome could be expected.[309]
3. When individual family is taken into serious consideration a desirable outcome could be expected because here the focus is specific and goal oriented.

Though Naga society is community oriented and people enjoy group activities, there are certain areas where people wish to keep it personal. Therefore this model is useful and relevant for such families.

2.5. Couple Counselling

In most family counselling, couple (husband and wife) plays an important role. One may ask why then distinguish between marriage counselling and family counselling. In this case it is content of the issue than the process of therapy that determines the model of counselling. At this juncture, we may ask certain consideration. (i) The problems being experienced are specified according to this relationship. (ii) The necessity to make the boundary of marital subsystem. (iii) Respect for the couple's privacy. (iv) How the issue affects the other family members. (v) Whether the issue or the solution is going to affect the other members of the family.[310]

2.5.1. Application of Couple Counselling in the Context of the Naga Families

1. After ascertaining these facts, the couple may be taken for counselling. The success of the family to large extend depend on the couple. Therefore, the couple should be taken into confidence. The family therapist's role is to act as a coach in guiding the couple toward meaningful life.
2. A healthy couple produces healthy functional family. If needed be regular couple counselling is initiated to further strengthen family relationship.
3. Alongside the above counselling intervention for family, the importance of creating Media Awareness programme and Gender Equality Awareness Porgrammes, could be introduced to the family so that every member in the family is aware of their responsibilities, rights, and privileges.

---

309 T. A., Sayger, Homrich, A. M., and Horne, *A. Working from Family Focus: The Historical Content of Family Development and Family Systems.* In A. Horne (ed.), *Family Counselling and Therapy*, (Itasca, IL: F.E. Peacock, 2000), 12-38.

310 R. L., Barker, H., Kessler, and J. M. Lehn, *Treating Couples in Crisis*, (New York: Fortress Press, 1984), 121-122.

2.6. Media Awareness[311] Model

Mass media is a very important part of life in today's context. If it is used for right purpose it enhances the effectiveness of life, however in this study we are dealing with the negative impact of media. Family in which there is unrestraint excessive use of media, like television, internet, mobile, and movies becomes a threat and hazardous for family life. The study result is obvious, as per the data analysis, it is found that families have been tremendously confronted and challenged by mass media. Naga families who were once considered to have strong believed in family values and uphold the family ethos and close ties are in a transition period. As a matter of fact, various mass media has impacted family life so much that family values are been neglected today.

In the recent past only radio and newspapers along with hardly two-three national television channels were accessible by both rural and urban families in Nagaland. But today, hardly any village is without connection of cable (satellite) TV, latest magazines, internet connection, smart mobile etc., which promote individualism and personalized lifestyle. As such even within the same family people don't have sufficient time to share their happiness or sorrow, which in turn affects the family fabric and ties.

The researcher is not all together rejecting the use of modern means of communication; rather it is highly recommended that these modern means of communication should be used for right purposes, also there should be strict monitoring by the parent on the usage of media especially by today's generation. Mass media play a crucial role in today's context. The impact of mass media in the life of family members is enormous. The research result shows that there is high significant correlation between family and mass media, the lesser the members of the family are exposed to the media, the higher the level of family life satisfaction. Whereas, random and uncontrolled usage of media have adverse impact on family life and family functioning.

Licensed Family and Marriage therapist H. L. Schwab[312] who has been practicing Media Model since 1989 in family counselling projected that media awareness by couples and family members is very crucial in the smooth functioning of the family. He endorses that family counsellor be well equipped with the impact of media on family life.

---

311 Media awareness is an understanding of the different methods for decoding information in newspapers, on television, on the internet, etc., and of the possible uses and dangers of these methods. Family should be told of the harmful effects of media when media is used without caution. Cf., Andersen, Neil, Carreiro, P & Sinclair, D. Responding to Media Violence: Starting Points for Classroom Practice K-6. Pembroke Publishing, 1998. A sensible, thoughtful approach to media violence with appropriate curriculum directed to elementary teachers.

312 H. Laurence Schwab, M.F.T., L.M.F.T. is known as the father of Intensive Couples Counseling with a Licensed Marriage and Family Therapist.

2.6.1. Application of Media Awareness Model

1. Churches, counsellors and educators must create awareness among the community, to sensitize the people on the harmful impact of excessive usage of media.
2. Educating the people on the right usage of mass media has become an urgent task. This way a lot of problems could be resolve, considering the multi-dimensional affects of the excessive usage of media among the Naga families.
3. There was a recent random analysis conducted among the Naga youths by the researches on mobile phone usages. It is found out that some Naga youth are using mobile phone for more than 10 hours a day. Which is actually a very unhealthy practice, and this could impact the individual as well as family life. In terms of time, money and career, when so much time is invested on mobile phone each day where is the real time to do something productive? This is a real problem.

The above issues could be resolve by organising seminar, consultation, and other such concerted activities, so that family life is preserved and strengthened.

2.7. Couples Group Counselling

Couples group therapy combines the principles of subsystems theory and group dynamics into a format for working with couples. Ian Alger[313] and Peggy Papp[314] are main proponents of this model. The couples group counselling might be conducted in a variety of ways. The format varies according to the choice of the counsellor. Here the format includes a lot of spontaneity.

Three to four couples comprise the optimal size group. Careful evaluation should be made of the appropriateness of a couple for group treatment. In this case the counselling team is made up one male one female (preferably), so that both the gender could be effectively addressed.[315] There is ample opportunity for the churches today, to be fully engaged and participate in the life of the family, especially the married couple whom the church have solemnised. The churches have access to the couples as they are members of the church. With this advantage, the couple could be grouped together with other couples who have similar issues so that such problems are effectively addressed. For eg. Families

---

313 Ian Ewart Alger was born on June 20, 1926, Oshawa, Ontario – February 21, 2009, New York City, was an innovative psychotherapist who was an early adopter of using videotape as a tool in therapy.[cf.] *Carey, Benedict (March 11, 2009).* "Ian Alger, Pioneer in Innovative Therapeutic Techniques, Dies at 82." The New York Times Retrieved June 23, 2018.

314 Peggy Papp, LCSW, was a senior faculty member of the Ackerman Institute for the Family. Currently she was the founder and Director of the Project for Adolescents and Their Families. This project has developed a family-based model for treating adolescents focused on bringing about a simultaneous transition in which the adolescent and family change together.

315 Joan Chunkapura and Antony Mannarkulam, *Psychotherapies and Counselling*, (Kottayam: TRADA Publications, 2007), 105-110.

with alcoholism or substance abuse could be grouped together, so that their real problem is appropriately resolved.

More than ever before, the need for couple counselling has been felt among the Nagas families. As a practicing counsellor, the researcher and few trained counsellors are actively involved among the Naga families with various needs.

2.8. Family Networking Model

Family networking model focuses on the natural and continuous relationship system of persons as individuals or in various groupings. Carolyn, Attneave and Rose Speck initiated this model.[316] The technique of incorporating persons from outside the family depends on the nature of the present problem and the counsellor style. Family networking is led by a team of three to six counsellors and may include as many as one hundred people.[317] Six distinct phases of the network process are delineated, including: Retribalization,[318] Polarization, Mobilization, Depression, Break through & Exhaustion - Elation. Notably, these phases happen in a recurring cycle and are present regardless of the frequency or duration of the network intervention process and even tend to repeat themselves within the course of single session.

In the Retribalization phase, the family calls together the network members, providing the setting while the intervention team is responsible for explaining the rationale and significance of the network meeting. A problem-solving explanation in which the difficulty or "problem" is redefined in terms of the functioning of the social network is utilized, and a blueprint for the different phases to occur is given to the entire network. In addition, the intervention team must reduce tension and promote a "we" feeling through encounter type experiences aimed at making the network visible and rebuilding ties or bonds between members. Although, all of the pressing problem may not be resolved as a result of the networking intervention, it may facilitate the creation of a more supportive context.

2.8.1. Relevance for Naga Family Counselling

1. Naga society is community oriented as such people enjoy being in the group. Learning, sharing and experiencing together.
2. Using this model may create interest among the participating families.

316 A model associated with Ross Speck, Carolyn and Attneave. Treatment includes People from the Client's Social Network (often a large group, including family, friends and neighbours) as well as a team of therapists that come together to solve the client or family problem. Treatment consists of six phases: retribalization, polarization, mobilization, depression, breakthrough, and exhaustion-elation.

317 Chunkapura and Antony Mannarkulam, *Psychotherapies and Counselling...*, 91-95.

318 Retribalization is the act of forming and returning to a tribal group or division. Cf., McLuhan concept of retribalization and the end of individualism can be a beautiful concept in the process of restructuring and reforming the Naga tribal community.

When various families are brought together, they enriched each other by sharing their experiences.

3. One of the effective tools in family counselling is learning from people's life experiences. It is expected that learning through observation and practical session with other family could help families gain new insights.

2.9. Group Family Counselling

Group family counselling is characterized by the application of the principles of group counselling to the treatment of family and thus, in this instance it is the underlying theory which distinguishes the therapy. The proponent of this is John Elderkin Bell.[319] It is his belief that action processes in families and the rules assumed by family members provide the keys to understanding and treating the problem.

The therapist acts in a pre-determined role of group leader and facilitator whose behaviours consists the following, as outlined by John Elderkin Bell in his work "A Theoretical Framework for family Group Therapy."[320]

1. Stating and legitimizing the leader's role
2. Concentrating attention on what is going on between family members
3. Bridging gap between the family members
4. Modelling the act of listening
5. Distributing opportunities for family members to speak
6. Firming up the boundaries around the family in a related way
7. Affirming the importance of each individual and of the family as a whole
8. Assisting the family in explaining the solution
9. Encouraging trails of new interaction
10. Facilitating termination of the session[321]

Depending on the receptiveness of the participating families group family counselling could be organized. Especially in the context of tribal community where socializing is rather a frequent events, this model of family counselling

---

319 John Elderkin Bell, who was known for his pioneering work in the field of family therapy. His work appeared in publications including *Projective Techniques: A Dynamic Approach to the Study of Personality* (1948), *Family Group Therapy: A Method for the Psychological Treatment of Older Children, Adolescents, and Their Parents* (1961), and *The Family in the Hospital: Lessons from the Developing Countries* (1969). In 1952 Bell served as president of the Society for Projective Techniques, and in 1970, he was one of two psychologists to whom the Division of Clinical Psychology presented its Distinguished Scientific Contribution Award.

320 John Elderkin Bell, "A Theoretical Framework for Family Group Therapy," in P. J. Guerin (Ed.), *Family Therapy*, (New York: Gardner Press, 1976), 147.

321 J., Lebow, What does the research tell us about couple and family therapies? *Psychotherapy in Practice, 56*, 2000, 1083-1094. cf. Bell, J. E. *Family Context Therapy: A Model for Family Change, Journal of Marriage and Family Counseling*, 1978, *4*, 111–126.

might be successful. Because of the fact that one family easily relates with another family, including sharing of their joy, happiness at the same time their problems, difficulties and hardship.

3. The Role of the Church in Caring the Family

The church acts as the caring and healing community. One of the cardinals concepts of New testament is the church as the "Beloved Community." It is the *koinonia* of those in communion with God and in loving fellowship with one another. Where then church becomes the redemptive-loving and healing fellowship is experienced. If there is any place where broken, strayed and confused people can find themselves refuge, the church should be that place where families and individuals can find true meaning and purpose of life.[322] The Church has always regarded the family as its special concern. In the tribal society it is the church that validated marriages and legitimated the birth of children. Religious rites associated with birth, marriage, and death continues to be modes of care that enable individuals and families to live through the stress that usually accompanies change and loss. The recent development of the family systems perspective has introduced new approaches to the care of individuals and families.

Naga community with strong church foundation where almost the entire population has embraced Christianity, it is anticipated that the church can impact and transform the life of the families through various programmes such as:

1. Conducting workshop, seminar and consultation on family issues with expert in the field, so that Naga families would be guided toward successful family life.

2. Teaching and educating the importance of family life as part of regular church programme so that every member of the family would value family life.

3. Engaging the families, especially those with family relationship problems so that they all feel valued and counted. Because often those families with problems feel neglected and sidelined. Such families should be identified and nurtured.

4. The Naga tribal churches have access to large masses of people during conference, jubilee, and other such gathering. The church can impart the family values and principles during such events, so that the entire members are made responsible in caring for the family of God.

5. Home Visitation. One of the effective ways of helping the family is through home visitation by the church team. Where there is breakdown in family life it is important to have some way of knowing what has gone wrong and to help them to regain their problem-solving abilities.[323] Many couples from dysfunctional families do not feel free to share their problems for counselling. In

322 Phanenmo Kath, *Human Sexuality: Endangered Morality in Cyber-sonic Era*, (Tribal Development and Communication Centre, Mokokchung, 2015), 177.

323 Clinebell, *Basic Types of Pastoral Care and Counselling...*, 294.

such cases home visitation can be better alternative, so that pastoral support team can guide and support the families in need.

6. Family Enrichment Programmes. Family enrichment programmes are designed to help families for better functioning and effective relationship. It focuses mainly on helping families to identify and develop their unused strengths and also to enhance their communication.[324] This may improve the quality of family life and successful family relationship.

7. Biblical Guidance for Good Christian Family. The Bible provides guidelines for good relations within the family. Regarding the teachings in the Bible Apostle Paul says" "they are written down to instruct us" (1 Cor 10:11). The first requirement for the Christian family is to have a true relationship with Jesus Christ. One of the ways to do so is to be in touch with the word of God in the Bible.[325] Jesus said; "If you continue in my word, you are truly my disciples, and you will know the truth, and the truth will make you free" (Jn 8: 31-32). In this challenging time the Naga families need to be nurtured with the word of God, so that meaningful family life is experienced by all.

8. Biblical model of Parent-children Relationship. Children need loving discipline. Parents are instructed to bring up their children in the training and instruction of the Lord: ...do not provoke your children to anger, but bring them up in the discipline and instruction of the Lord" (Eph 6:4).

Parents are responsible for teaching their children. "And these words which I command you this day shall be upon your heart; and you shall teach them diligently to your children, and you shall talk of them when you sit in your house, and when you walk by the road and when you lie down, and when you rise" (Deut 6:6-7).

Children are given two primary responsibilities in the family: *to obey their parents and to honour them* (Eph 6:1-3). Children are to obey their parents as God promises his blessing on those who honour their parents: "Children, obey your parents in the Lord, because this is right" (Eph 6:1).

Children are to honour their parents. The first commandment that has a promise attached to it is: Honour your father and your mother, so that you may have a long life in the land that your Lord God is giving you "(Exo 20:12). Further, children are to learn from their parents;" Listen my son (sic) to your father's instruction, and do not reject your mother's teaching (Pro 1:8).[326]

9. Conducting Family Bible Study. Raising Godly children in today's society is not easy. God promised that if you "train up a child in the way he should go... when he is old he will not depart from it" (Prov 22:6). It is important for the

---

324 Clinebell, *Basic Types of Pastoral Care and Counselling...*, 258-259.

325 Thomas Manjaly, "The Bible and Family Catechesis" in *Kristu Joyti* 31, 1 & 2 (2015), 17.

326 Thomas Manjaly, "The Bible and Family Catechesis" in *Kristu Joyti...*,18.

family to take some time out to sit down as a family and study the word of God.[327] As a result the following could be achieved.

9.1. It opens the door for parents to share their faith with their children. Most Christian children hear more about Christ from priest than they do from their parents, but they trust parents the most. That is why, when parents sit down and share their heart with their children it really brings God's word home.[328]

9.2. It helps the family grow in faith and stay close to each other. Family Bible study will help family grow close, and stay close. In the favourable atmosphere of family Bible study every family member is encouraged to share and reveals oneself: their sadness, their discouragement, their hopes and aspirations, above all their experiences of Christ. Starting this simple tradition is a great way to ensure that family will always stay together.

9.3. It will open up channels of communication. In that atmosphere favourable for conversation, the time of family Bible study also provides an opportunity for children to open up and ask questions that they would not have felt comfortable asking in a larger group. But in the safety of the home circle, they can find out what God's word really says about the important issues they are facing.[329] They get the answers from parents rather than a schoolmate or television.

9.4. The Church as Advocate for the Family. So far as we know, there has been something like what is call the family to protect and nurture those who are young. Only, recently, however, we have begun to explore the ways in which the whole human history might be told in terms of household events. The history of Israel is often carried by family stories. Although the continuity of the church as the new Israel is not dependent on family lineage, the early Christian community is often described in family metaphors.[330] The Bible everywhere assumes the significance of the family as a context for criticism and care even though its importance is modified by the claims of discipleship.

The church has sought throughout its history to establish and maintain the sanctity of the home. It has taught that the family is the vehicle for God's continual creation and rule. In ways that have ignored the diversity across cultures, the church has sometimes declared that there is only one family structure that fulfills the plan of God. Within some branches of Christianity, it is still claimed that questions about sexual expression and procreation are the province of the

---

327 Joseph Pamplany, "The Great Mystery: The Concept of Family in The Bible" in *Word and Worship*, 47/4 (2014), 308-330.

328 Liberating is a concept used by Carolyn Osiek. Cf., Carolyn Osiek, "The Family in Early Christianity: Family Values Revisited," *Catholic Quarterly*, 58/1 (1996), 1-24.

329 Thomas Manjaly, "The Bible and Family Catechesis" in *Kristu Joyti* ..., 42.

330 H. Anderson, "Pastoral Care and Counseling of Family" in *Dictionary of Pastoral Care and Counseling*, Rodney J. Hunter ed. (Bangalore: Theological Publication of India), 416.

church and not the family.[331] Nonetheless, the church continues to be an advocate for family life and a context in which questions about the purpose of the family can be examined and debated.

Family Counsellors and Naga Church ministers must join hands in helping the Naga families. Church based ministry must promote means to provide systematic Biblical teaching to the families so that every member of the church would care for the family life and value it as an important institution.

4. The Role of Pastoral Care

The analysis result reveals that there is an urgent need of Pastoral care for the Naga families. If there is anything lacking in the Naga society, it is the pastoral care aspect that need to be provide in all the Naga Churches and society. The word "care" expresses concerns and the word "Pastoral" gives direction to that concern. In classical study of pastoral care, the church historians identified *Healing Guiding, Sustaining, Reconciling and Nurturing,* Emmanuel Y. Lartey have added two more important cardinals *Liberating and Empowering.* They are discussed as follows:

4.1. Healing. Healing is an indispensible part of caring ministry. Today Naga families need healing from various problems. They need to be restored to functional wholeness from impaired family relationship.

4.2. Sustaining. The aspect of the therapeutic perspective that emphasises "standing by." The Naga families need to be sustained in their family relationship, and spiritually in their relationship with God as well. In this Sustaining is the ministry of comforting. Wayne E. Oates put it beautifully the pastoral task as "to heal sometimes, to remedy often, but to comfort always."[332] As Oates implicates the pastoral team must comfort at all time, when healing and remedy is not possible.

4.3. Guiding. Proper guidance about the meaning of family life among the Naga families is needed. There are times when they want to decide what to do in their life, so they search from the pastor to guide them.[333] At such a time, the pastor should guide them and direct them towards right direction.

4.4. Nurturing. Nurturing is known in the historical expression as "training new members in the Christian life, or religious education. In the present usage it is an educational counselling and care through developmental Crisis."[334]

4.5. Reconciling. Reconciling is the process of rebuilding or mending strained relationship between people in the family and society and between human and God. This could be achieved through forgiveness, discipline,[335]

331 Anderson, "Pastoral Care and Counseling of Family" in *Dictionary of Pastoral Care and Counseling*, 416.

332 Wayne E. Oates , *Pastoral Counseling*, (Philadelphia : Westminster Press, 1974), 9.

333 Harold Taylor, *Applied Theology 2 "Tend My Sheep"* (Delhi: ISPCK, 1999), 72.

334 Murry, *Introduction to Pastoral Care and Counselling...*, 41.

335 Murry, *Introduction to Pastoral Care and Counselling...*, 40.

respect, honesty, and empathy shown to the client by the therapist. Emmanuel Y. Lartey has added two more important cardinals such as, *Liberating and Empowering*, as an essential part of pastoral caring ministry.

4.6. Liberating.[336] Nagas in spite of embracing and practicing Christianity, many still suffer due to superstition and ignorance of certain truths. Therefore, they need to be liberated from all such wrong teachings and superstitious beliefs, for example (the concept of women as weaker sex). A society where people are fully liberated, then only they can experience full potential for growth and development in every aspect of their life.[337]

Even among the so called matured Christians there are certain superstitious beliefs and practices that continue to hinder people's life. This need to be address so that people are not blinded by such practices.

4.7. Empowering.[338] Another important aspect of pastoral care is to empower people from every walk of life. The tribal society though a classless society, there has been always the division between rich and poor, ruling class and the common people etc. Such concept must be eradicated in today's progressive society otherwise the Nagas families would continue to remain stagnant and unprogressive.

4.8. Pastoral Care and the Family Life Cycle. The family is an organism of change. Some of that change is unexpected. Some of it is inevitable as individuals within the family grow up and grow older. Because the family is always changing, adaptability is one of its essential characteristics. To believe God who is always making new means that change is an unavoidable dimension of each family structure.[339]

One can assumed that individuals change throughout the entire life cycle according to relatively predictable phases. So do families. Every individual life cycle crisis is also a family crisis. Individual transitions into and out of different family roles-such as leaving home, getting married, becoming parents coping with widowhood- are interrelated with changes in the family as a system.

These life cycle ceremonies provide a framework for families to change as well. They are "hinges of time" on which doors can open or close for several generations.[340] The church's access to families at these nodal events is a privilege and an opportunity for a ministry with individuals and with entire families for the growth and stability.

336 Immanuel Y. Lartey, In *Living Color An Intercultural Approach to Pastoral Care and Counseling* Second Edition, (New York/London: Jessica Kingsley Publishers, 2003), 73.

337 Charlotte Holt Clinebell, *Counselling for Liberation* (Philadelphia: Fortress Press, 1976), 197.

338 Lartey, In *Living Color An Intercultural Approach to Pastoral Care and Counseling* Second Edition..., 73.

339 Robert Leslie, *Sharing Groups in the Church* (Nashville: Abington Press, 1971), 187.

340 James L. McCary, *Freedom and Growth in Marriage* (Santa Barbara, California.: Hamilton, 1975),

Pastoral care is valuable instrument by which the Church stay relevant to the family needs. They are ways of translating the good news into language of relationship.

4.8.1. Small Change Makes Large Change

It is often said from a family system perspective that a small change will make for a large change. Although families (like individuals) seek help, thinking that a major overhaul of their family is the only solution, a seemingly small change in the family's structure, rules, allocation of role responsibility, distribution of power, or pattern of communication may be enough to unstuck the system. The first and the most difficult task, is to reframe the family's problem in terms of the whole. The pastor's ability to think interactionally may be the small change that will make large change in the family system.[341] Expertise in family therapy techniques is less capacity to think systematically and to be close to families without being caught up in their emotional swirl.

4.8.2. Taking Initiative

The Introduction of family therapy intervention into the practice of pastoral ministry has emphasised anew the importance of pastoral initiative in general. In contrast to the non-directive or Rogerian approach that has dominated pastoral care for some time, the family systems perspective encourages greater activity on the part of the helping person.[342] As a result there is less emphasis on the presumed neutrality of the helper and more deliberately and open use of the subjective reactions of the helper. This greater activity on the part of the helper in the therapeutic process presupposes clarity about one's authority and a willingness to use one's power in appropriate ways.

4.8.3. Home Visitation

Since the contexts in which one live are important, family therapists have used home visit as a regular part of assessment and treatment.[343] Visiting a family's home provide and unparallel opportunity to learn about interactional patterns, values, how conflicts are dealt with, individual styles of living and ways being together as a family that can best be learned by observing families in their natural habitat.[344] A pastor who approaches his or her ministry from interactional or

341 Sherod Miller et al., *Alive and Aware: Improving Communication in Relationships* (Minneapolis: Interpersonal Communication Program, 1975), 117.

342 Herbert Anderson, *The Family and Pastoral Care* (Philadelphia: Fortress Press, 1984), 128. Cf. *Finding God at Home: Family* Life as Spiritual Discipline. San Francisco: Harper... Journal of Marriage and the Family 47 (1985): 395-405.

343 J. Patton and B. H. Childs, *Christian Marriage and Family: Caring for Our Generation* (Dayton OH: NACFLM, 1988), 118.

344 J. C. Wynn, *Family Therapy in Pastoral Ministry* (New York: Crossroad Publishing Co., 1982), 112.

systemic perspectives will be committed to and comfortable with the traditional privilege of calling on parishioners in order to understand them more clearly and help them more effectively.

4.8.4. Differentiated Pastoral Leadership

The emphasis on the whole in the family systems thinking does not diminish the importance of the differentiation of its parts. A family function best when the boundaries that separate that parts that are clear but permeable. Leaving home is the process of differentiating the self in the interest of autonomy and for the sake of the possibility of intimacy anew family. The differentiation of the self is equally important in the pastoral leadership in general and the care of families in particular. An organism tends to function best when its "head" is well differentiated.[345] The effectiveness of one's pastoral ministry with congregation and with the families finally depends more on the leader's capacity for self-definition than on the ability to motivate or change others.

4.9. Family Pastoral Care and Larger Social Systems

Although, the church regards itself as a guarantor of family well-being, it has not always functioned effectively as an advocate for public policy favourable to the family.[346] As a result, family structures in the present day society have been significantly influenced by the implicit values of values factors such as media, liberal views etc. The concern for the larger social, economic, and political context of the family is an extension of systems thinking. The church needs to add its voice to debate about a public policy for the family, particularly families that have been disenfranchised by society.

Religious congregations continue to have opportunities to strengthen the families through programmes in the parent education or marriage enrichment, through support groups for families with special needs, and other forms of assistance, and through the creation of communities that provide a substitute extended family for the people who have been cut off from their roots.[347] In all this efforts the church need to be careful lest its effort of support reinforces an already diminishing sense of competence in families today. Alongside its programmes that are intended to promote family well-being, the church needs to provide a conducive atmosphere for families who are discouraged or fearful or who fail to be all they would like to be or who have experienced more stress than they were able to endure.

---

345 Edwin Howard Friedman, *Generation to Generation: Family Process* in *Church and Synagogue* (New York: Guilford Press, 1985), 181.

346 Anderson, *The Family and Pastoral Care...*,129.

347 H. Cox, *Religion in the Secular City: Toward a Post Modern Theology* ((New York: Simon and Schuster, 1984), 155.

4.10. The Family and Christian Discipleship

The family is a necessary component of creation. Despite wide diversity of form and function throughout human history, the family has fulfilled God's intent to provide a context for creation and care in order to ensure the continuity of humankind.[348] From the perspective of Christian discipleship, however, the family can never be an end itself.[349] In order to be a vital human organism, the family is always moving outside itself for the sake justice, peace, and freedom in ever-widening human communities.

The fundamental paradox is: the family is necessity for human life to continue and its significance is always limited. The systems perspective on family life enables one to acknowledge that growth toward autonomy is most likely to occur in families where the rules are flexible, the roles interchangeable, and the rituals dependable. It is the call to discipleship, however, that vitalizes family life by pushing the family out of nurturing contexts into those ever-enlarging circles of human interaction in which God continues to make all things new.

5. Pastoral Counselling

Counselling intervention is an important aspect of helping the families. Here the researchers suggest some the relevant counselling techniques as part of counselling intervention is helping the Naga families.

5.1. Rewriting the Life Script. A script is one's life plan, written by a person's own early decisions which the person follows for the rest of his/her life. A person can formulate a script about himself/herself in accordance to the messages (strokes) he/she received from the parents and the society. Scripts may be constructive (winner), destructive (losers), or going nowhere (banal).[350] The goal of script analysis is to change nonproductive scripts into winners scripts through deep level re-decision for personal autonomy. In pastoral work such re-decisions have been compared to the process of repentance and conversion. As a script is a decision it can be changed by a new decision. A person's negative script can be replaced by a constructive script (Counter-Script).[351] To improve and enhance the quality of the Naga family life, it is important that the pastoral counsellor help people to rewrite their life scripts from nonproductive scripts to productive scripts because over the years Nagas have incorporated many nonproductive scripts in to their life that hampers in their quality of life.

---

348 E. Beck-Gersheim, *Reinventing the Family: In Search of New Lifestyle* (Malden: MA: Blackwell, 2002), 117.

349

350 J. C., Landrud "Script Analysis," in *Dictionary of Pastoral Care and Counselling,* Rodney J. Hunter ed., (Bangalore, Theological Publications in India, 2017), 1283.

351 Falkenberg, "The Holy Spirit in the Counselling Process" in *Pastoral Psychology,* Nov. 1964, 11. Cf. Ezamo Murry, *An Introduction to Pastoral Care and Counselling*..., 159-160.

5.2. Gestalt Therapy. The emphasis in Gestalt therapy is working with the whole person. The focus of therapy is "in the now' and on the "how." In the Gestalt approach the therapist set up experiments or exercises to help clients see and accept what they are doing and how they are doing it.[352] The therapist gives importance to the awareness of the current by the client. The person is also seen as an organism living in close relation to the environment. Therefore, gestalt therapists seek to help the person improve the quality of their relationship.[353] One of the variables under consideration is on family relationship, therefore Gestalt formation process (becoming wholeness) will strengthen family ties and relationship among the Naga families, as each member feels whole, it can also change their perception about other as whole and complete.

5.3. Client-Centred-Therapy. Rogers, an important figure in the *Human Potential Movement* recognizes an inborn capability in every human to develop and to grow to maturity. Rogers, by his acquaintance with the Biblical view of humans *as created in God's image*, he feels that humans are worth respecting and accepting. From this derived his three basic conditions for therapeutic relationship: congruence, empathy and respect.

5.3.1. Congruence - here refer to genuineness, honesty with the client by the therapist.

5.3.2. Empathy - is the ability to feel what the client feels.

5.3.3. Respect - is the acceptance, unconditional positive regard towards the client.

6. Important Conclusions

7. Observation on the Select Correlates

The following are the important conclusions that are emerging from the present investigation on the impact of select correlates on Naga family system:

7.1. Family Communication

Family communication has an important role in the healthy functioning of family life. Families that practices healthy, open and frank communication experience higher-level of family satisfaction than families where couple and family members hardly open up. Therefore, Naga families should be encouraged for better communication within the family, so that family life will be exciting, enriching and functional. The researcher as family counsellor uses day briefing model.[354]

352 V. Vande Reit, "Psychotherapy and Gestalt Therapy" in *Dictionary of Pastoral Care and Counselling,* Rodney J. Hunter ed., (Bangalore, Theological Publications in India, 2017), 458.

353 Ezamo Murry, *An Introduction to Pastoral Care and Counselling...*, 183

354 Day briefing, in family relationship is the quality time a husband and wife spend together at the end of the day, after completing their day activities. sharing each other's excitement and hardship they each faces that day. This would make them to support each other so that they could face the coming day more prepared and equipped.

7.2. Mass Media

The adverse effect of mass media on family and culture is everywhere, not only on Naga families. However, it is surprising to note that 82% (percent) of the respondents agreed that there is not strict timing or monitoring of the watching of the television, usage of internet, watching late night movies among the families that responded on the impact of mass media on Naga families. To sustain healthy and functional family, Naga families should be guided in maintaining and monitoring of strict timing for the usage of media, like watching television and light night movies, internet usage or mobile phone. The adverse effect of media on family should be properly guided to the family so that media is use to the right purpose.

Mass media has become a crucial factor in every individual's life. Almost every affairs of life is controlled by mass media in the present day scenario. There is a significant correlation of the impact of mass media and family. Families that don't maintain set time for watching television, excessive internet usage and exposed to unrestrained mass media experienced disharmony in family life.

7.3. Religious Adherence

Religious adherence has high significant correlation to family. Family that spend enough time together for prayer, reading the word of God, and attending religious functions and rituals enjoy better family bonding than those family that do not gives importance to religious activities. Because of the fact that the research was done among the married Christian couple, families that do not maintain their loyalty and allegiance to religious activities might be disturbed of not doing so. As a result it could diminish their happiness in life, and ultimately affects their families.

7.4. Levels of Education

It is revealed that level of education has significant impact on family. People with higher educational qualification determine the quality of life they live. The nitty-gritty of family life depends on the kinds of life they share and live day-to-day to the fullest, because people who are well informed and well read apply their learning and knowledge into practical life, as a result they do better in their family relationship. Naga educated, should use their knowledge and learning in helping and guiding the Nagas so that vibrant society is created among the Naga community.

7.5. Place of Residence

Place of residence has no significant correlation with family. Tribal society whether in the urban or rural setting still maintain and hold on to same value system. In contrary to what is believed that people shifting from rural to urban setting tend to loss their culture and value system, the study result revealed that people from rural and urban settings have similar perception, belief and practices in regard to family life and family functioning. Therefore, people shifting from rural villages to urban do not change their perception and notion about their cultural and traditional practices.

7.6. Level of Income

It is found out that level of income has significant correlation to family. Level of income here primarily means the income level monetarily. However, level of income also has several other implications. People with higher income are people who are also actually successful in their professional life. Accordingly, level of income has significant correlation to family life. People with higher income among the Naga families are able to enjoy better family relationship, because of the fact that they are in a position to help themselves and extend help to others.

7.7. Gender Difference

It is revealed that gender difference has a significant correlation to family. In families where female enjoy equal freedom, rights and privileges attains higher level of family than those family where woman are look down and their roles limited to kitchen works, child-rearing, and being horse for the family. Ezamo Murry expressed that "parents themselves sex-type their children, e.g., 'girl must behave like girls', 'boys should not speak like that' etc. making children remain within the gender bound behaviour."[355] It is therefore important that parents and church should be aware of the language they used while guiding and educating their children.

8. Suggestions for Further Research

Here, an attempt is made to highlight certain pertinent suggestion for further research.

8.1. A study on examining the impact of select correlates on Marital Satisfaction will be worthwhile for a deeper understanding of the present family life.

8.2. A similar study including Naga Family hailing from outside of the present state of Nagaland would also enrich the quality of research in the area.

8.3. An intervention study which includes family and quality of life among married couple could be undertaken.

8.4. A case study on the impact of alcoholism on family could be undertaken to better understand its impact on family relationship.

---

355 Email correspondence with Professor Rev. Dr. Ezamo Murry (6-7-18).

8.5. A comparative study on traditional family model vis-à-vis contemporary family will be worthwhile for a better understanding on the changing trends in family lifestyle.

8.6. An intervention study which includes family and quality of life from the feminist Perspective could be an important area of consideration.

9. Reflection

Family is a gift of God to human community. We must accept this gift thankfully and live gratefully. Family is an ideal type that transcends time and also gets transcend by the time. In this fast changing society, families need to be equipped to face the realities of today and tomorrow.[356] The strength of the society or for that matter the future of human community depends on how families survive the onslaught of the present pathos. We live in a globalized world where we seem to have many choices and vast space with modern gadgets and other channels of communication. The irony of our time is that we lost much of our creativity to choose good and evil.

The hallmark of a Christian family is 'unity and love.' All members of the family are knit together and held together in the cord of love to live and celebrate. In the context of family, values are treasured and harnessed. In theological terms, a family is a local unit of the kingdom of God, where the kingdom values are transacted without any hitch or hamper. Family has gone through change from a joint system to nuclear families. The ideals and ideas of traditional family system are considered to be old fashioned and outdated by today's generation.

It is high time that the church and family therapists must consciously think of helping families to develop healthy and meaningful families. If family has to be maintained and sustained, there should be effective family counselling models that could meaningfully address the need of the present day families. Change is the only constant in the world today, and it is happening at an increasing pace in every society. Many inventions and discoveries in the fields of science and technology, facilitation of education for all, advancement in information technology and mass media, widespread industrialization, expanded trade and commerce, women's liberation, the acceptance of democratic ideals, and the impact of western civilization – all have had a tremendous influence on marriage and family life. Accordingly, age-old notions and values regarding family and marriage have undergone a sea change. Thus, every effort must be made to enable young men and women to meet life with more adequate knowledge and resources, especially with regard to the establishment and maintenance of their marriage and family life. This can best occur through education on a widespread scale. In earlier times people in times of trouble they would go to their parents, teachers, gurus, relatives or intimate friends for comfort and enlightenment. But in today's

356 Joseph, Mar Thoma, "Forward," in *Christian Family, in Transition: Continuity and Discontinuity*, Koshy P. Varughese ed., (Faridabad: Dharma Joyti Peeth, 2011), 8.

generation, people struggle to begin and maintain happy homes with a sturdy sense of independence. As the generation gap increase, young people feel that their elders are incapable of understanding their particular problems. However, all family members, no matter how young or old, have much to offer one another. And, each of them faces their own unique set of problems and challenges at each phase of life. Hence, family members, supported by their local communities, are in the best position to remedy their own ills and prevent difficulties before they have a chance to develop. Truly, therefore, it is time for family life education in India and particularly the family counsellors and family therapist to "come of age" and to help the families maintain healthy relationship.

Problem within a family unit affect all members. Families with problems have certain needs, require specific coping skills, and therefore, may be considered 'high risk' families. When couples have strained relationships, children feel the effects, even when parents try to hide the conflicts. In the same way, chronic illness, disability in a family member, unemployment, divorce, death or any member of other family member family problems disturbed the whole family system.

In this demanding and challenging era "Family the bedrock and heart of a strong society" should be nurtured and given utmost support. If Naga society has to move forward and experience progress and development, they must first address the issues of every family than only the society can experience real change and progress because family is the most basic unit and the bottom most block of the society's foundation.

It is expected that the findings and results of the present analysis may provide deeper understanding on the tenets of family life, and may give insights in maintaining healthy functional families.

10. Conclusion

The concluding chapter has provided the summary of the research along with major findings, tenability of the research, implications for Church in caring the family, pastoral care and counselling towards the family by adopting some of the classical models of family counselling, at the same time the researcher has made a humble attempt in suggesting some of the new models. Considering the limitation of the present research and the magnitude of the subject, the researcher has also suggested various themes on the subject for further research. Although, the research cannot claim for drastic result, it is expected that to certain extend some of the models suggested would be essential in dealing with Naga family issues in particular and wider family context in general.

Bibliography

Books

Abrol, Usha, Thapar Vandana, Khan, and Srinivastava, Paul. *Television Viewing Among Children of Delhi School.* New Delhi: National Institute of Public Corporation and Child Development, 1991.

Aier, Anungla. "Ministry to Naga Families with Youth." *Doing Youth Ministry in a Naga Context.* Edited by Soren Oestergaard and Adela Mero. Dimapur, Nagaland: Project Nehemiah NBYF, 2002.

Amanto, Paul R., and Alan Booth. *A Generation at Risk: Growing Up in An Era of Family Upheaval.* Cambridge/London: Harvard University Press, 2000.

Anderson, ham, and Ozment, Steven, E. *Families in the Greco-Roman World.* Louisville, London Westminster John Knox Press. 1989.

Anderson, Herbert., Don Browning., et al. eds. *The Family Handbook: The Family Religion and Culture.* Louseville, kentucky: Westminster John Knox Press, 1998.

Anderson, R. S., & Guernsey, D. B. *On Being Family.* Grand Rapids, MI: Eerdmans. 1985.

Antony, D., John. *Psychotherapy in Counselling.* Dindagul: Anugraha Institute for Counselling, (2003), 2005.

Antony, D., John. *Family Counselling: The Classical Schools.* Dindagul: Anugraha Institute for Counselling, (2003), 2005.

Aparajit, Chowdhury. *Family Life Education in India: Perspective, Challenges and Application.* Jiapur/New Delhi/Bangalore/Mumbai: Rawat Publications, 2006.

Atkin, C. K., Anderson, J. A., et al. "Research Evidence of Mass Mediated Health Communication Campaign." In *Communication Year Book* (ed.) D. Nimo. Newbury Park, CA: Sage Publications, 1979.

Augustine, J. S., and Murmi. *The Indian Family in Transition.* New Delhi: Vikas Publications, 1982.

Balch, David. *Let Wives Be Submissive: Domestic Code of 1 Peter*. Atlanta: Scholars Press, 1983.

Balswick, J. O., and Judith K. Balswick. *The Family: A Christian Perspective on the Contemporary Home.* Third Edition. Grand Rapids, MI.: Baker Publishing Company, 2007.

Balswick J. O. and J. K. Balswick. *Family in Pain: Working through the Hurts.* Grand Rapids: Ravell, 1997.

Balswick, J. O. and J. K. Balswick. *A Model for Marriage: Covenant*, Grace, Empowering, and Intimacy. Downers Grove, IL: InterVarsity, 2006.

Baral, J. K., and Bishoyee, A. P. *Family in Transition: Some Theoretical and Methodological Questions*. In J. K. Baral and, A. Chowdhury (eds.), *Family in Transition: Power and Development* (pp.1-15), New Delhi: Northern Book Centre. 1999.

Barker P. *Basic Family Therapy*. London: Collins.1986.

Barker, R. L., Kessler, H., and Lehn, J. M. *Treating Couples in Crisis*. New York: Fortress Press, 1984.

Barton S. "Biblical Hermeneutics and the Family." In *The Family in Theological Perspectives*, S. Barton ed., Edinburgh: T&T Clark, 1996.

Batson, C. D. *The Religious Experience: A Social-Psychological Perspective*. New York: Oxford University Press, 1983.

Beck-Gersheim, E., *Reinventing the Family: In Search of New Lifestyles,* Malden, MA: Blackwell, 2002. 105.

Bell, J. E. "Family System Theory." In *Baker Encyclopedia of Psychology and Counselling*. David G. Benner and Peter C. Hill, eds. Grand Rapids, Michigan: Baker Books, 1999, 442-443.

Bell, John Elderkin. *A Theoretical Framework for Family Group Therapy*. In P. J. Guerin (Ed.), *Family Therapy*, New York: Gardner Press, 1976.

Bell, Margaret, and Kate Wilson, eds. *The Practitioner's Guide to Working with Families*. Norfolk: Palgrave, Macmillan, 2003.

Bcit-Hallahimi, and Argyle, M. *The Psychology of Religious Belief, Behaviour and Experiences*. London: Routledge, 1997.

Bendangyapang, A. *History of Christianity in Nagaland: Social Changes 1872-1972*. Bangalore: Shalom Ministry Publication, 2004.

Bendroth, Margaret. *Fundamentalism and Gender: 1875 to the Present.* New Haven: Yale University Press, 1994.

Berger, Brigitte, and Peter L. Berger. *The War Over the Family: Capturing the Middle Ground.* New York: Anchor City, 1993.

Bergin, A. E., & Garfield, S. L. (Eds) *Handbook of Psychotherapy and Behavioral Change*, 2004.

Bertalanffy, L. V. *General System Theory*. New York: Braziller, 1968.

Bhagat, R. B. and S. Mohanty. "Emerging Pattern of Urbanization and the Contribution of Migration in Urban Growth in India." *Asian Population Studies*. Vol. 5 no. 1 (2011): 5-20.

Bhusan Vidya and D. R. Sachdeva. *An Introduction to Sociology*. Allahabad: Kitab Mahal, 2008.

Bradley, K. R. *Discovering the Roman Family*. New York: Oxford University Press, 1991.

Bowen, Murray. *Family Therapy in Clinical Practice*. New York: Jason and Aronson Publication, 1987.

Borrowdale, Anne. *Restructuring Family Values*. London: SPCK, 1994.

Browning, Don, Bonnie Miller-Mclemore at.el. *From Culture Wars to Common Ground: Religion and the American Family Debate*. Louisville: Westminster John Knox Press, 1997.

Brown, L'Engle, and Kenneavey *Multi-dimensional Effects of Media on Family*. Grand Rapids, Michigan: Baker Books, 2006.

Burke, S. *The Heart of Pastoral Counselling: Healing Through Relationship*. Grand Rapids: Ministry through Resources Library, 1989.

Burton, Graeme. *Media and Behavioral Change*. Louisville: Westminster John Knox Press, 2005.

Carbo, Richard. et.al. eds. *Retelling Naga Narratives: More Than Thrice-Told Tales*. Dimapur: Heritage publishing House, 2014.

Carr, A. *Family Therapy: Concepts, Process & Practice*. New Delhi: Wiley and Sons, 2000.

Carson, David K., et.al. "Developing Resiliency in Contemporary Indian Families." *Family Life Education in India: Perspective. Challenges, and Applications*. Edited by Chowdhury, Aparajita, et. al Jiapur/New Delhi/ Bangalore/Mumbai: Rawat Publications, 2006.

Casey, James. *The History of the Family*. Oxford: Basil Blackwell, 1989.

Chadha, Neerja, Girishwar Misra, and Ratra Amiteshwar, eds. *Counselling and Family Therapy: Basic Concepts and Theoretical Perspectives*. New Delhi: IGNUO, 2011.

Chatterji, S. "Rise in Female-Headed Families." In S. Chatterji, ed. *The Indian Women's Search for an Identity*. New Delhi: Vikas, 1988.

Chauhan, S. S. *Advanced Educational Psychology* 6th ed. New Delhi: Vikas Publishing House, 2001.

Chekki, D. A. *Modernization and Kin Network*. London: E. J. Brill, 1974.

Cherian, Jacob. "Pastoral Counselling: Family Research and Family Therapy: Issues and Methods." In *Methodological Issues in Theological Discipline*. Samson Prabhakar, ed. Bangalore: SATHRI, 2002. 56-74.

Cherian, Jacob. "Marital Relationship in the Context of Family of Origin Issues." In *Christian Family in Transition: Continuity and Discontinuity*. Edited by Koshy P. Varughese. Faridabad/Haryana: Dharma Joyti Vidya Peeth, 2012.

Chowdhury, Aparajita, David K. Carson et.al, eds. *Family Life Education in India: Perspective, Challenges, and Applications*. Edited by Chowdhury, Aparajita, David K. Carson et.al, Jiapur/New Delhi/Bangalore/Mumbai: Rawat Publications, 2006.

Chowdhury, Rita. "Understanding Family Life in India." *Family Life Education in India: Perspective, Challenges, and Applications*. Edited by Chowdhury, Aparajita, David K. Carson et.al, Jiapur/New Delhi/Bangalore/Mumbai: Rawat Publications, 2006.

Chunkapura, Joan and Antony Mannarkulam. *Psychotherapies and Counselling*. Kottayam: TRADA Publications, 2007.

Clapp, Rodney. *Families at the Crossroad: Beyond Traditional and Modern Options*. Downers Grove, Illinois, USA/Leicester, England: InterVarsity Press, 1993.

Clarke, David. *The Impact of Social Media on Children, Adolescent, and Family*. Washington D.C.: Routledge, 2007.

Clinebell, Howard J. *Basic Types of Pastoral Care and Counselling*. London: SCM Press Ltd., 1984.

Colapinto, Jorge. *Structural Family Therapy.* Itasca, Illinois: F. E. Peacock, 1982.

Colapinto, Jorge. *Structural Family Therapy*. In A. M. Horne & M. M. Ohlsen (Eds.), *Family Counseling and Therapy*. Illinois: F. E. Peacock Publishers, Inc, 1981.

Das, R.C. *Marriage in Transition: A Biosocial Approach*. New Delhi: Northern Book Centre. 1999.

David, J. Atkinson and David H. Field, eds. "Family Therapy." *New Dictionary of Christian Ethics and Pastoral Theology*. Nottingham, England: InterVarsity Press, 2005, 375-376.

David, Larson. *Religious Survey of American Family*. Minneapolis: National Institute of Healthcare Research/Fortress Press, 1996.

Davis, Mari. *Discovering What Works for Families*. Melbourne: The Australian Institute of Family Studies, 1987.

Dixon, Suzanne. *The Roman Family*. Baltimore: Johns Hopkins University Press, 1992.

Douglas, Ann. *The Feminization of American Culture*. New York: Alfred A. Knopf, 1997.

Dozo, P. "The Prophetic Role of The Church." In *Crusade on Naga Morality*. Compiled by V. K. Nuh. Kohima: Research Wing, Council of Naga Baptist Churches, 1996.

Dube, Leela. *Sociology of Kinship in India*. Bombay: Popular Prakashan Publication, 1974.

Duhl, F. S., Kantor, D., & Duhl, B. S. *Learning Space and Action in Family Therapy: A Primer of Sculpting.* In D. Bloch (Ed.), *Techniques of Family Psychotherapy*. New York: Norton.1973.

Breunlin, D., Schwartz, R., & MacKune-Karrer, B. *Meta Frameworks for Psychotherapy: Transcending the Models of Family Therapy.* San Francisco: Jossey Bass, 1992.

Emmons, Robert A., and Paloutzian, Raymond F. *Psychology of Religion.* California: Department of Psychology, University of California, 2003.

Falola, Toyin. *Media and African Culture*. Nairobi: Oxford Publishing House, 2000.

Farge, James K. *Marriage, Family and Law in Medieval Europe*. Toronto/Buffalo: University of Toronto Press, 2010.

Fisch, R., J. H., Weakland, & L. Segal. *The Tactics of Change: Doing Therapy Briefly*. San Francisco: Josey-Bass, 1982.

Fernandes, M. *Marriage: A Life Long Partnership' in Alive*. New Delhi: Low Price Publication, 1997.

Frymer-knesy, Kensey. *Studies on Families in the Bible.* Louisville, London: Westminster John Knox Press, 1998.

Framo, James L. *Family of Origin Therapy: An Intergenerational Approach.* New York: Brunner/Mazel Publishers. Tenth Edition, 2010.

Gay, L. R. *Education Research: Competencies for Analysis and Organization (3rd Ed.)*. New York: Merrille Publication Co. 1990.

Gladding, S. T. *Family Therapy: History, Theory, and Practice (6th Ed.)*. San Francisco, CA: Pearson Higher Ed., 2014.

Godwin, Ekhayeme. *Media and the Changing Trends in Socio-cultural Life*. Nairobi: Print Well Publishing House, 2012.

Gong, Honge, Rebecca Cassells, and Marcia, Keegan. "*Understanding Life Satisfaction and the Education in Australia: A Profile from HILDA Wave 9.*" National Centre for Social and Economic Modelling, 2011.

Gore, M. S. *Urbanization and Family Change*. New Delhi: Popular Prakashan, 1968.

Gorey, Gerald. *Theory and Practice of Counselling and Psychotherapy*. Singapore: Brooks/Cole, 1996.

Gurman, A. S., & Kniskern, D. P. (Eds.). *Handbook of Family Therapy*. New York, NY: Routledge, 2014.

Gurman, A. S., Lebow, J. L., & Snyder, D. K. (Eds.). *Clinical Handbook of Couple Therapy (5th Ed.)*. New York, NY: Guilford Publications, 2015.

Hauser, Stuart, T. *Adolescents and their Families*. New York: The Free Press, 1991.

Heward-Mills, Dag. *Model Marriage: A Marriage Counselling Handbook*. Chennai: Vasant Prints and Packs, 2011.

Holeman, Virginia Todd. *Theology for Better Counselling*. (Find author) InterVarsity Press Academics. 2012.

Horam, M. "Naga Religion: A Case Study" *Religion and Society of the North East India*. New Delhi: Vikas Publishing House, 1980.

Horam M. *Naga Polity*, Delhi: Low Price Publications, 1975.

Horam, M. *Social and Cultural Life of the Nagas*, Delhi: P. R. Publishing, Co., 1977.

Horam, M. *Nagas: Old Way New Trends*. New Delhi: Cosmo Publications. 1988.

Hood, R. W., Spilka, Hunsberger B, Gorsuch, H. I. *The Psychology of Religion: An Empirical Approach*. New York: Guilford, 1996.

Humbert, Stephen. "Gender Difference and Life Satisfaction." *Journal of Happiness Studies*. Vol. 1 No. 1 (2013): 1-22.

Impett, Malamuth. *Media and its Impact on Personality.* Nashville: Oxford University Press, 2001.

Ivey, Allen E, Michael D' Andrea, et al. 5th ed. *Theories of Counseling and Psychotherapy: A Multicultural Perspective.* Boston, MA: Allen & Bacon, A Pearson Education Company, 2002.

James, Lovely Awomi. *Tribal Theology: Reviewing Naga Traditional Worldview.* New Delhi: Christian World Imprints, 2017.

John, Santhosh. *Spirituality of Marriage*. Delhi: ISPCK, 2011.

Kanuga, Rosenfeld. *A Study on Today Media*. New York: Guilford Press, 2004.

Kapadia, K. M. *Marriage and Family in India*. Bombay: Oxford University Press, 1972.

Kapur, P. *Marriage and Working Women in India.* New Delhi: Vikas Publishing House, 1972.

Karve, I. *Kinship Organization in India*. Poona Deccan P. G. College and Research Institute, 1953.

Kath, Kenilo. *Traditional Religious System of the Rengma Nagas.* Kolkata: Anshah Publications, 2005.

Kolenda, P. *Regional Differences in Family Structure in India*. Jaipur: Rawat Publications, 1987.

Laxminarayan, H. D. "The Rural Family in Transition." In J. K. Augustan, ed. *The Indian Family in Transition*. New Delhi: Vikas, 1982.

Laquar, H., Peter. *Multiple Family Therapy*. Florence, South Carolina: Multiple Family Therapy Resource Centre, 1977.

Longchar, Wati, "The Continuity of Indigenous People in Today's World." In *Garnering Tribal Resources for Doing Tribal Christian Theology*. Edited by Razouselie Lasetso. Jorhat: ETC Programme Coordination, 2008.

Longchar, A. Wati. *The Tribal Religious Traditions*. Jorhat: Tribal Study Centre, ETC, 1991.

Longchar, Imtijungla. *Restore Our Family*. Dimapur: S. Wati Aier and Sons, 2006.

Longkumer, Limatula, "Naga Women in Theological Education: Problems and Perspectives." In *Side by Side: Naga Women Doing Theology in Search of Justice and Partnership*. Edited by Limatula Longkumer and Talijungla Longkumer. Jorhat: CCA-EGY/Naga Women Theological Forum, 2004.

Longkumer, Limatula. *Christian Education for Transformation: Foundations, Approaches and Effective Teaching*. Kolkata: Limatula Longkumer/ESPAGE, 2017.

Longkumer, Limatula. *Christian Education for Adults in Tribal Context*. Jorhat: Eastern Theological College, 1998.

Lora, Eduardo, and Juan Camilo Chaparro. *The Conflictive Relationship between Family Life Satisfaction and Income Level*. New York Avenue/Washington, D.C.: Inter-American Development bank, 2008.

Maldonado, Jorge. *Even in the Best of Families: The Family of Jesus and other Biblical Families Like Ours*. Geneva/Switzerland: WCC Publications, 1997.

Margolis, Rachel, and Mikko, Myrskyla. *Income: Regional Difference in the Determinants of Family Life Satisfaction*. London: Department of Sociology, University of Western Ontario, Social Sciences Center/Max Planck Institute for Demographic Research, 2012.

Mascarenhas, Marie Mignon. *Family Life Education: Value Education*. Bangalore: Centre for Research Education Service and Training for Family Life Promotion, 1993.

Mar Thoma, Joseph. "Forward." In *Christian Family in Transition: Continuity and Discontinuity* edited by Koshy P. Varughese. Faridabad, Haryana: Dharma Jyoti Vidya Peeth, 2012.

Mar Philoxenos, Isaac. "Forward." In *Family God's Design and Destiny* edited by Simon, K. V. Hyderabad: Authentic Book, 2009.

McGoldrick, M., Pearce, J. K., & Giodano, J.(Eds.). *Ethnicity and Family Therapy*. New York: Guilford Press, 1982.

McGoldrick, M., Gerson, R., & Schellenberger, S. *Genograms in Family Assessment 2nd Ed*, New York: Norton, 1998.

Meier, Johnson. *Study of Religion and Family*. Maryknoll/New York: Orbis Books, 2003.

Mero, Adela. "The Naga Home and Youth." In *Doing Youth Ministry in a Naga Context*. Edited by Soren Oestergaard and Adela Mero. Dimapur/Nagaland: Project Nehemiah NBYF, 2002.

Mills, J. P. *The Rengma Nagas*. Guwahati: Spectrum Publications,1980.

Minuchin S. *Families and Family Therapy.* Cambridge, MA: Harvard University Press, 1974.

Minuchin, Salvador and H. Charles Fishman. *Family Therapy Techniques.* Cambridge, Massachusetts/London: Harvard University Press, 1981.

Misra, Girishwar, Neerja Chadha, and Ratra Amiteshwa, eds. *Counselling and Family Therapy: Applied Aspects.* New Delhi: IGNUO, 2011.

Moslener, R. W. "Family Systems Theory," In *Baker Encyclopedia of Psychology and Counseling* Second Edition. Edited by David G. Benner and Peter C. Hill. Grand Rapid, Michigan: Baker Books, 1999. (442-444).

Morries, Pam, David Luries and Racha, Jain. *Changing Media, Changing Families.* Minneapolis, Fortress, Press, 2010.

Mullati, L. *The Bhakti Movement and Status of Women: A Case Study of Veerasaivism*. New Delhi: Abhinava Publications, 1989.

Murmu, D. "The Tribal Family in Transition." In J. S. Augustine, ed. *The Indian Family in Transition*, New Delhi: Vikas, 1982.

Murry, Ezamo. *An Introduction to Pastoral Care and Counselling.* New Delhi: ISPCK, 2009.

Newman, Jay. *Biblical Religion and Family Values: A Person in the Philosophy of Religion.* New York: Ballantine Press, 2001.

Nichols, Michael P. *The Essentials of Family Therapy*. (Fourth edition) Pearson Education: Boston, New York, San Francisco, 2009.

Nichols Michael P. *Inside Family Therapy*. Boston: Allyn and Bacon, 1999.

Nichols, Michael P. *Family Therapy: Concepts and Methods.* Boston/London/ Sydney/Tokyo /Singapore/Toronto: Allyn and Bacon, 2001.

Nichols Michael P. *The Self in the System.* New York: Brunner/Mazel, 1987.

Nichols, M., & Schwartz, R. *Family Therapy Concepts and Methods (4th Ed.).* Cambridge, MA: Allyn and Bacon,1998.

Nichols Michael P., and Richard C. Schwartz. *Family Therapy Concepts and Methods*. New Jersey: Allyn and Bacon, 1995.

Nshonga, A. *Traditional Naga Village System and Its Transformation.* New Delhi: Anshah Publishing House. 2009.

Oestergaard, Soren and Adela Mero, eds. *Doing Youth Ministry in a Naga Context.* Dimapur, Nagaland: Project Nehemiah NBYF, 2002.

O J, Boab. 'Marriage', *The Interpreter's Dictionary.* New York: Abington Press, 1962.

O'Leary, Charles J. *Counselling Couples and Families: A Person-Centred Approach.* New Delhi/London/Thousand: SAGE Publication, 2004.

Ozment, Steven E. *When Fathers Ruled: Family Life in Reformation Europe.* Cambridge, Massachusetts: Harvard University Press, 1983.

Packer, Lana. *Women Making a Difference in Marriage.* Nashville: Tennessee: Lifeway Press, 2003.

Paul W. Henshaw, Harold E. Weemhoff, *Worship in Our Family.* Nashville, Tennessee: The Upper Room. 1981.

Pfuhl, Reimer. "Cultivate Viewers and Readers: A life-style Perspective." In Signorielli and M. Morgan (eds.), *Cultivation Analysis: New Direction in Media Effects Research.* Newbury Park, CA. Sage, 1990.

Pongener, Mar. *Morung Speaks: Cultural Values, Elements for the Enrichment of the Naga Community.* Mokokchung: Tribal Development and Communication Centre, 2011.

Poster, M. "Christian Theology and Ethics of Family." In *Dictionary of Pastoral Care and Counselling* edited by Rodney J. Hunter. Bangalore: TPI, 2007, (406-411).

Pradhan, H. *Family Life and Indian Society.* New Delhi: Anshah Publishing House, 2006.

Rai, B. C. *Sociological Foundation of Education.* Lucknow: Prakashan Kendra, 1998.

Randall T., Frost. "Challenges of Conducting Bowen Family Systems Research on Differentiation of Self." In *Differentiation of Self: Bowen Family Systems Theory Perspectives*, ed. Peter Titelman. New York: Routledge, 2014.

Rath, Arundhati. "Family Life Enrichment: Some Practical Consideration." *Family Life Education in India: Perspective, Challenges, and Applications.* Edited by Chowdhury, Aparajita, David K. Carson et. al Jiapur/New Delhi/Bangalore/Mumbai: Rawat Publications, 2006.

Rao, P. R. and Manu, Rao. *A Sociological Study of Indian Family Life.* Mumbai: Rawat Publications. 1982.

Rao Shankar. *Sociology: Principles of Sociology with An Introduction to Social Thought*, First Ed. New Delhi: S. Chand and Company, 2009.

Rawson, Beryl, ed. *The Family in Ancient Rome: New Perspective.* Ithaca, N.Y.: Cornell University Press, 1986.

Regnerus, Mark D. "Research on Religion and Family." Research conducted at the University of Texas at Austin, 2007.

Resnick, Chandy & Blum. *Religious Survey of American Family.* Minneapolis: Fortress Press, 1996.

Richard, Mathew. *Study on Family Structure.* Nashville: Abington Press, 1994.

Rivett, Mark. and Eddy, Street. *Family Therapy in Focus.* London/Thousand Oaks/New Delhi: SAGE Publications, 2003.

Rostosky, Sharon. *Why Religion Matters Even More: The Impact of Religious Practice on Social Stability.* Wisconsin: University of Wisconsin Press, 2004.

Sadgrove, Michael. "Theological Images of Marriage" in *Rethinking Marriage: Public and Private Perspective*. Edited by Christopher Clulow. London: Karnac Books, 1993.

Sahayaraj, L. *Marriage and Family in the Plan of God: Reflections of Saint John Paul II.* New Delhi: Christian World Imprints, 2014.

Samuel, George. "Preface." In *Family God's Design and Destiny*. Edited by K. V. Samuel. Hyderabad: Authentic Books, 2009.

Saradamani, K., (ed.). *Women, Work, and Society: Proceeding of First Symposium*. Calcutta: Indian Statistical Institute, 1985.

Saraswati, T. S. and Pai, S. "Socialization in Indian Context." In *Asian Perspectives in Psychology,* H. Kao and D. Singh, eds. New Delhi: Sage (Methodology Series), 1997.

Satir, Virginia. *The Satir Model: Family Therapy and Beyond.* Palo, Alto, CA: Science and Behavior Book,1991.

Sayger, T. A., Homrich, A. M., and Horne, *A. Working from Family Focus: The Historical Content of Family Development and Family Systems.* In A. Horne (ed.), *Family Counselling and Therapy*, Itasca, IL: F. E. Peacock, 2000.

Schawartz, Richard. *Internal Family Systems Therapy.* New York/London: The Guilford Press, 1995.

Schwad, H. L. *Couple Counselling in Media*. Pennsylvania: Media House, 1989,

Searle, David. *Truth and Love in a Sexually Disordered World.* Carlisle, Cumbria, UK: Paternoster Publishing, 1997.

Sema Z., Boholi. *Parent-Children Relationship among the Naga Society Towards Family Enrichment*. Naharbari, Dimapur: Shikhu Scholastic Press, 2012.

Sharfanske, E. P. (ed). *Religion and the Clinical Practice of Psychology*. Washington D.C: American Psychological Association, 1996.

Sherman, R., & N. Fredman. *Handbook of Structural Techniques in Marriage and Family Therapy*. New York: Brunner/Mazel, 1986.

Shimray, Shimreingam, "Globalization Process and Tribal People." In Narola Imchen, ed. *Tribal Women and Globalization*. Jorhat: Tribal Women Study Center, 2008.

Shimray, R. R. *Origin and Culture of Nagas*. New Delhi: Pamleiphi Shimray, 1985.

Simon, K. V. *Family God's Design and Destiny*: Hyderabad: Authentic Book, 2009.

Sinha, D. "The Family Scenario of Developing Country its Implications for Mental Health." *Health and Cross-Culture Psychology: Towards Application*. New Delhi: Sage Publications. 1984.

Smith, R. S. *Theories of Psychotherapy and Counselling*, Pacific Grove, CA. Brooks/ cole 2004.

Smith R. L. and Stevens. *Basic Techniques and Marriage and Family Counsellingand Therapy*. Eric Digest. ERIC Clearinghouse on Counselling and Personal Service. Anne Arbor MI. 1992-04-05.

Srinivas, M. N. *Social Change in Modern India*. New Delhi: Orient Longman Pvt., 2007.

Stinnet, Nick, and John DeFrain. *Family Strength and Adolescent Wellness*. Montgomery: The International Family Life Institute, Inc. 1980.

Soji, Alabi. *The Influence of Television on Family Institution in Nigeria*. Nairobi: Print Well Publishing House, 2010.

Steinglass, P. "The Conceptualization of Marriage from a Systems Theory Perspetive." In .J. Paolino and B. S. McCrady. Eds., *Marriage and Family Therapy.* 1978.

Stewart, Charles. *The Ministers as Family Counsellor*. Nashville: Abington Press, 1970.

Takuyaba. "Witnessing the Truth in The Society." In V. K. Nuh ed. *Crusade on Naga Morality*. Kohima: Research wing, CNBC, 1996.

Thomas, Darwin L. and Gwendolyn C. Henry. *Religion and Family Studies*. Brigham Young University's Department of Sociology, 2009.

Thomas, Jacob, P. "Stewardship in Family." In *Christian Family in Transition: Continuity and Discontinuity*. Edited by Koshy P. Varughese. Faridabad/ Haryana: Dharma Joyti Vidya Peeth, 2012.

Thampu, Valson. Faith and Family: Signposts to Fullness of Life. New Delhi Kalpana Printing House, 2005.

Thong, S. Joseph and Phanenmo Kath. *Glimpses of Naga Legacy and Culture*. Kottayam: Society for Naga Welfare Society, Kerala, 2012.

Thong, S. Joseph. *Head-Hunter Culture: Historic Culture of Nagas*. Tseminyu, Nagaland: Khinyi Woch, 1997.

Thornton, Arland, and Donald Camburn. *The Negative Impact of Media*. Nashville: Abington Press, 2010.

Varghese, G. "Formation of Christian Values in a Family." Thomas, Jacob P. "Formation of Christian Values in Family." In *Christian Family in Transition: Continuity and Discontinuity*. Edited by Koshy P. Varughese. Faridabad/ Haryana: Dharma Joyti Vidya Peeth, 2012.

Varughese, Koshy P. ed. *Christian Family in Transition: Continuity and Discontinuity*. Faridabad/Haryana: Dharma Joyti Vidya Peeth, 2012.

Vinson, Tony, and Mathew Ericson. *Life Satisfaction and Happiness*. Richmond, Australia: Jesuit Social Service, 2012.

Wadkar, A. J., Gerbner et.al., *The Impact of Television on its Viewer and the Family Environment*. Pune: Pustak Publications, 1998.

Weaver, James B. and Stephanie Lee Sargent. *Study on Media Effects and Family Interaction*. Louisville, Ky.: Westminster John Knox Press, 2005.

Weiss, P. L. "The Conceptualization of Marriage from a Behavioural Perspective." In T. J. Paolino and B. S. McCrady, eds., *Marriage and Family Therapy* (1978).

Witte, John, Jr. *From Sacrament to Contract: Marriage, Religion and Law in the Western Tradition*. Louisville, Ky.: Westminster John Knox Press, 1997.

Wood, Beulah. *Families in the Plan of God: A Theology from South Asia*. Bangalore: SAIACS Press, 2010.

Wood, Beulah. *Building Stronger Families.* Bangalore: SAIACS, 2005.

Wright, H. Norman. *The Premarital Counseling Handbook.* Chigaco: Moody Press, 1992.

Wright, H. Norman. *The Family that Listens: Keys to developing a Healthy Family Climate through Communication*. Wheaton, Illinois: Victor Books, 1984.

Wuthnow, R. *After Heaven: Spirituality in America Since the 1950's*. Berkeley: University of California Press, 1998.

Journals and Periodicals

Adam, B, "Families and Family Study in International Perspective." In *Journal of Marriage and Family*. 66: 2004, 1076-1088.

Aponte, H. J. and J. M. Van Dusen, Structural Family Therapy in A. S. Gurman, and D. P. Kniskern, eds. *The Handbook of Family Therapy: Vol 1.* New York: Brunner/Mazel, 1981, 310-316.

Arles, Nalini. "Restructuring Pastoral Care in India: Shades of the Past in Shaping the Future" *Bangalore Theological Forum* Vol. XXXVII, No.1 (June), 2005: 27-57.

Ball, Armistead, & Austin. "Impact of Religion on family and Society." A study survey conducted at Department of Sociology at Brigham Young University, 1985, 167-169.

Batson, C., and Raynor-Prince, L. "Religious Orientation and Complexity of Thought about Existential Concerns" *Journal for the Study of Religion and Family*, 22/1 (1983): 38-50.

Bharat, S. "Family Socialization of the India Child." *Trends in Social Science Research*, Vol. 4, No.1, June, (1991): 106-110.

Bharat, S. "Single-Parent Family in India: Issues and Implications." *The Indian Journal of Social Work*, 49/4 (1986): 367-376.

Call, Vaughn R. A. and Tim B. Heaton "Impact of Religion of Family Life." In *Journal for the Scientific Study of Religion*, Vol. 112/04 (1997): 19-27.

Cassel, J. "The Contribution of the Social Environment to Host Resistance." *American Journal of Epistemology*. 104 (1996): 107-122.

Carta, M. G. Koveas, V., Hardy, MC., et al "Life Satisfaction: Urban-Rural Difference" in *Clinical Practice Epistemology*. Vol. 8. No. 2 (2012): 102-109.

Chasie, Rocus. "Significance of Family Catechesis Today." In *Kristu Jyoti: A Pastoral Theological Catechetical Journal.* Vol. 31, No. 1 & 2 (March & June 2015): 1-16

Coldwell, Kevin J. "Impact of Religion in Family Life." In *Survey Conducted at the University of Wisconsin*, Madison, (2012): 115-125.

Conklin, G. H. "The Influence of Economic Development on Pattern of Conjugal Power Extended Family Residence." *Journal of Comparative Family Studies.* 19 (1988): 187-206.

Dean, A. and Lin, N. "The Stress-Buffering Role of Social Support: Problems, Prospects and Systematic Investigation." *Journal of Nervous and Mental Disease.* 1997:31-39.

George, Joseph. "Partnership: A Quest for Integration in Family." *NCCR*. 856. 1994.

George, Joseph. "The Changing Pattern of Family in India. Exploration in Postmodern Age." *Ripples.* 1/1. (2008): 11-19.

Gorai, D.C. A Sociological Perspective of Indian Family." *NCCR*: 815/10. 1994.

Gulati. L. "Male Migration to the Middle East and the Impact on the Family: Some Evidence from Kerala." *The Economic and Political Weekly*, 22/44 (1983): 41-46.

Hill, P. *Religious Experience and their Relation with Happiness and Personality. The International Journal for Psychology of Religion.* 10 (2000): 157-172.

Jacobvitz, Deborah B. and Nell F. Bush. "Reconstruction of Family Relationships: Parent-Child Alliances, Personal Distress, and Self Esteem." *Developmental Psychology* Vol. 32, No. 4.732-743. 1996.

Jang-Young, Lee, Byoung Mohk, Choi. "Life Satisfaction Comparison Between Urban and Rural People in Korea." Paper presented *at XII World Congress of Rural Sociology of the International Rural Sociology Association*, July, 6-11 (2008): Goyang, Korea.

Jehad M. Alaedein. "Is Bowen Theory Universal? Differentiation of Self among Jordanian Male and Female College Students and between them and a Sample of American Students through Bowen's Proposition" in *Educational Sciences*. Vol. 35. No. 2. 2008. 193-197.

J. E., Bell. *Family Context Therapy: A Model for Family Change, Journal of Marriage and Family Counseling*, 1978, *4*, 111–126.

Johnson, S. M., Hunsley, J., Greenberg, L., & Schindler, D. Emotion focused couples therapy: Status and challenges. *Clinical Psychology: Science and Practice, 6*. 1999. 67-79.

Kath, Phanenmo. "Understanding the Shift in Contemporary Indian Family Life: Challenges for Family Therapy" in *SATHRI Journal* Vol. VII, No.1 (2013): 13-38.

Kate, Levin, Dallago Lorenzo; and Currie, Candace. "The Association between Gender-Difference and Family Life Satisfaction" *Social Indicators Research* April 2012, Vol. 106, No. 2 (2012): 287.

Lebow, J. *What does the Research Tell us About Couple and Family Therapies? Psychotherapy in Practice, 56*, 2000. 1083-1094.

Light, Harriett K. and Doris Hertsgaard. "Education: Significant Factor in Family Life Satisfaction." *Research in Rural Education*, Vol. 3/1 (2010): 7-15.

Lopez, Shiela. "Impact of Television of Family." In *Journal of Comparative Family Studies*. (2010): 141-145.

Mahoney, A. R., & Knudson-Martin, C. Will Old Gender Scripts Limit New Millennium Families' Ability to Thrive. *Michigan Family Review, 5* (1). (2000), 41-52.

McAdams, C. R., Avadhanam, R., Foster, V. A., Harris, P. N., Javaheri, A., Kim, S., ... & Williams, A. E., The Viability of Structural Family Therapy in the Twenty-first Century: An Analysis of Key Indicators. *Contemporary Family Therapy. 38*(3), . (2016). 255-261.

McLeod, Morgan, Shanahan et. al "Television and Family Value." In *Mass Communication and Society*, Vol. 2. 1/2 (1972): 47-63.

Mc cree, Millers. "Religion and Family." In *Journal of Comparative Family Studies*. 42/04 (2003): 291-297.

Milavsky, Shapiro, M., and Lang, A. "Making Television Reality: Unconscious Processes in the Construction of Social Reality." In *Communication Research*, 18/5 (1982): 685-705.

Mishra, G. "Reflection on Continuity and Changes in the Indian Family System."*Trends in Social Research*. 2 (1), 1995. 27-30.

Mullati, L. "Families in India: Beliefs and Realities." *Journal of Comparative Family Studies*, 26/1 (1995): 11-25.

N. S. Jacobson, & Addis, M. E. Research on Couples and Couple Therapy: What do we Know? *Journal of Consulting and Clinical Psychology. 61*, (1993). 85-93.

Napoliello, A. L., and Sweet, E. S "Bowen Theory: A Study of Differentiation of Self, Social Anxiety, and Physiological Symptoms," in *Contemporary Family Therapy* June 2002, Vol., 24 Issue 2, 355-369.

Obi, Obioma Des. "African Understanding of Family Values and Struggle." *Ephrem's* 13/2 (2009): 134-140.

O'keeffe, Gwenn Schurgin and Kathleen Clarke. *The Impact of Social Media on Children, Adolescent and Family*. Paediatrics Vol. 127 No. 4 April 1 (2011): 800-804.

Oshio, Takashi. "Gender Differences in the Association with Family Life Satisfaction." *Journal of Cross-Cultural Gerontology* Vol. 27 No. 3 (2012): 259-274.

Pargament, K. I., and Park, C. L. Merely a Defense? The Variety of Religious Means and Ends. *Journal of Sociology*, Issue 51 (1995): 95-107.

Parsuraman, S. "Migration and Its Effect on the Family." *The Indian Journal of Social Work*, 47/1 (1986.): 1-14.

Pearlman, S. D., and P. R. Abraham, "Sexual Satisfaction among Married and Cohabiting Individual," in *Journal of Marriage and Family*, Vol. 32, 54-67.

Phatak, and Singh. "Television in Indian Adolescents' Lives: A Member of the Family." In *Journal of Youth and Adolescence*, Vol. 31/3 June (1986): 177-183.

Paulraj, S. C. "Social Change and Family: A Post-modern Concern." *AETEI*. 04/02 (1991): 10-21.

Prasada Rao, B. D. "A Sociological Perspective of Indian Family." *NCCR* Vol. CVIV/01 (1994): 521-533.

Parven Karkhaneh at.el. "The Study of the Effectiveness of the Bowen Self – Differentiation Counselling on Marital Conflicts on Married Women." in *International Journal of Life Science and Pharma Research*. Vol., 6. Issue 4, October 2016. 193-197.

Ramu, G. N. "Marital Roles and Power: Perception and Reality in an Urban Setting." In *Journal of Comparative Family Studies*. 19/2 (1988): 207-227.

Ramu, G. N. "Untouchability in Rural Areas." *The Indian Journal of Social Work*, 29 (1998): 147-158.

R., Sherman, & Fredman, N. *Handbook of Structural Techniques in Marriage and Family Therapy*. New York: Brunner/Mazel, 1986.

Sinha, D. Some Recent Changes in the Indian Family and their Implications for Socialization. *The Indian Journal of Social Work*, 45, 1984. 271-286.

Singh, D. *New Trends in India Family Life. The Indian, Journal of Social Work*, 107, 2001. 632-638.

Sinha, M. "Reflection. *Social Welfare"*, Vol. 45, No. 11, February, 1999.

Singh, L. B., Singh, A. K. "Alienation: A Symptomic Reaction of Educated Employed Youth in India." *International Journal of Psychology*, 3/12 (1996): 101-110.

Sighal, R. and Mishra, R. Achievement Goals: A Situational Contextual Analysis. *International Journal of Intercultural Relations*, 18(2), 1994, 239-258.

Sivamurthy, M. Household Headship in India: Trends and Implications. *The Journal of Family Welfare*, 34(4), 1999, 3-11.

Slaught, J. "Towards a Biblical Theology of Family." *Family Life Ministry*. Classroom Handout, Concordia University, NE, 2010.

Sriram, R. and Bakshi, A. "Family Violence against Married Women."*Social Change* 18(3), 1998, 45-48.

South, Scott J, Katherine Trent, and Sunita Boss. "Mate-selection: Demographic Opportunity and Mate-selection Process in India." In *Journal of Comparative Family* Studies. Volume XLVII, Spring No. 2, (2016): 221-246.

Toda, Akihito. "Satisfaction Levels (Qualitative Data): Family Life Satisfaction" *Japan Labour Review* Vol.10. No. 4, (2013): 1-41.

Toth, John F, Ralph B. Brown and Xiaohe Xu. "A Comparison of Rural-Urban Difference in Relation to Family Life Satisfaction." *Work, Community, and Family*. Vol. 5. Issue 2. (2010): 181-202.

Waliszewski, Bob. "Impact of Media of Family." *Focus on Family*. 105/05 (2013): 110-119.

W. M. Pinsof, & Wynne, L. C. The Efficacy of Marital and Family Therapy: An Empirical Overview, Conclusions, and Recommendations. *Journal of Marital and Family Therapy, 21*, (1995). 585-613.

Webliography

Jenny Brown, "Bowen Family System Theory and Practice: Illustration and Critique," New Zealand Journal of Family Therapy 20, No. 2 (June 1999), Under "The Process," http//www.thefsi.comau/wp-content/uploads/2014/01/Bowen-Family-System-Theory-and Practice-Illustration-and-Crtiques.pdf (accessed April 25, 2018).

William M. Fleming, "Family Systems Theory-Challenges and Future Derictions," J Rak http://family.jrank.org/pages/598/Family-Systems-Theory-Challenges-Future-Direction.html (accessed April 30, 2018).

Rakesh K. Chadda and Koushik Sinha. "Indian Family Systems, Collectivistic Society and Psychotherapy." Indian Journal of Psychiatry 55, No. 2 (January 2013) under "Introduction." https://.www.ncbi.nlm.nih.gov/pmc/article/PMC3705700/ (accessed June 12, 2018).

Robert R. Green and Robert G. Blundo. "Postmodern Critique of Systems Theory in Social Work with the Aged and their Families." *Journal of Gerontological Social Work* 31, No. 3-4 (1999) 95. http://www.tandfonline.com/doi/abs/10.1300/J083v31no3_06 (accessed 13, June 2018).

https://www.ukessays.com/essays/sociology/key-concepts-of-structural-family-therapy-sociology-essay.php (accessed June 12, 2018)

Essays, UK. (November 2013). Key concepts of structural family therapy. Retrieved from https://www.ukessays.com/essays/sociology/key-concepts-of-structural-family-therapy-sociology-essay.php?vref=1(accessed June 12, 2018).

Thesis

Adjustment and Correlates in the Early Adulthood and Its Impact on Pastoral Counselling, Varghese, Cherian, BD, 1999.

Adjustment and Its Correlates Among Children of Missionaries in Boarding Homes: Implication for Pastoral Care and Counselling.

Adjustment and Its correlates Among the Widows in Nagaland: Implications for Pastoral Care and Counselling, H. V. Toli FFRRC, MTh, 2016.

Sexual Behaviour in Adolescent: A Study on the Ecological Correlates, Saji Kumar, K.P. Ph.D. Thesis submitted to M.G. University, Kottayam, Kerala, 2013.

Appendix-I

Personal Data Sheet

1. Qualification	: Matric and Undergraduate Graduate ( )				
	: Graduate and Post Graduates ( )				
2. Place of Residence	: Urban ( )				
	: Rural ( )				
3. Gender (Sex)	: Male ( ) Female ( )				
4. Family Monthly Income	: Below Rs. 24,000 ( )				
	Above Rs. 25,000 ( )				
5. Tribe	: Angami	( )	Ao	( )	
	Chakhesang	( )	Chang	( )	
	Khiamngam	( )	Konyak	( )	
	Mao	( )	Lotha,	( )	
	Phom,	( )	Pochury	( )	
	Poumai	( )	Rengma	( )	
	Sangtam	( )	Sema	( )	
	Yimchinger	( )	Zeliang	( )	

Appendix-II

Family Rating Scale

Family Rating Scale [Bernice S. and Rudolf H. Moos (2009) and Thelma, Debby and Richard, 2011]
Standardized by Phanenmo Kath January (2012)

Given below are some of the statements to identity the communication level that impact family life. Read the statement carefully and put a tick [√]mark against any one of the alternatives that suits you most. The options are 1-Strongly agree, 2-Agree, 3-Don't Know, 4-Disagree, 5-Strongly Disagree. Make sure not to omit any of the statement. Your responses will be kept confidential and used only for research purposes. Thanking you for your participation.

1. A close relationship should be maintained with parents of both couples for maintaining a good family system.
   ( ) Strongly agree ( ) Agree ( ) Don't know
   ( ) Disagree ( ) Strongly disagree

3. A family which maintains a healthy family system will hosts community feasts occasionally.
   ( ) Strongly agree ( ) Agree ( ) Don't know
   ( ) Disagree ( ) Strongly disagree

5. Accommodating Guest and relatives occasionally in my house helps me maintain good family ties. ( ) Strongly agree ( ) Agree
   ( ) Don't know ( ) Disagree ( ) Strongly disagree

7. I must maintain a healthy communication with my in-laws in order to keep a healthy family system.( ) Strongly agree ( ) Agree ( ) Don't know
   ( ) Disagree ( ) Strongly disagree

8. It is always necessary to receive advices from elders in order to keep a healthy family system.
( ) Strongly agree ( ) Agree ( ) Don't know
( ) Disagree ( ) Strongly disagree

10. Young couple must never feel hesitant to receive guidance from elders of the village though elders are not educated as youngsters.
( ) Strongly agree ( ) Agree ( ) Don't know
( ) Disagree ( ) Strongly disagree

11. I never feel belittled to sacrificially help my partner in his/her responsibility.
( ) Strongly agree ( ) Agree ( ) Don't know
( ) Disagree ( ) Strongly disagree

12. In spite of fast changing trends among the contemporary Naga Society, elders in the clan, village and community still receives enough respect from the youngsters.
( ) Strongly agree ( ) Agree ( ) Don't know
( ) Disagree ( ) Strongly disagree

13. Common interest and community welfare is always a priority and plays a crucial role against individuals' interest among the Naga families.
( ) Strongly agree ( ) Agree ( ) Don't know
( ) Disagree ( ) Strongly disagree

14. Rich and poor Families (Haves and have-not) alike enjoy equal status among the Naga families as Naga maintain Classless society. ( ) Strongly agree
( ) Agree ( ) Don't know ( ) Disagree ( ) Strongly disagree

16. Naga youngsters maintain high respect for their parents and elders in the community, and always seek their permission before taking any major decision.
( ) Strongly agree ( ) Agree ( ) Don't know
( ) Disagree ( ) Strongly disagree

17. Nagas still maintains me first when it comes to work and duties and you first when it comes to food or other such privileges.
( ) Strongly agree ( ) Agree ( ) Don't know
( ) Disagree ( ) Strongly disagree

18. Simplicity, dignity of labour and honesty (no lock system for private or public property is still the trade mark.
( ) Strongly agree ( ) Agree ( ) Don't know
( ) Disagree ( ) Strongly disagree

19. Cheating, stealing and forgery were never the way of life for the Naga families, and one who practices it is look down by people till today, and the practice is almost nil.
( ) Strongly agree ( ) Agree ( ) Don't know
( ) Disagree ( ) Strongly disagree

20. Attentiveness and relatedness is so strong among the Naga family members that occasions such as sickness, death, marriage, feasts etc. are collectively share by members of the family.
( ) Strongly agree ( ) Agree ( ) Don't know
( ) Disagree ( ) Strongly disagree

Deleted Items

2. Having close friends around will hinder a good family system.
( ) Strongly agree ( ) Agree ( ) Don't know
( ) Disagree ( ) Strongly disagree

4. It is always dangerous to reveal family secrets to relatives.
( ) Strongly agree ( ) Agree ( ) Don't know
( ) Disagree ( ) Strongly disagree

6. If any members of my clan struggle in life, it is my duty as a family to reach out to help.
( ) Strongly agree ( ) Agree ( ) Don't know
( ) Disagree ( ) Strongly disagree

9. Staying in a city never mean that somebody forget values learned from the village life.
( ) Strongly agree ( ) Agree ( ) Don't know
( ) Disagree ( ) Strongly disagree

15. Family value system of the Nagas' is still intact and have not been influenced by the so called modern culture (globalised culture).
( ) Strongly agree ( ) Agree ( ) Don't know
( ) Disagree ( ) Strongly disagree

Appendix-III

Item Analysis

(Family Rating Scale)

Table 1. Rank, Item Number and 't' – values of Family Rating Scale

Rank	Item No.	t- value
	17	-5.471
	08	-5.358
	16	-5.229
	14	-4.978
	12	-4.702
	05	-4.673
	18	-4.515
	03	-4.219
	19	-3.955
	13	-3.775
	11	-3.763
	01	-3.488
	20	-3.459
	10	-3.250
	07	-3.236
	15	-2.420*
	09	-2.900*
	02	-2.350*
	06	-2.305*
	04	-1.905*

't'-value of < -2.470 is significant

*Not significant: Deleted

Appendix-IV

Table 7.0. Cronbach's Alpha of the Family Rating Scale

Item Number	Scale Mean if Item Deleted	Scale Variance if Item Deleted	Corrected Item-Total Correlation	Cronbach's Alpha if Item Deleted
FRS 1	49.910	44.184	0.341	0.716
FRS 3	48.730	43.330	0.320	0.717
FRS 5	47.720	41.876	0.444	0.704
FRS 7	47.090	44.204	0.396	0.712
FRS 9	47.460	41.988	0.406	0.708
FRS 10	47.290	45.097	0.282	0.721
FRS 11	47.220	45.253	0.294	0.720
FRS 12	47.970	42.959	0.320	0.717
FRS 13	48.230	43.310	0.266	0.724
FRS 14	49.050	42.250	0.327	0.717
FRS 16	48.740	41.507	0.410	0.707
FRS 17	49.090	41.780	0.464	0.702
FRS 18	48.880	44.309	0.217	0.729
FRS 19	48.080	42.972	0.268	0.725
FRS 20	47.280	45.072	0.302	0.719

Appendix-V

Media Influence Rating Scale (Dohnt and Tiggemann (2006) and S. Lucita and Saji KP (2011)

Standardized by Phanenmo Kath (2012)

Following are some items to measure the Impact of Mass Media on Family system. Indicate your opinion and experiences by using a tick [√] mark. The options are 1-Strongly agree, 2-Agree, 3-Don't Know, 4-Disagree, 5-Strongly Disagree. Your answers will be kept confidential and used only for research purposes. Thanking you for your participation.

1. My family usually set apart considerable time to watch Television.
   ( ) Strongly agree ( ) Agree ( ) Don't know
   ( ) Disagree ( ) Strongly disagree
2. Usually I discuss with my friends the things that I watch and learn from the Television.
   ( ) Strongly agree ( ) Agree ( ) Don't know
   ( ) Disagree ( ) Strongly disagree
3. I never miss my favourite serial in Television, even at the cost of family prayer or other important issues.
   ( ) Strongly agree ( ) Agree ( ) Don't know
   ( ) Disagree ( ) Strongly disagree
4. Mass media has changed people's perspective and brings chaotic situation to family environment.
   ( ) Strongly agree ( ) Agree ( ) Don't know
   ( ) Disagree ( ) Strongly disagree

5. There are lots of TV programmes which a family cannot comfortably watch together because of suggestive and provocative acts.
( ) Strongly agree ( ) Agree ( ) Don't know
( ) Disagree ( ) Strongly disagree

6. I feel that I spent more time before Television than the time spent with family members and friends.
( ) Strongly agree ( ) Agree ( ) Don't know
( ) Disagree ( ) Strongly disagree

7. I have a habit of watching Movies as soon as they are released.
( ) Strongly agree ( ) Agree ( ) Don't know
( ) Disagree ( ) Strongly disagree

8. Youngsters pick up many new lifestyles from movies and television which were actually alien to Naga way of life.
( ) Strongly agree ( ) Agree ( ) Don't know
( ) Disagree ( ) Strongly disagree

9. Movie and Television culture has replaced the legacy of morung system where all the basic information related to life were imparted.
( ) Strongly agree ( ) Agree ( ) Don't know
( ) Disagree ( ) Strongly disagree

10. Mass media promotes unhealthy family lifestyle as a result `many young couples are opting for divorce and separation.
( ) Strongly agree ( ) Agree ( ) Don't know
( ) Disagree ( ) Strongly disagree

11. I have a habit of talking long hours on Mobile phone, and spent huge amount on recharge even affecting my family budget.
( ) Strongly agree ( ) Agree ( ) Disagree
( ) Strongly disagree ( ) Don't know

12. I regularly listen to Radio, as it promotes educational, informative and culturally based programmes.
( ) Strongly agree ( ) Agree ( ) Disagree
( ) Strongly disagree ( ) Don't know

13. I am addicted to Newspaper and Magazines, that I hardly get time to talk to family members.
( ) Strongly agree ( ) Agree ( ) Don't know
( ) Disagree ( ) Strongly disagree

14. I spent a great amount of time every day to use internet at the cost of my official responsibility.
( ) Strongly agree ( ) Agree ( ) Don't know
( ) Disagree ( ) Strongly disagree

17. I cannot imagine living without an internet connection at home, as I spent lot of time on chatting with friends and even with stranger occasionally.
    ( ) Strongly agree ( ) Agree ( ) Don't know
    ( ) Disagree ( ) Strongly disagree

Deleted Items

6. Mass media has adverse impact on Naga culture.
    ( ) Strongly agree ( ) Agree ( ) Don't know
    ( ) Disagree ( ) Strongly disagree

8. My family usually is interested to watch Television programmes that present creative talk and informative programmes.
    ( ) Strongly agree ( ) Agree ( ) Don't know
    ( ) Disagree ( ) Strongly disagree

10. It is unimaginable to live without Television at home, as TV has become like lifeline for people.
    ( ) Strongly agree ( ) Agree ( ) Don't know
    ( ) Disagree ( ) Strongly disagree

16. If there is a new music album published, I will try to purchase it as soon as possible.
    ( ) Strongly agree ( ) Agree ( ) Don't know
    ( ) Disagree ( ) Strongly disagree

20. Cultural values, ethos and traditions are at the verge of extinction due to mass media.
    ( ) Strongly agree ( ) Agree ( ) Disagree
    ( ) Strongly disagree ( ) Don't know

Appendix-VI

Item Analysis
(Media Influence Rating Scale)

Table 2. Rank, Item Number and 't' – values of Media Influence Scale

Rank	Item No.	t-value
1	16	-6.402
2	14	-5.391
3	13	-5.115
4	04	-4.620
5	18	-4.443
6	17	-4.364
7	03	-3.872
8	01	-3.647
9	12	-3.517
10	09	-3.376
11	02	-3.376
12	07	-3.157
13	19	-2.700
14	11	-2.682
15	05	-2.470
16	20	-2.390*
17	10	-2.320*
18	15	-2.210*
19	06	-1.900*
20	08	-1.801*

't'-value of <-2.470 is significant

*Not significant: Deleted

Appendix-VII

Table 9.0. Cronbach's Alpha of the Media Rating Scale

Item Number	Scale Mean if Item Deleted	Scale Variance if Item Deleted	Corrected Item-Total Correlation	Cronbach's Alpha if Item Deleted
MIS1	49.750	41.927	0.217	0.727
MIS 5	49.220	42.315	0.286	0.721
MIS 6	49.220	40.638	0.337	0.712
MIS 7	49.180	40.230	0.443	0.706
MIS 9	50.530	39.989	0.362	0.713
MIS 10	50.310	40.964	0.181	0.738
MIS 11	49.670	39.536	0.304	0.720
MIS 12	50.100	39.667	0.365	0.712
MIS 13	50.180	40.533	0.256	0.725
MIS 14	49.840	39.990	0.377	0.712
MIS 15	50.510	38.931	0.377	0.711
MIS 17	50.590	39.990	0.494	0.873
MIS 18	61.29	215.40	0.360	0.877
MIS 19	61.72	208.99	0.559	0.871
MIS 20	61.56	213.83	0.437	0.874

Appendix-VIII

Religious Adherence Scale

Pfeifer and Waelty, 1995 and Sujita and Saji KP, (2011)
(Standardized by Phanenmo Kath 2013)

Given below are some of the statements to measure one's Religious Adherence and its impact on family life. Indicate your opinion and experiences by using a tick [√] mark. The options are 1-Strongly agree, 2-Agree, 3-Don't Know, 4-Disagree, 5-Strongly Disagree. Your responses will be kept confidential and used only for research purposes. Thanking you for your participation.

1. My family spends quality time together for prayer everyday in spite of busy schedules.
   ( ) Strongly agree ( ) Agree ( ) Don't know
   ( ) Disagree ( ) Strongly disagree

5. I do spend time in religious prayers before engaging in any duties or responsibilities.
   ( ) Strongly agree ( ) Agree ( ) Don't know
   ( ) Disagree ( ) Strongly disagree

1. I think it is important to be religious for the betterment of our life and prosperity.
   ( ) Strongly agree ( ) Agree ( ) Don't know
   ( ) Disagree ( ) Strongly disagree

2. I have a great respect for the religious leaders, because they are God's representatives on earth.
   ( ) Strongly agree ( ) Agree ( ) Don't know
   ( ) Disagree ( ) Strongly disagree

9. I have a habit of watching or listening to religious programmes in the Television.
( ) Strongly agree ( ) Agree ( ) Don't know
( ) Disagree ( ) Strongly disagree

1. I do believe that there is life after death, but at the moment I am not ready to face death because I still have long life to live.
( ) Strongly agree ( ) Agree ( ) Don't know
( ) Disagree ( ) Strongly disagree

2. Only religious faith and adherence helps us to please God and achieve proximity to God.
( ) Strongly agree ( ) Agree ( ) Don't know
( ) Disagree ( ) Strongly disagree

3. I am always interested to actively participate in practices, rites and rituals of my religion.
( ) Strongly agree ( ) Agree ( ) Don't know
( ) Disagree ( ) Strongly disagree

4. I believe religion and culture are two different entities, therefore if I want to be religious person I cannot observe most of my cultural practices which may displease God.
( ) Strongly agree ( ) Agree ( ) Don't know
( ) Disagree ( ) Strongly disagree

5. I have had a powerful religious/spiritual experience.
( ) Strongly agree ( ) Agree ( ) Don't know
( ) Disagree ( ) Strongly disagree

6. I do have a habit of discussing religious matters with my friends.
( ) Strongly agree ( ) Agree ( ) Don't know
( ) Disagree ( ) Strongly disagree

17. I never like to miss religious meetings, even at the cost of my official responsibilities.
( ) Strongly agree ( ) Agree ( ) Don't know
) Disagree ( ) Strongly disagree

18. I give a great importance to my religious rules in making moral judgements.
( ) Strongly agree ( ) Agree ( ) Don't know
( ) Disagree ( ) Strongly disagree

19. The success of family life depends on how close each member of the family is to God.
( ) Strongly agree ( ) Agree ( ) Don't know
( ) Disagree ( ) Strongly disagree

20. Given a chance, I want to make every atheist (Nonbeliever) converted to be religious people.
( ) Strongly agree ( ) Agree ( ) Don't know
( ) Disagree ( ) Strongly disagree

Deleted Items

2. I usually rely on religion when I have any problem.
( ) Strongly agree ( ) Agree ( ) Don't know
( ) Disagree ( ) Strongly disagree

3. I am not interested to read Scripture that is the duty of religious leaders and moral educators.
( ) Strongly agree ( ) Agree ( ) Don't know
( ) Disagree ( ) Strongly disagree

4. I do not feel it necessary to go to the church regularly because God resides in one's heart.
( ) Strongly agree ( ) Agree ( ) Don't know
( ) Disagree ( ) Strongly disagree

3. Since my church pastors and religious leaders are always praying for us we don't have to pray regularly.
( ) Strongly agree ( ) Agree ( ) Don't know
( ) Disagree ( ) Strongly disagree

16. I am interested to propagate the precept of my faith, though I am not a religious leader.
( ) Strongly agree ( ) Agree ( ) Don't know
( ) Disagree ( ) Strongly disagree

Appendix-IX

Item Analysis
(Religious Adherence Rating Scale)

Table 3. Rank, Item Number and 't' -values of Religious Adherence Rating Scale

Rank	Item No.	t-value
	17	-5.692
	06	-5.669
	12	-4.889
	20	-4.485
	09	-4.443
	07	-4.413
	13	-4.128
	11	-3.988
	14	-3.890
	15	-3.887
	18	-3.787
	05	-3.449
	10	-3.246
	19	-3.164
	01	-3.066
	16	-2.390*
	04	-2.330*
	08	-2.305*
	02	-2.200*
	03	-2.150*

't'-value of < -2.470 is significant

*Not significant: Deleted

Appendix-X

Table 11. 0. Cronbach's Alpha of the Religious Adherence Scale

Item Number	Scale Mean if Item Deleted	Scale Variance if Item Deleted	Corrected Item-Total Correlation	Cronbach's Alpha if Item Deleted
RAS 1	49.750	41.927	0.217	0.727
RAS 5	49.220	42.315	0.286	0.721
RAS 6	49.220	40.638	0.377	0.712
RAS 7	49.180	40.230	0.443	0.706
RAS 9	50.530	39.989	0.362	0.713
RAS 10	50.310	40.964	0.181	0.738
RAS 11	49.670	39.536	0.304	0.720
RAS 12	50.100	39.667	0.365	0.712
RAS 13	50.180	40.538	0.256	0.725
RAS 14	49.840	40.336	0.377	0.712
RAS 15	40.510	39.990	0.470	0.704
RAS 17	50.590	38.931	0.377	0.711
RAS 18	49.740	40.376	0.339	0.715
RAS 19	48.810	42.014	0.301	0.719
RAS 20	49.410	38.305	0.452	0.702